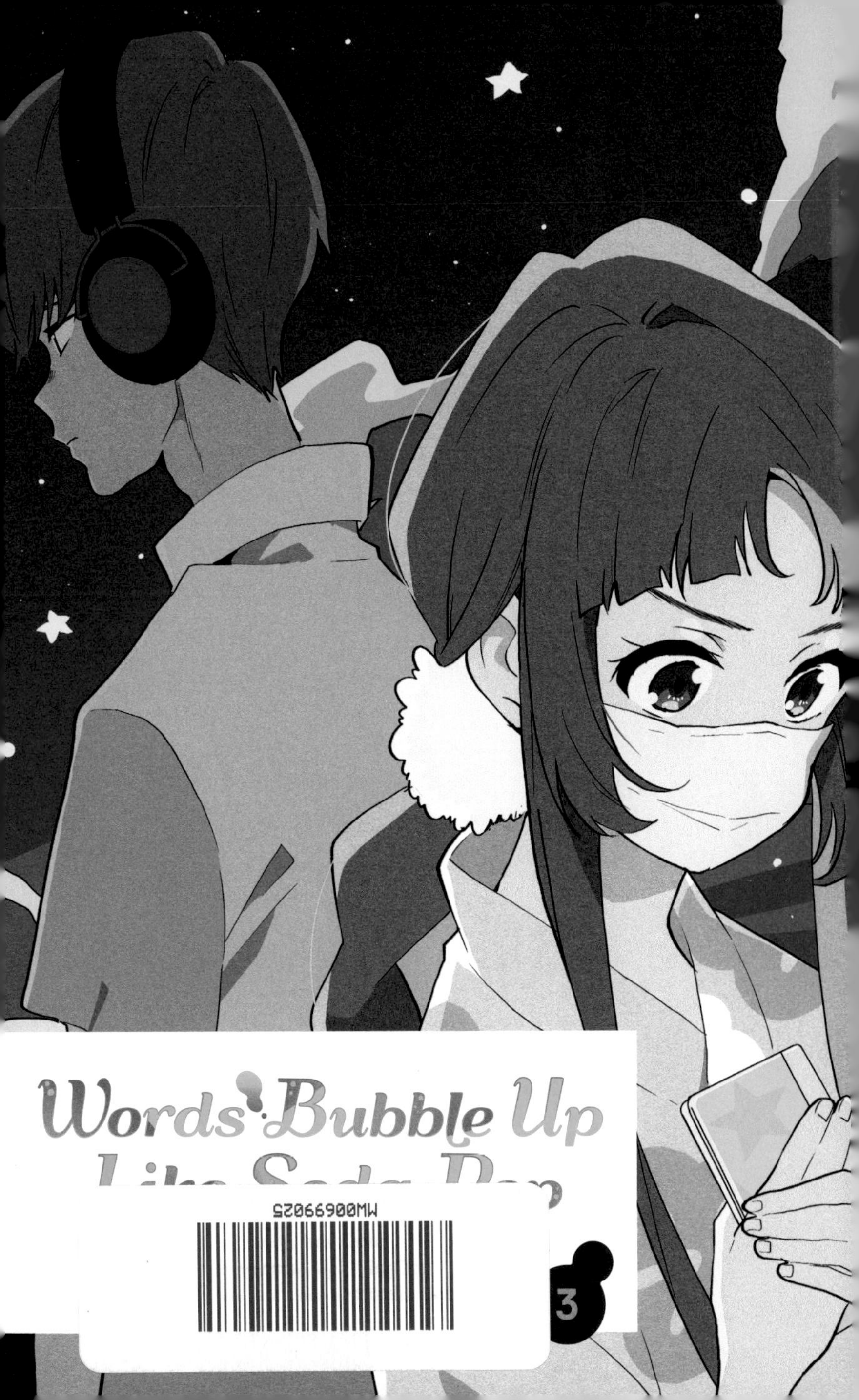

Words Bubble Up

3

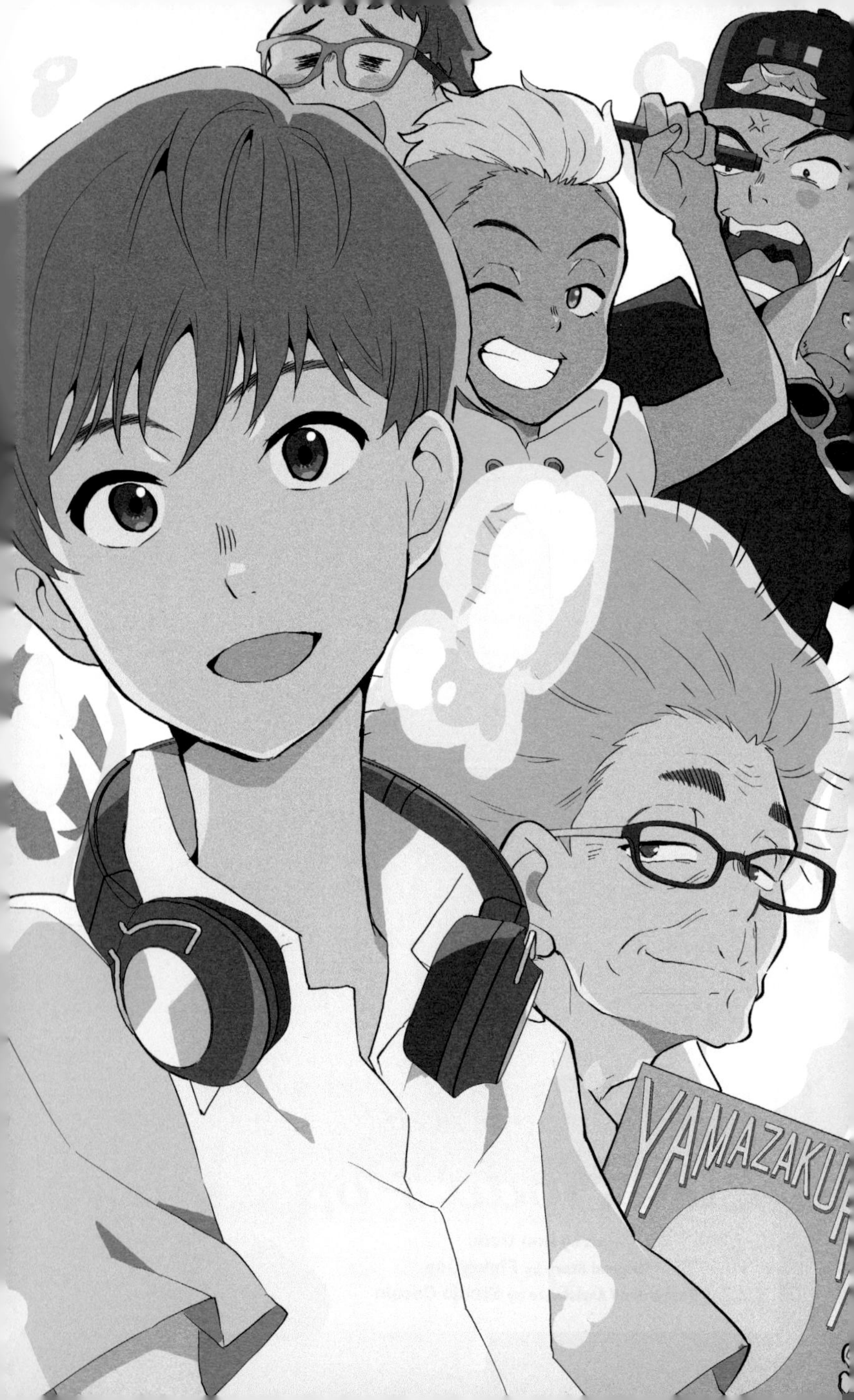
YAMAZAKU

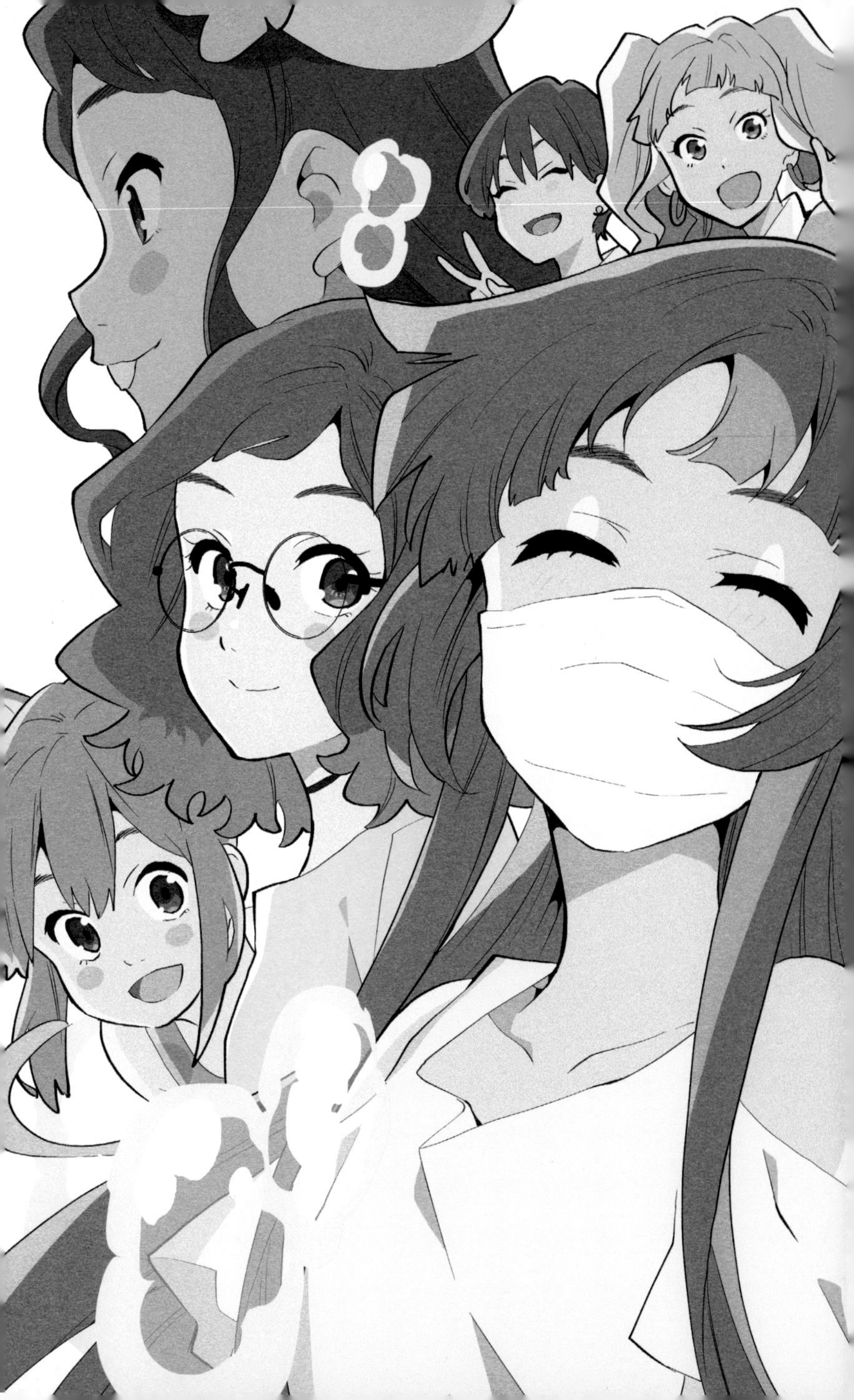

c o n t e n t s

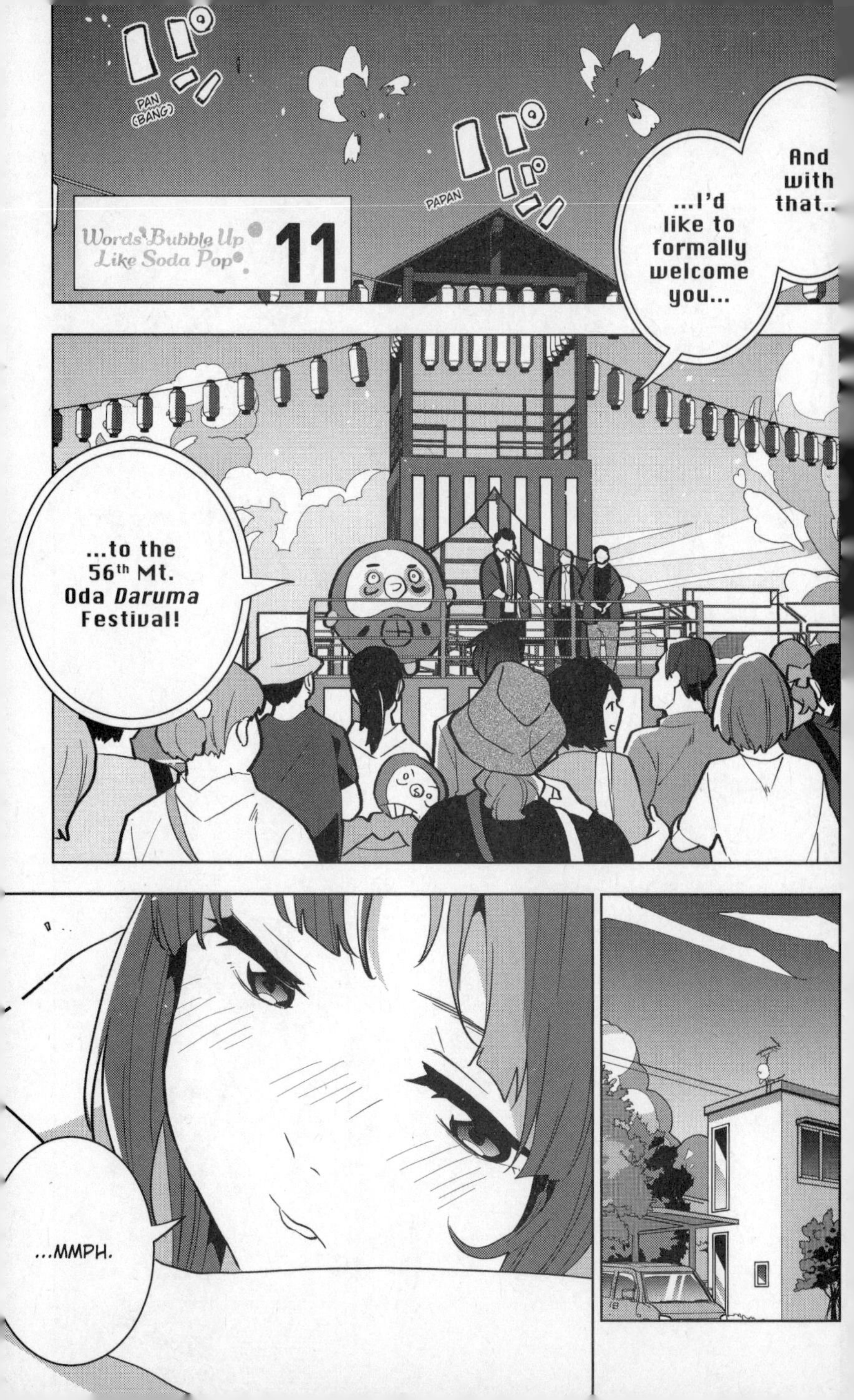
And with that...
...I'd like to formally welcome you...
PAPAN
PAN (BANG)
Words Bubble Up Like Soda Pop
11
...to the 56th Mt. Oda *Daruma* Festival!
...MMPH.

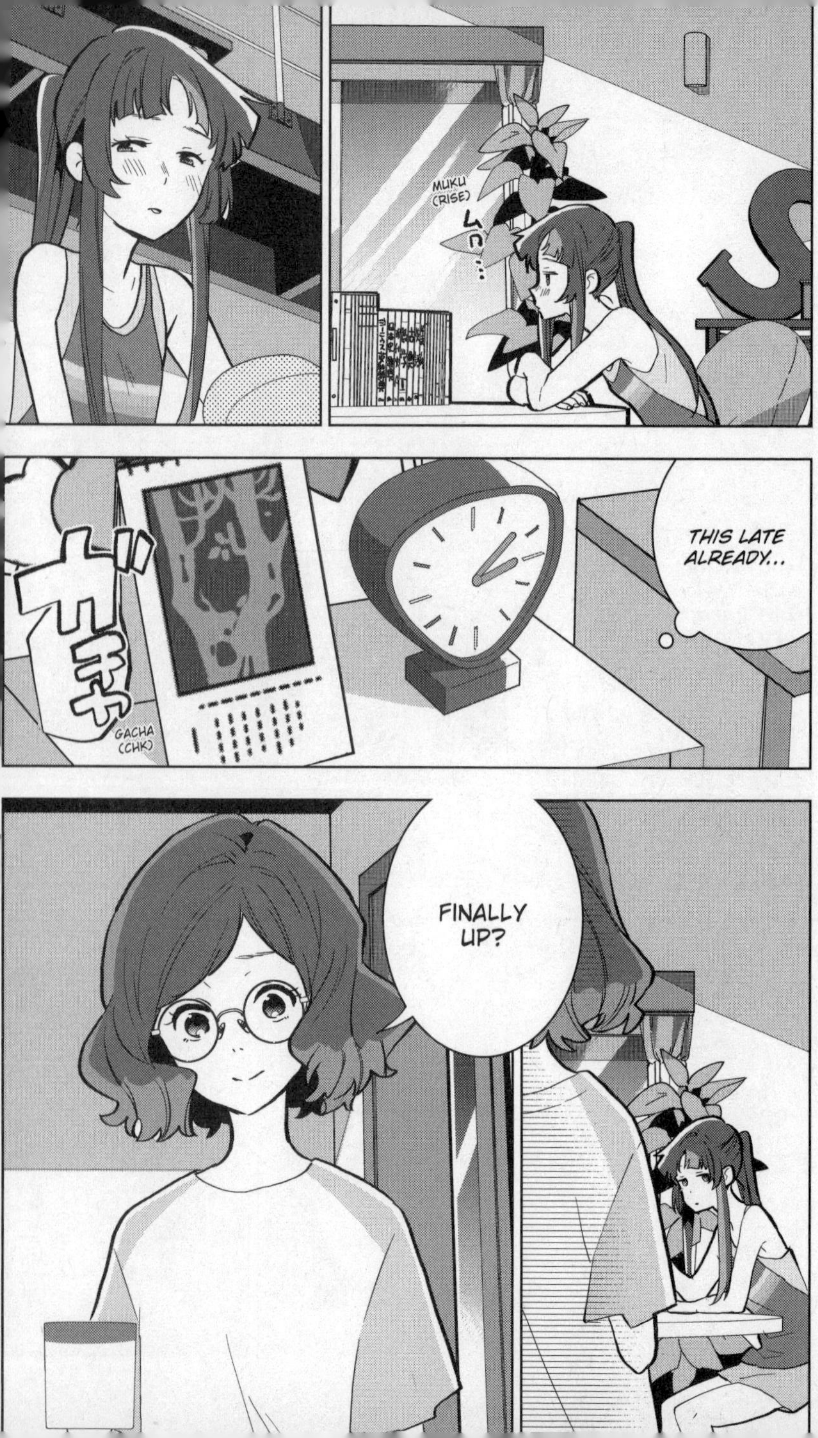
MUKU (RISE)
ムク…
THIS LATE ALREADY...
ガチャ
GACHA (CHK)
FINALLY UP?

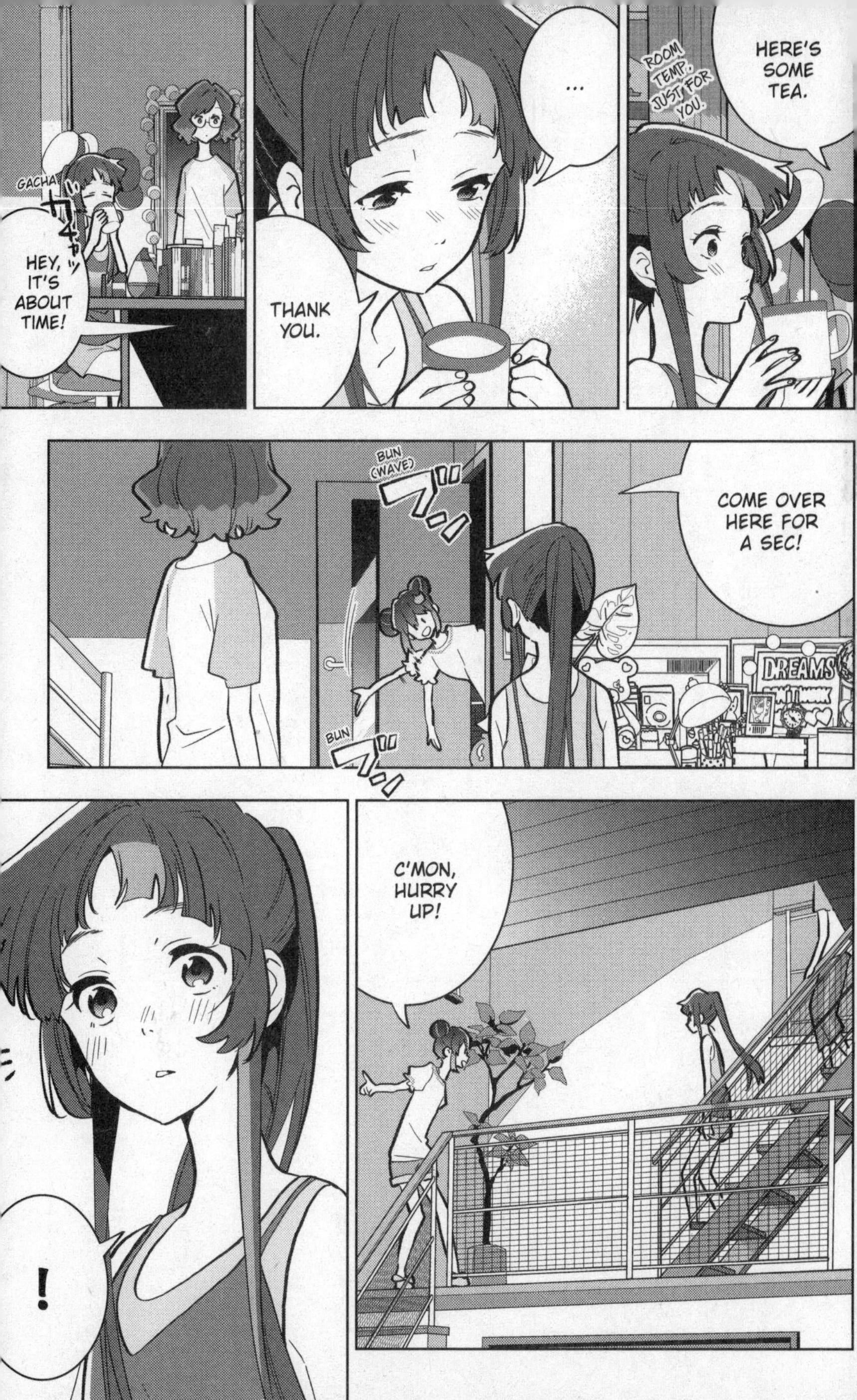
HERE'S SOME TEA.
ROOM TEMP. JUST FOR YOU.
...
THANK YOU.
GACHA
HEY, IT'S ABOUT TIME!
COME OVER HERE FOR A SEC!
BUN (WAVE)
BUN
DREAMS
C'MON, HURRY UP!
!

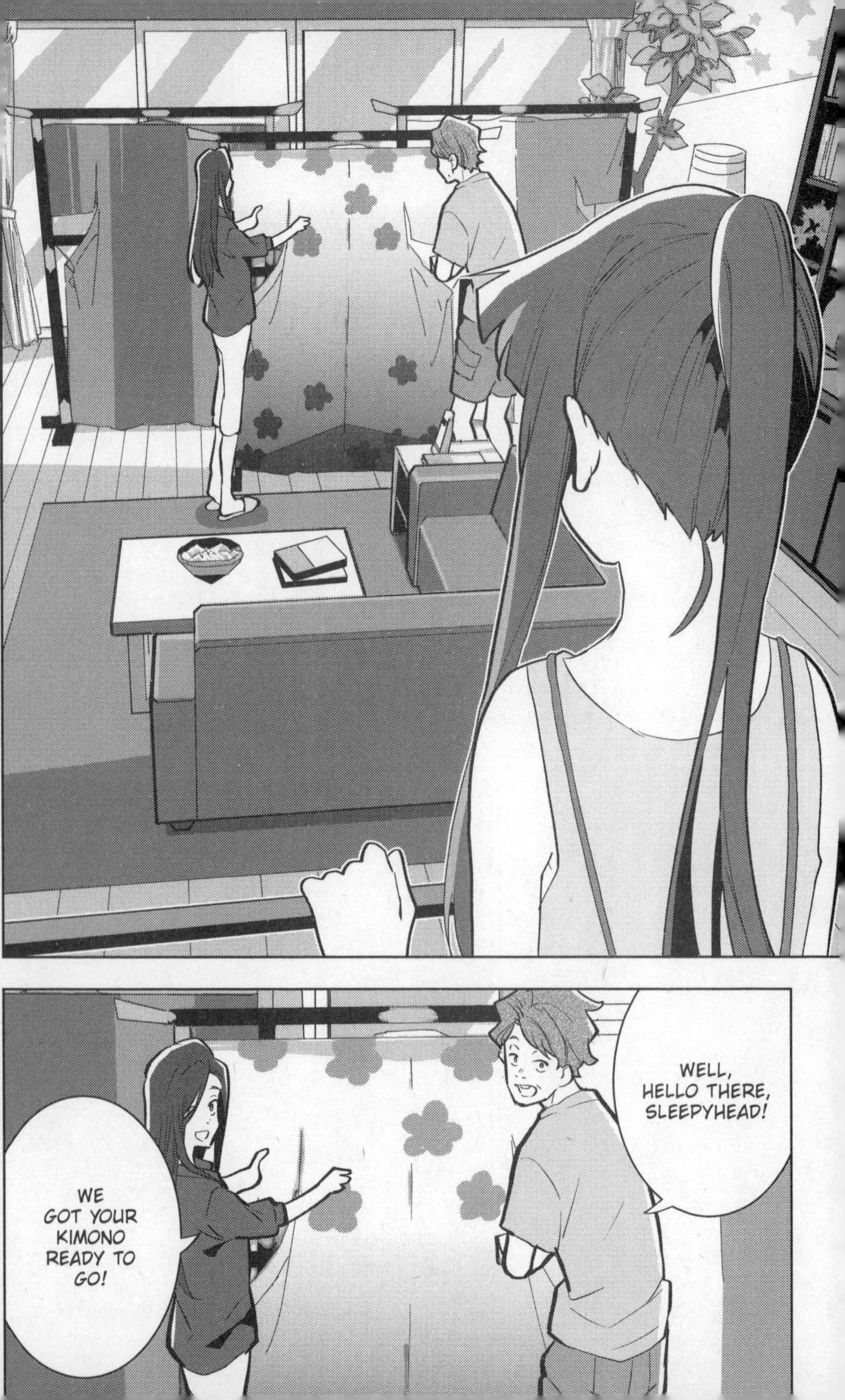
WELL, HELLO THERE, SLEEPYHEAD!
WE GOT YOUR KIMONO READY TO GO!

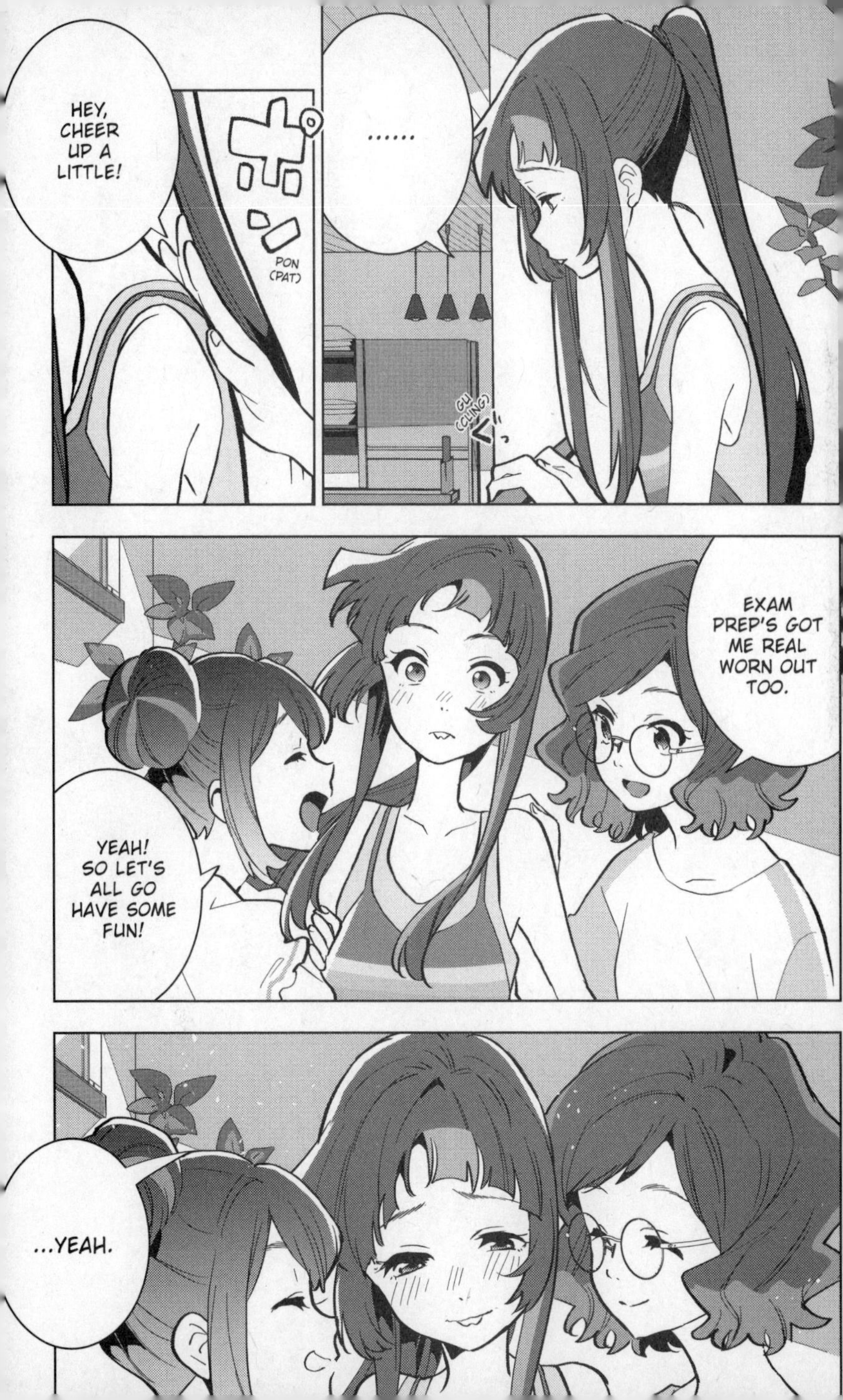
......
GU (CLING)
HEY, CHEER UP A LITTLE!
PON (PAT)
EXAM PREP'S GOT ME REAL WORN OUT TOO.
YEAH! SO LET'S ALL GO HAVE SOME FUN!
...YEAH.

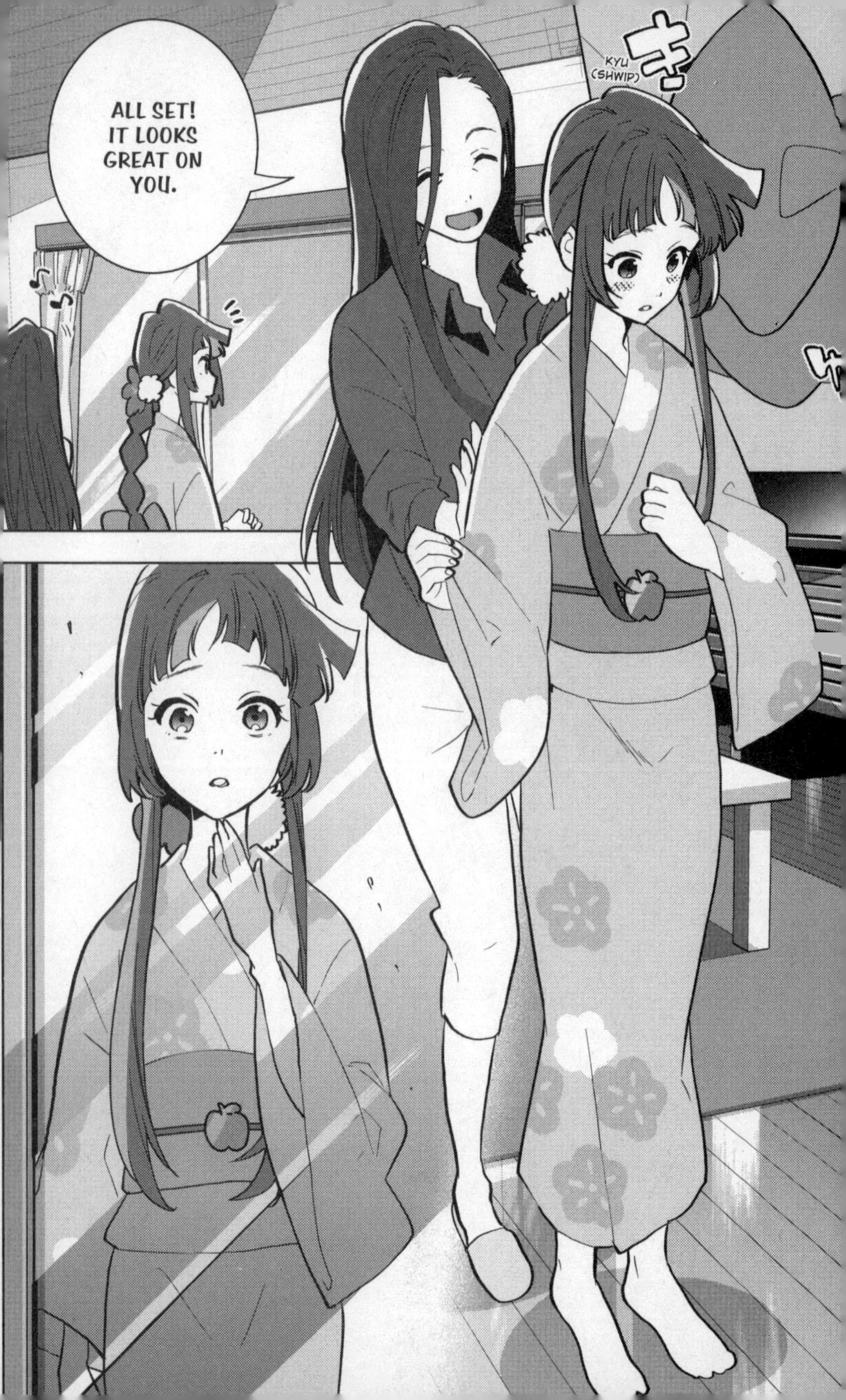
KYU
(SHWIP)
ALL SET! IT LOOKS GREAT ON YOU.

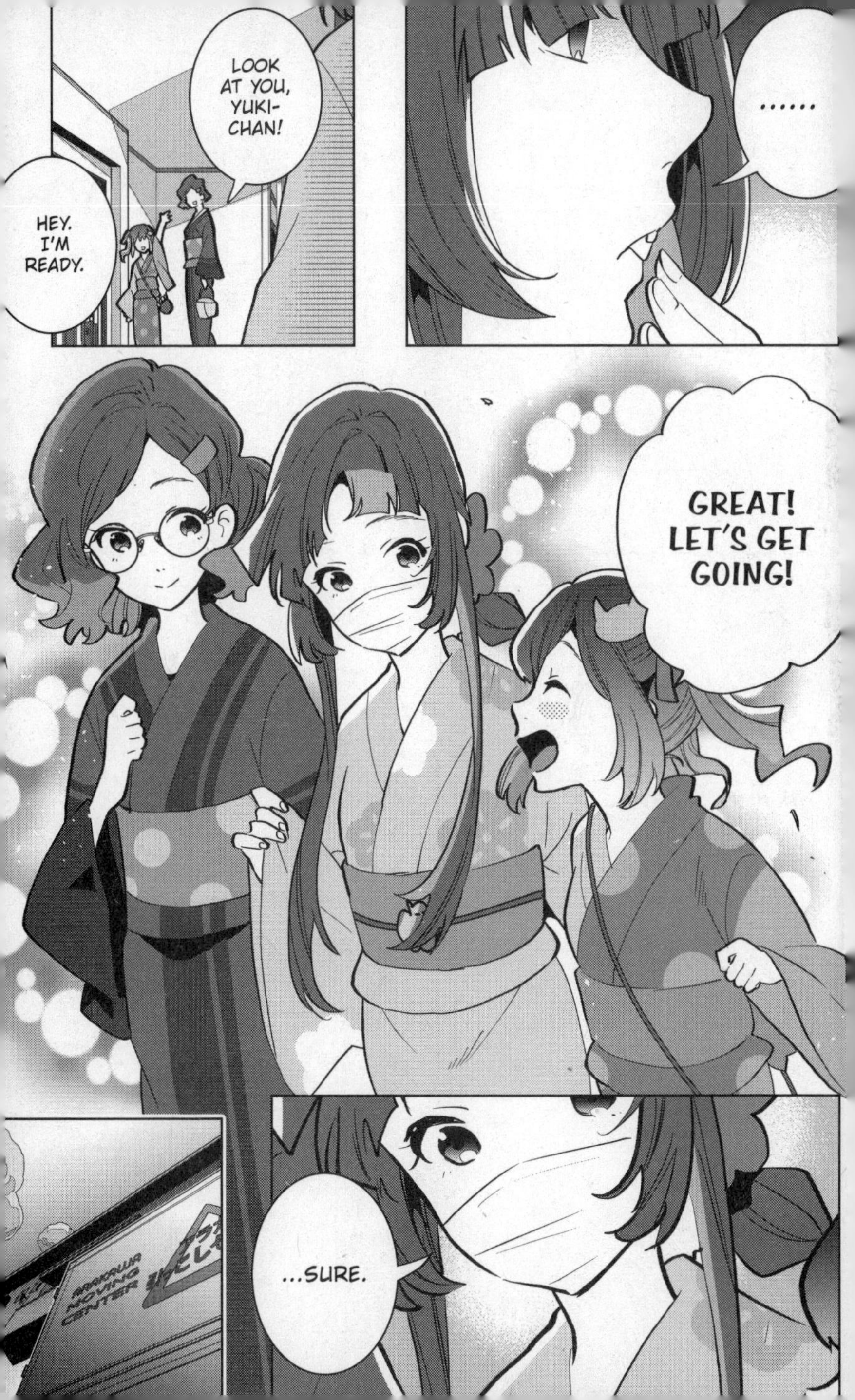
......
LOOK AT YOU, YUKI-CHAN!
HEY. I'M READY.
GREAT! LET'S GET GOING!
...SURE.
ARAKAWA MOVING CENTER

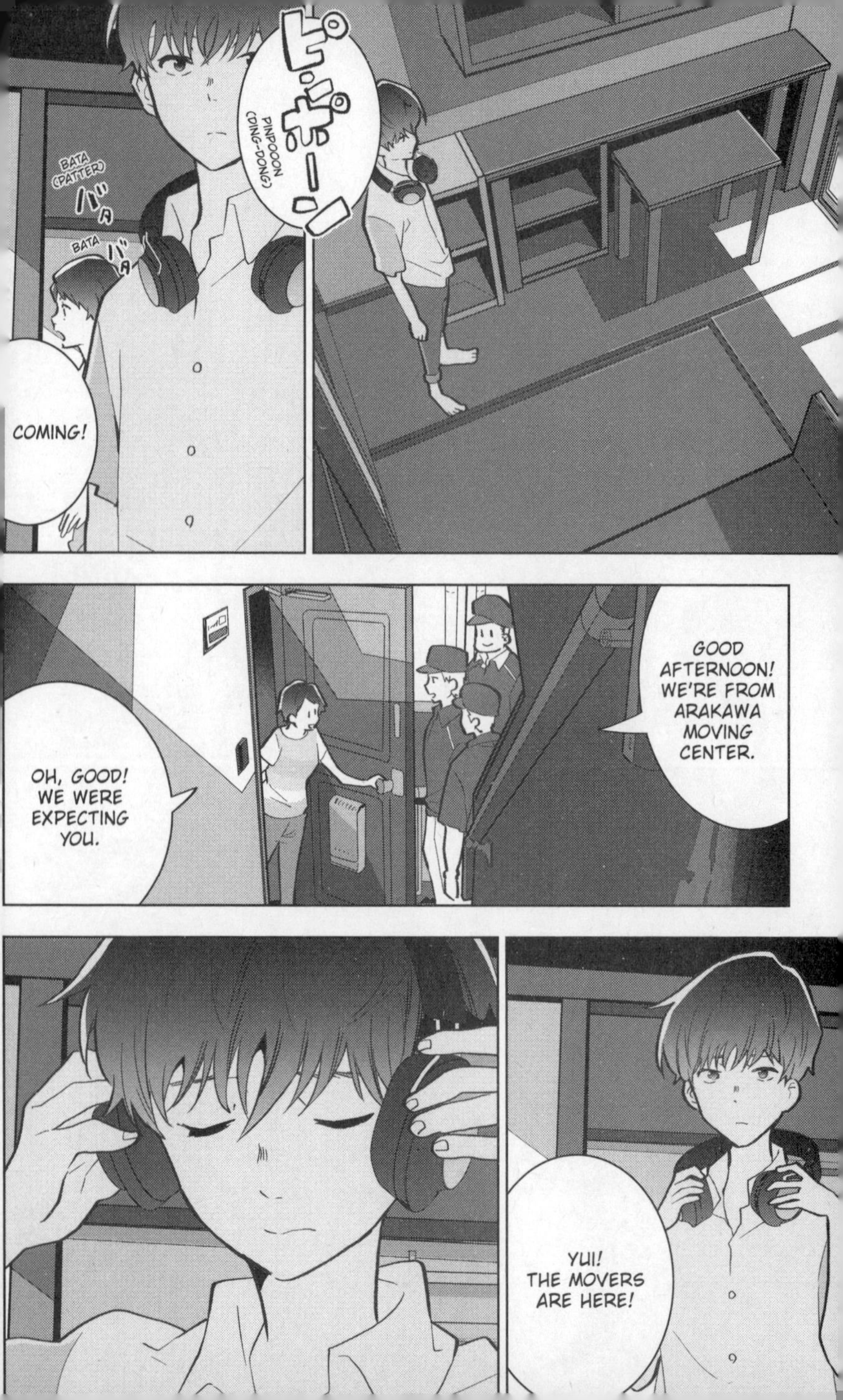
ピンポーン
PINPOOON (DING-DONG)
バタ BATA (PATTER)
バタ BATA
COMING!
GOOD AFTERNOON! WE'RE FROM ARAKAWA MOVING CENTER.
OH, GOOD! WE WERE EXPECTING YOU.
YUI! THE MOVERS ARE HERE!

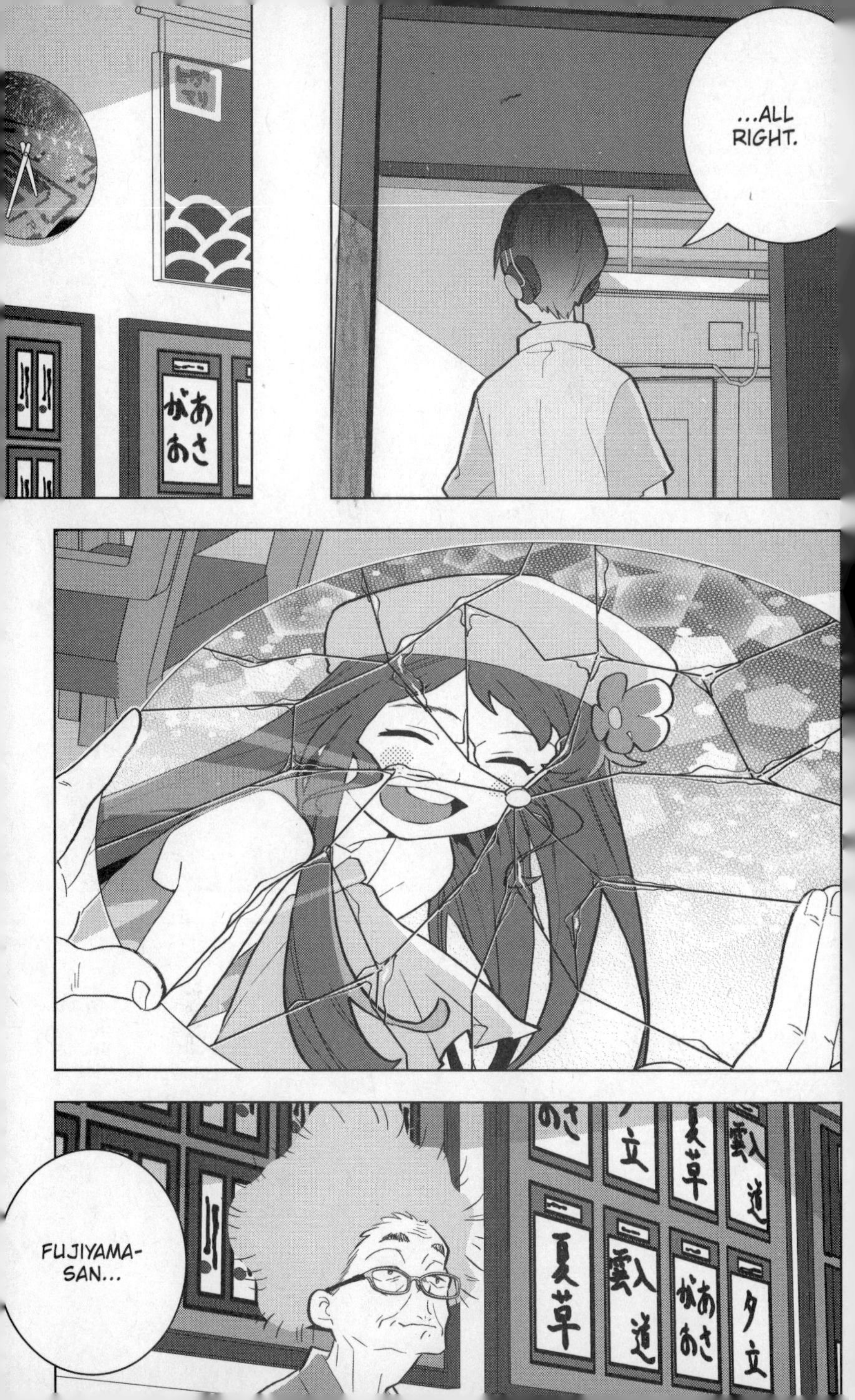
...ALL RIGHT.
FUJIYAMA-SAN...

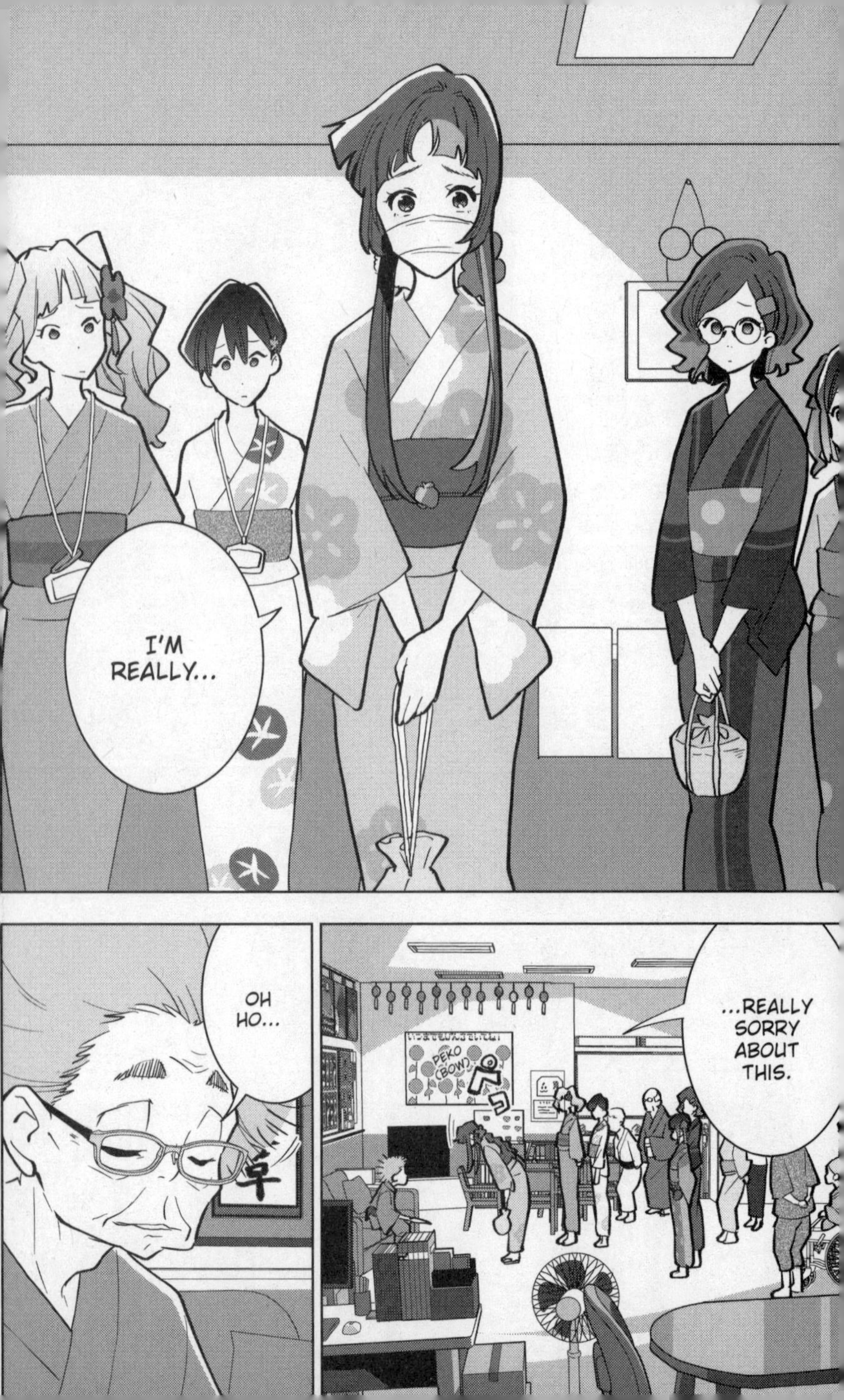
I'M REALLY...
...REALLY SORRY ABOUT THIS.
PEKO (BOW)
OH HO...

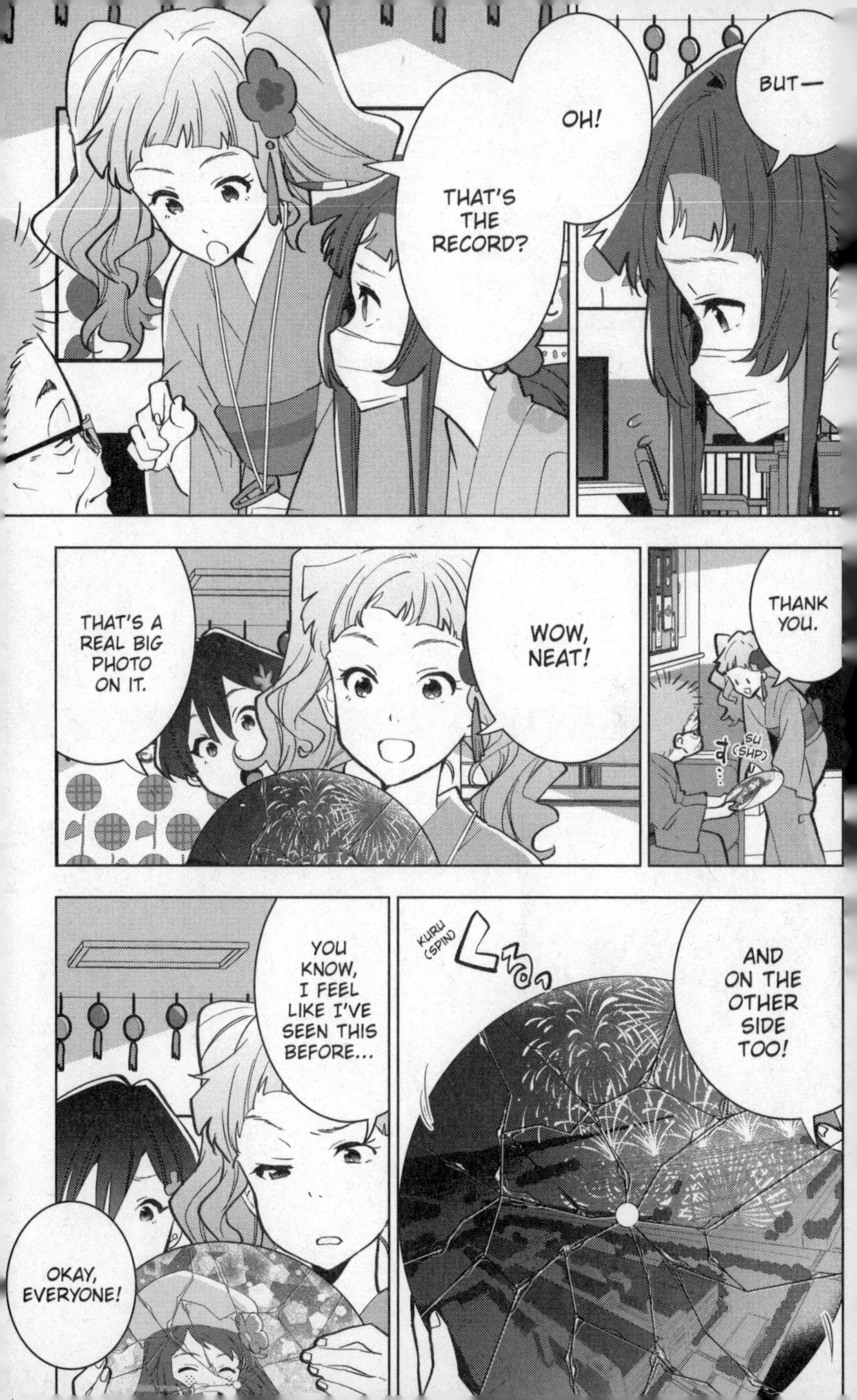
BUT—
OH!
THAT'S THE RECORD?
THANK YOU.
SU (SHP)
す…
WOW, NEAT!
THAT'S A REAL BIG PHOTO ON IT.
KURU (SPIN)
くるっ
AND ON THE OTHER SIDE TOO!
YOU KNOW, I FEEL LIKE I'VE SEEN THIS BEFORE...
OKAY, EVERYONE!

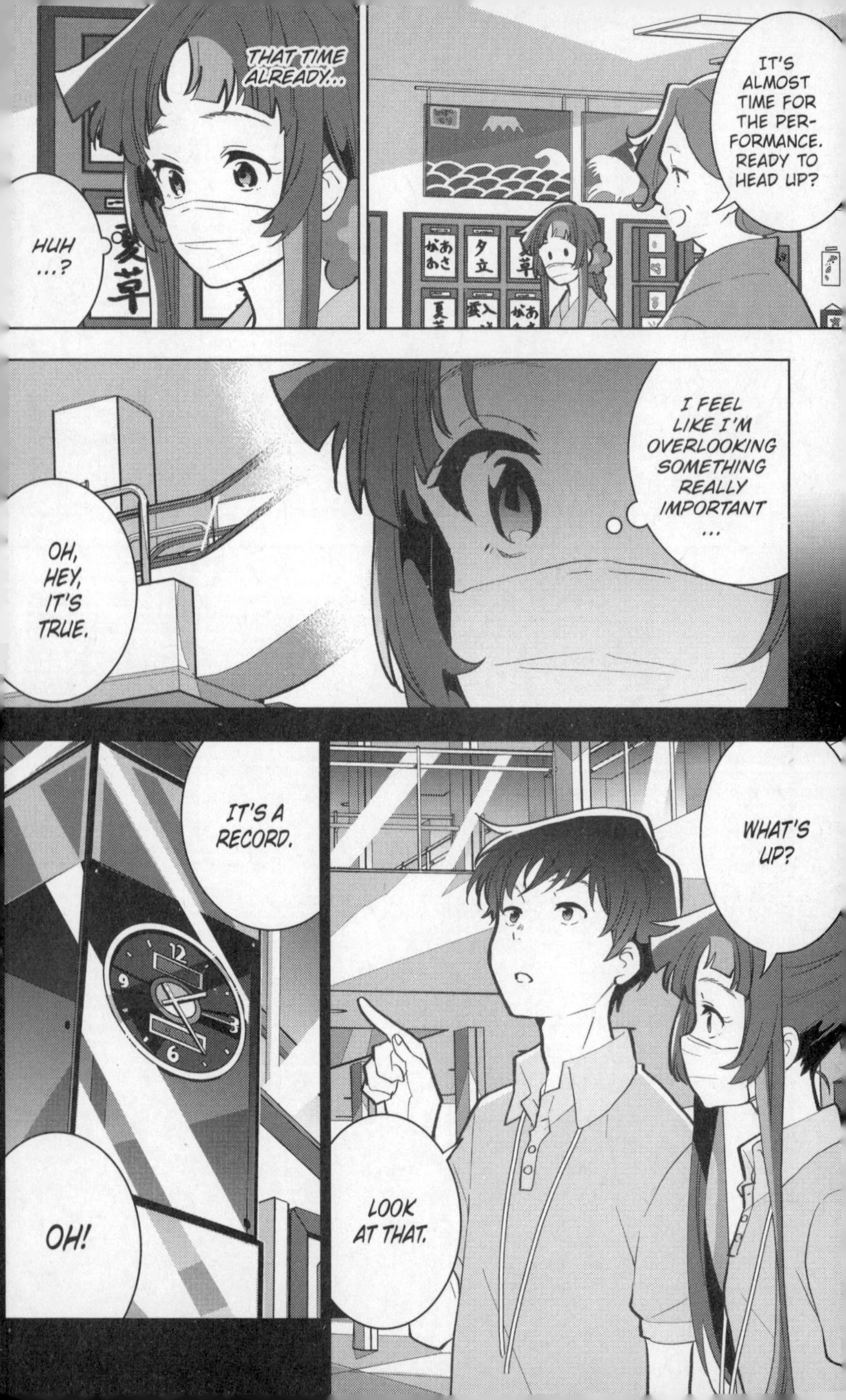
IT'S ALMOST TIME FOR THE PER-FORMANCE. READY TO HEAD UP?
THAT TIME ALREADY...
HUH ...?
I FEEL LIKE I'M OVERLOOKING SOMETHING REALLY IMPORTANT ...
OH, HEY, IT'S TRUE.
WHAT'S UP?
LOOK AT THAT.
IT'S A RECORD.
OH!

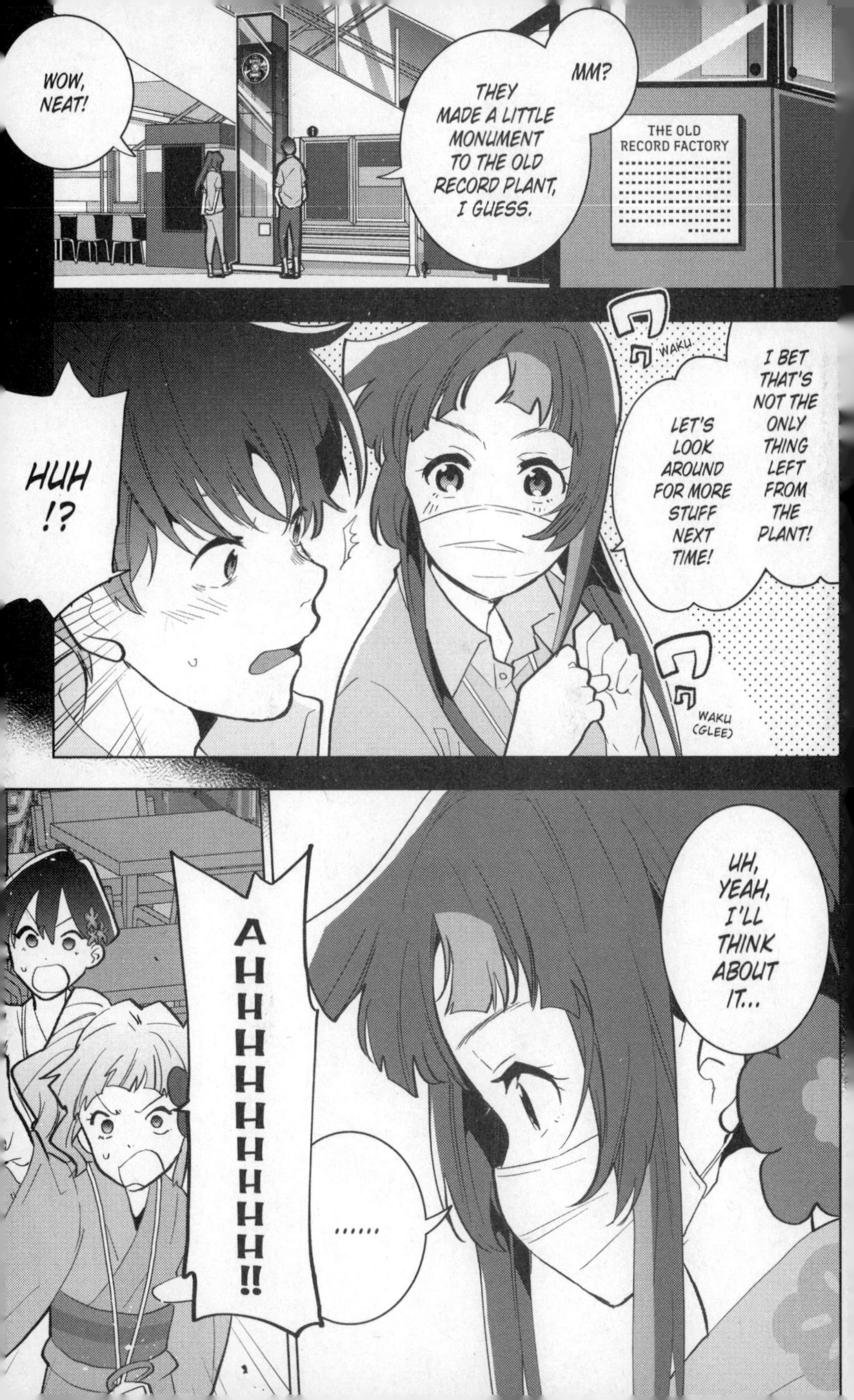
MM?
THEY MADE A LITTLE MONUMENT TO THE OLD RECORD PLANT, I GUESS.
THE OLD RECORD FACTORY
WOW, NEAT!
I BET THAT'S NOT THE ONLY THING LEFT FROM THE PLANT!
LET'S LOOK AROUND FOR MORE STUFF NEXT TIME!
WAKU
WAKU (GLEE)
HUH!?
UH, YEAH, I'LL THINK ABOUT IT...
......
AHHHHHHHHHH!!

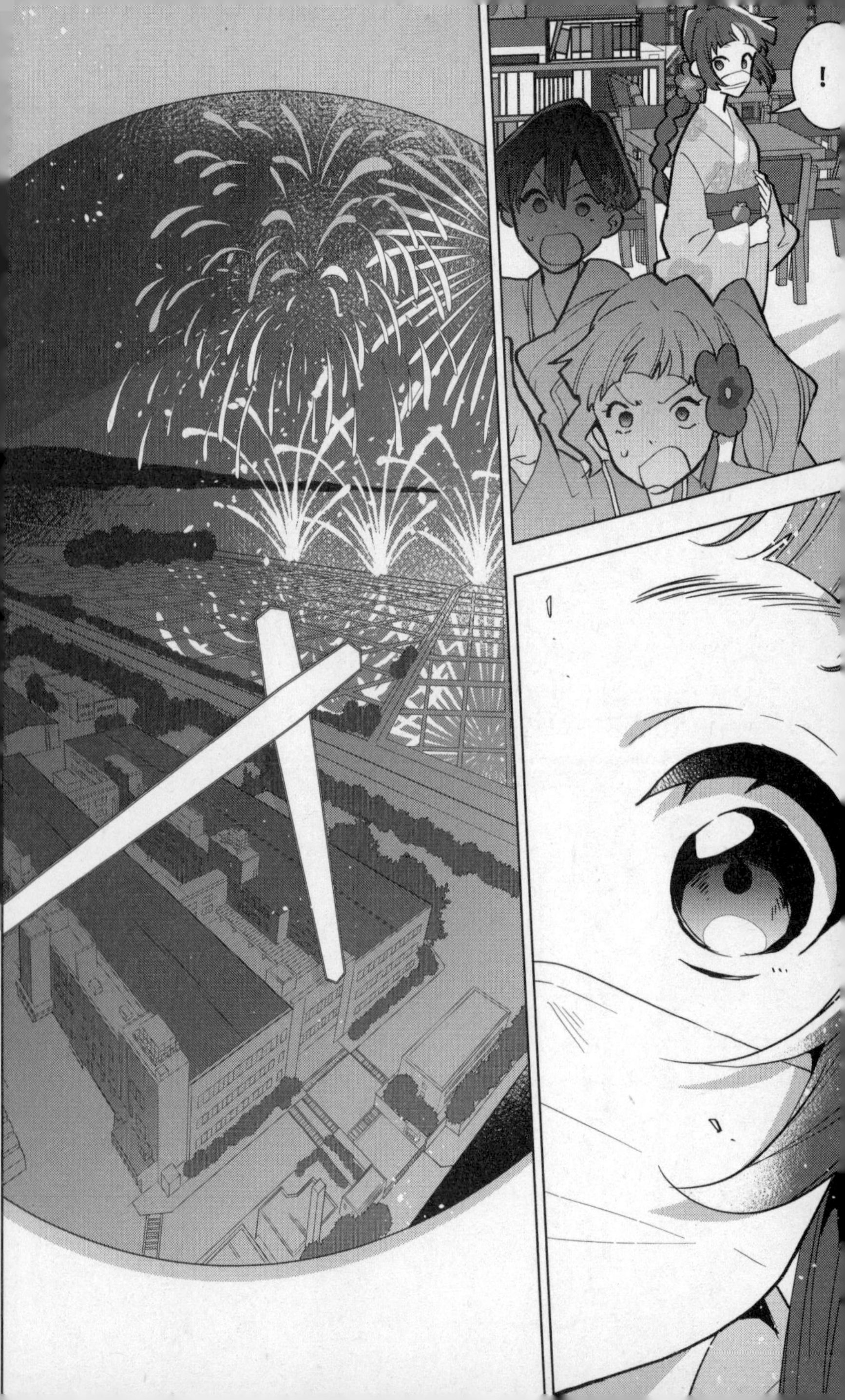
!

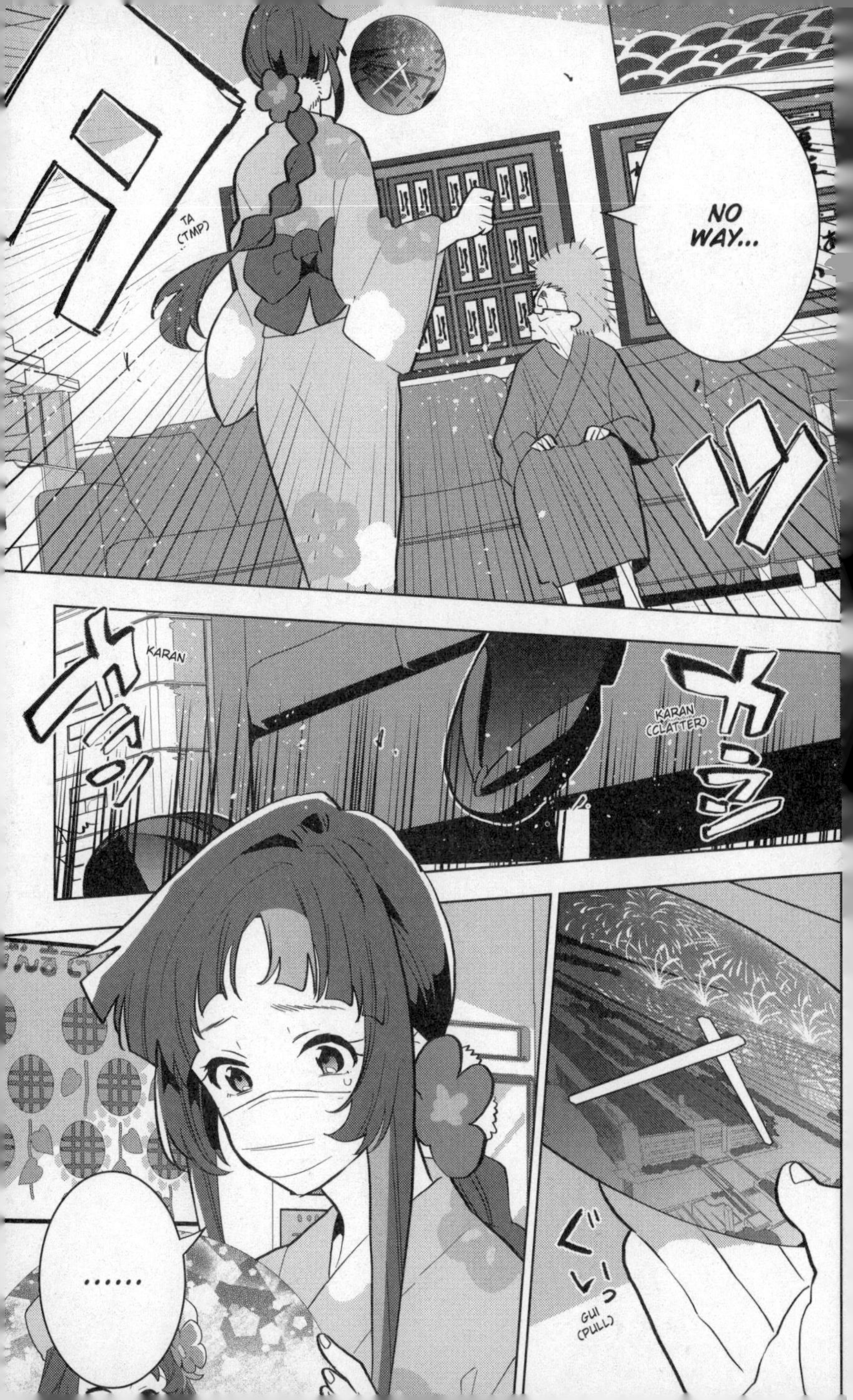
NO WAY...
TA (TMP)
KARAN (CLATTER)
KARAN
GUI (PULL)
......

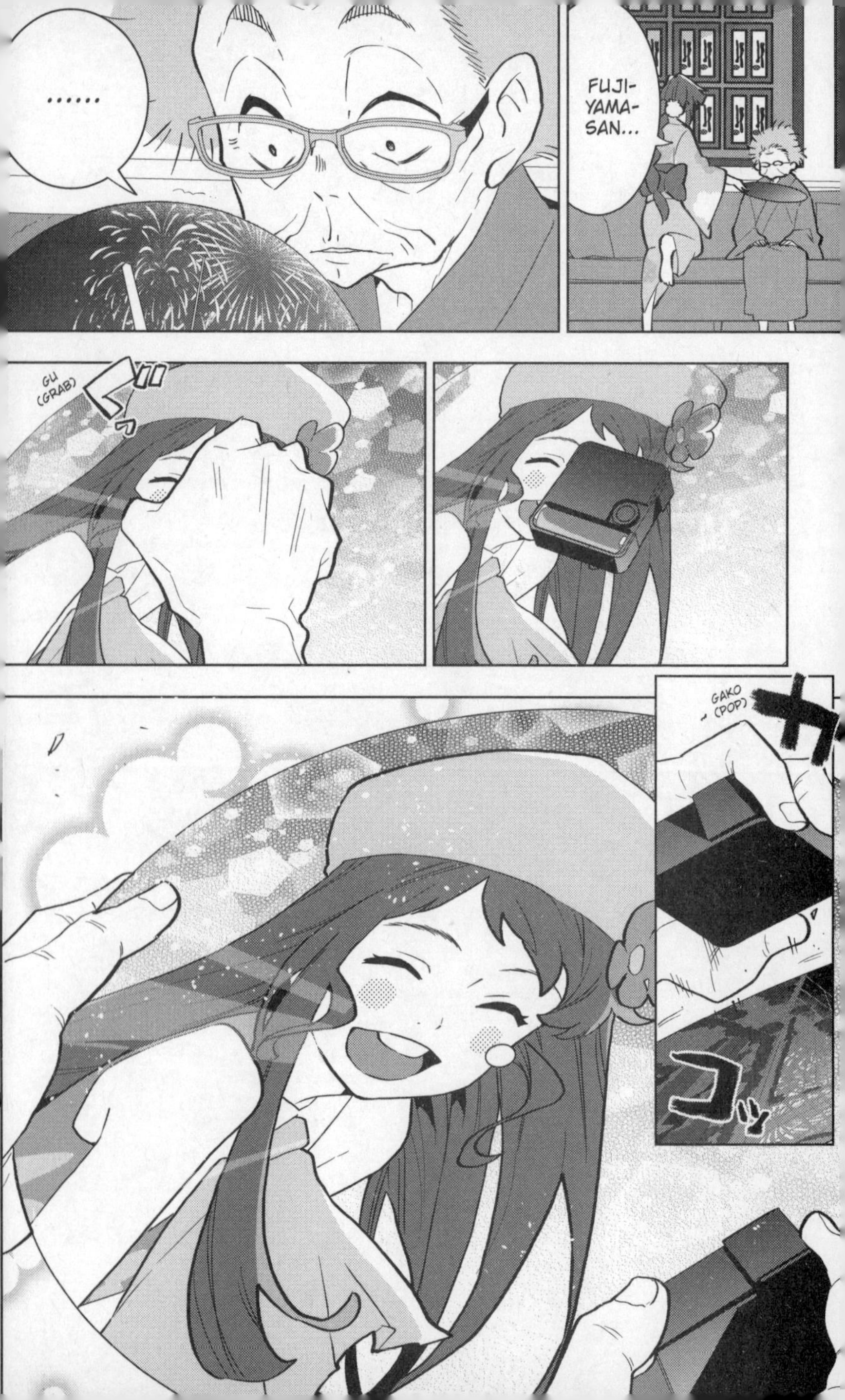
FUJI-YAMA-SAN...
......
GU (GRAB)
GAKO (POP)

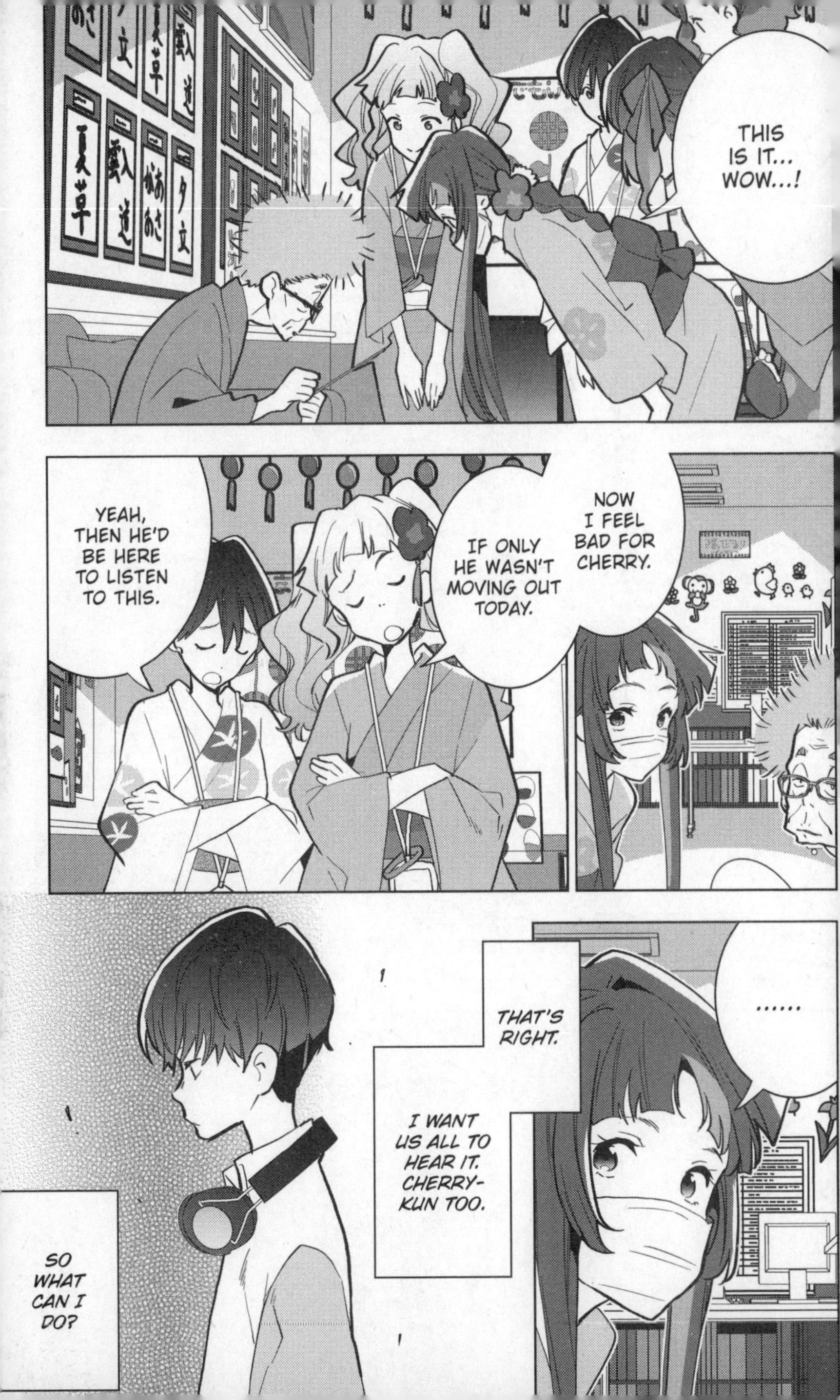
THIS IS IT... WOW...!
NOW I FEEL BAD FOR CHERRY.
IF ONLY HE WASN'T MOVING OUT TODAY.
YEAH, THEN HE'D BE HERE TO LISTEN TO THIS.
......
THAT'S RIGHT.
I WANT US ALL TO HEAR IT. CHERRY-KUN TOO.
SO WHAT CAN I DO?

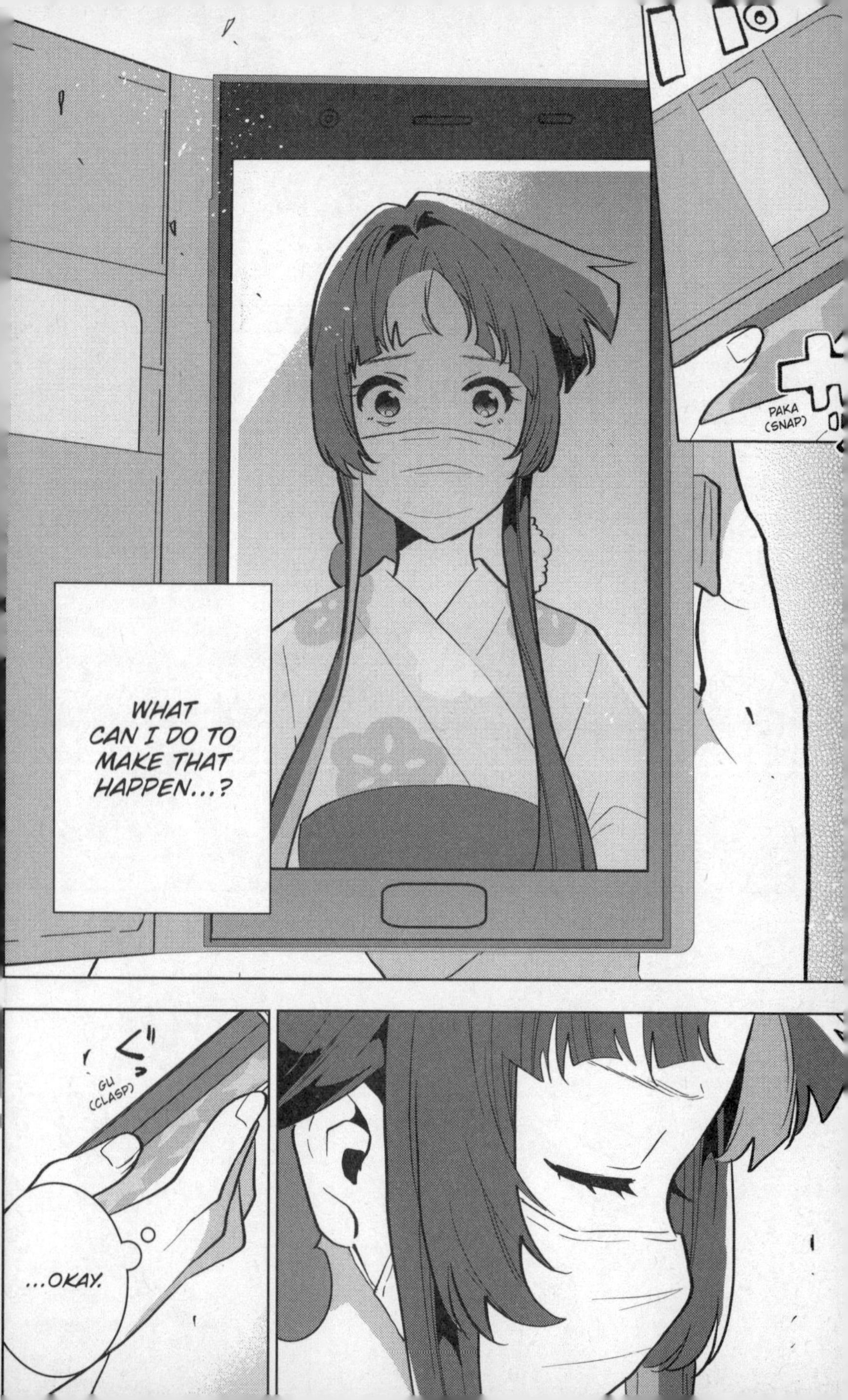
PAKA (SNAP)
WHAT CAN I DO TO MAKE THAT HAPPEN...?
GU (CLASP)
...OKAY.

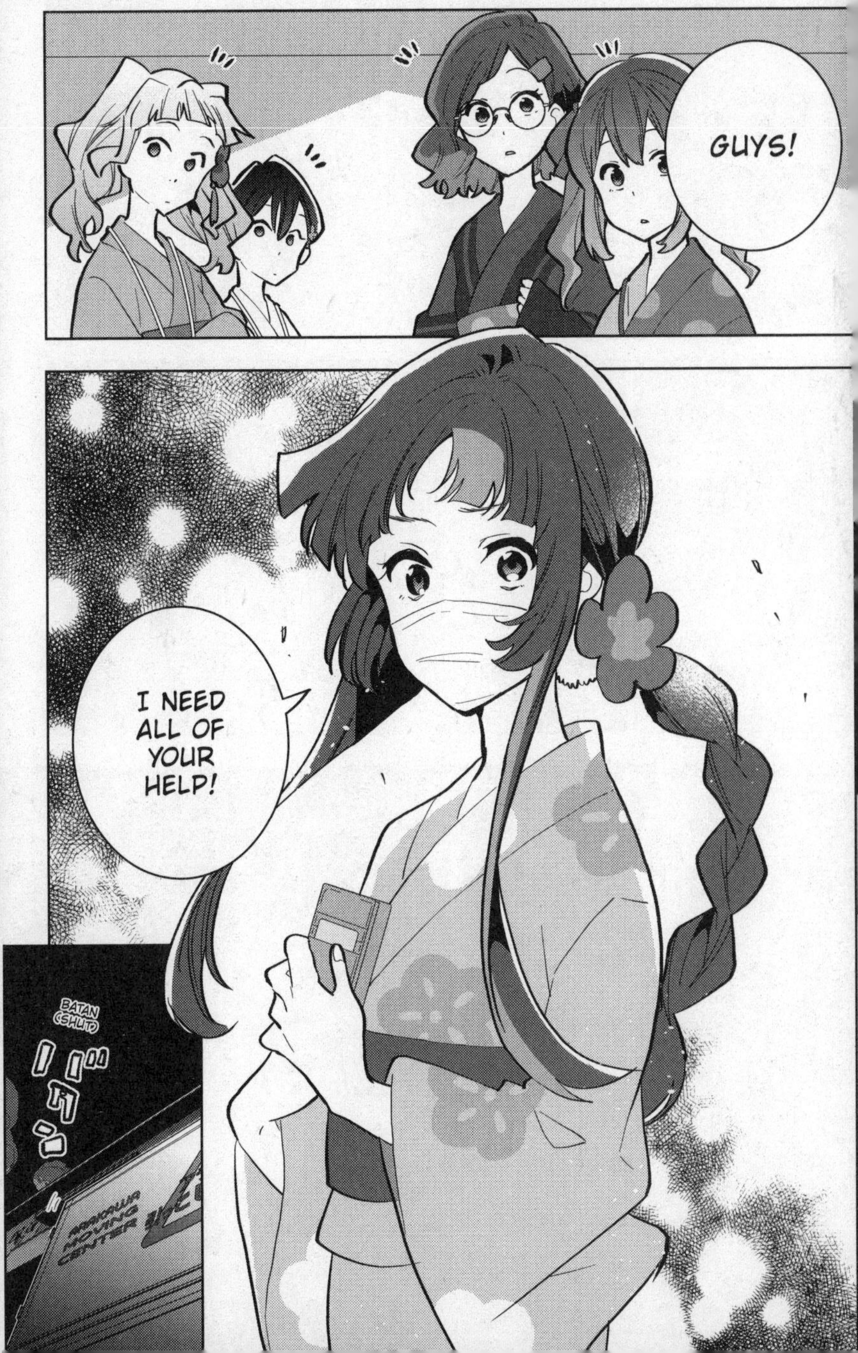
GUYS!
I NEED ALL OF YOUR HELP!
BATAN (SHUT)
MOVING CENTER

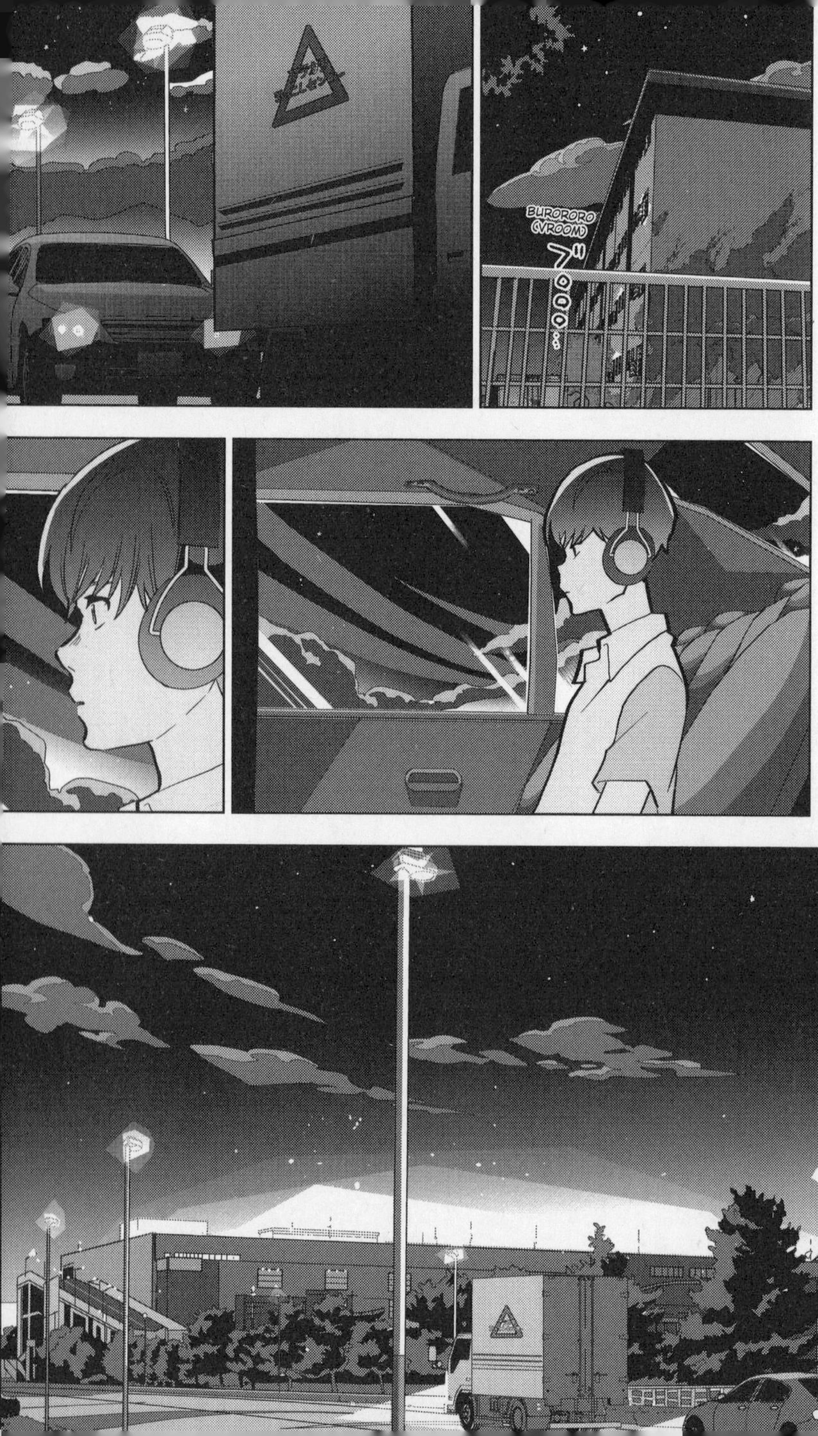
BURORORO (VROOM)
ブロロロ…

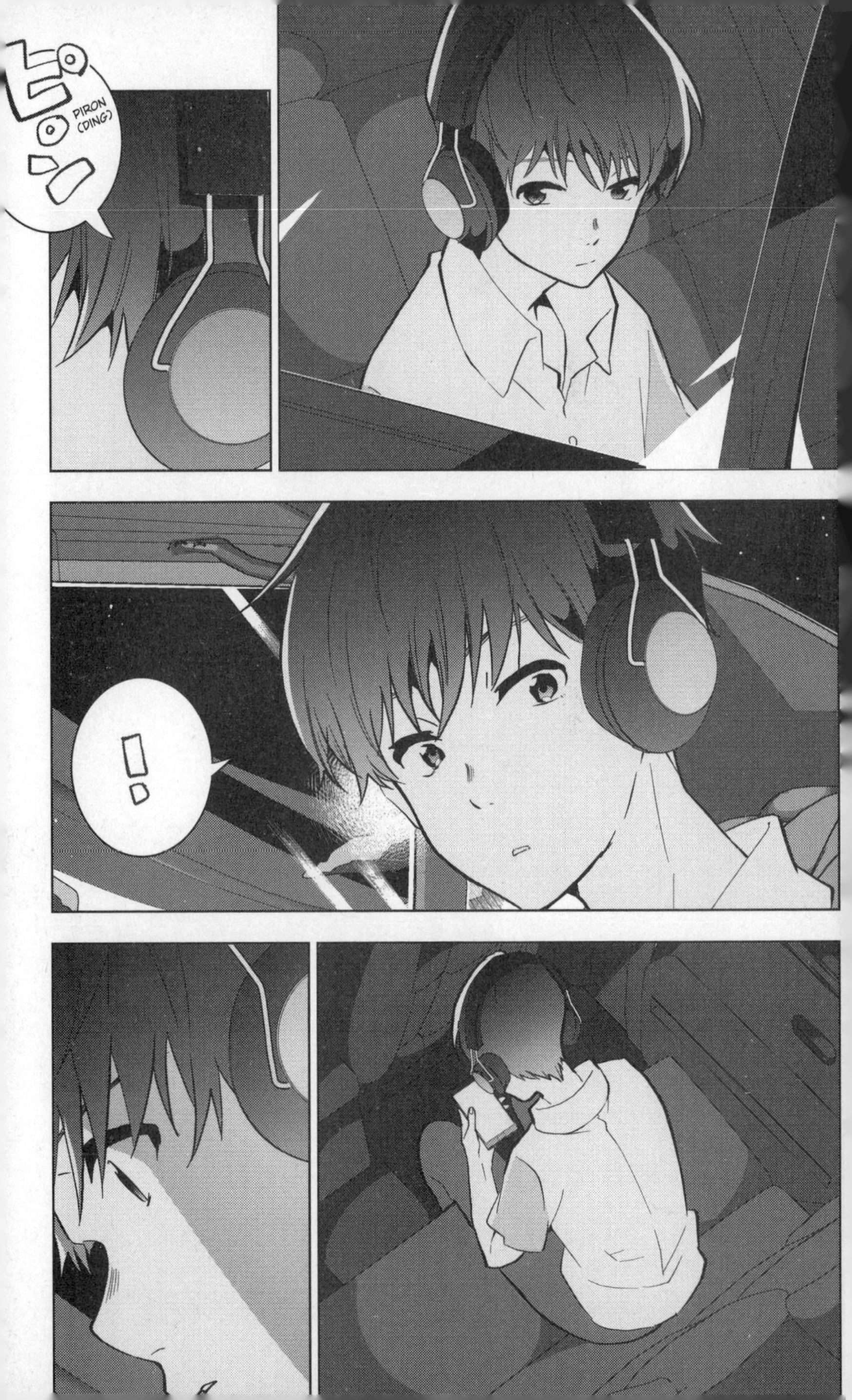
PIRON (DING)
!

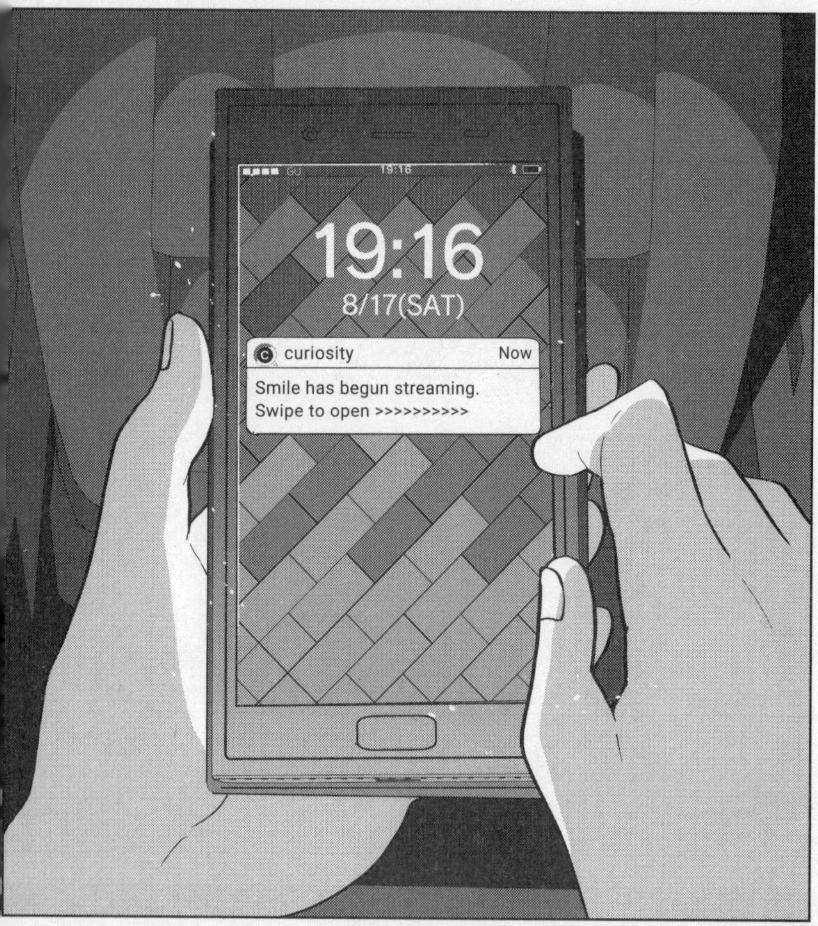
19:16
8/17(SAT)
curiosity
Now
Smile has begun streaming.
Swipe to open >>>>>>>>>>

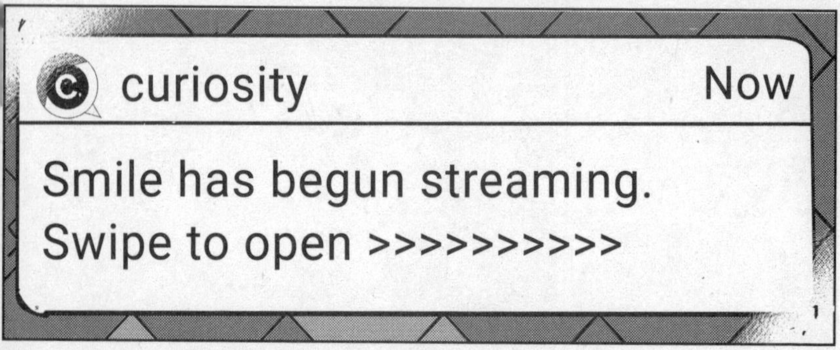
curiosity
Now
Smile has begun streaming.
Swipe to open >>>>>>>>>>>

Words Bubble Up
Like Soda Pop

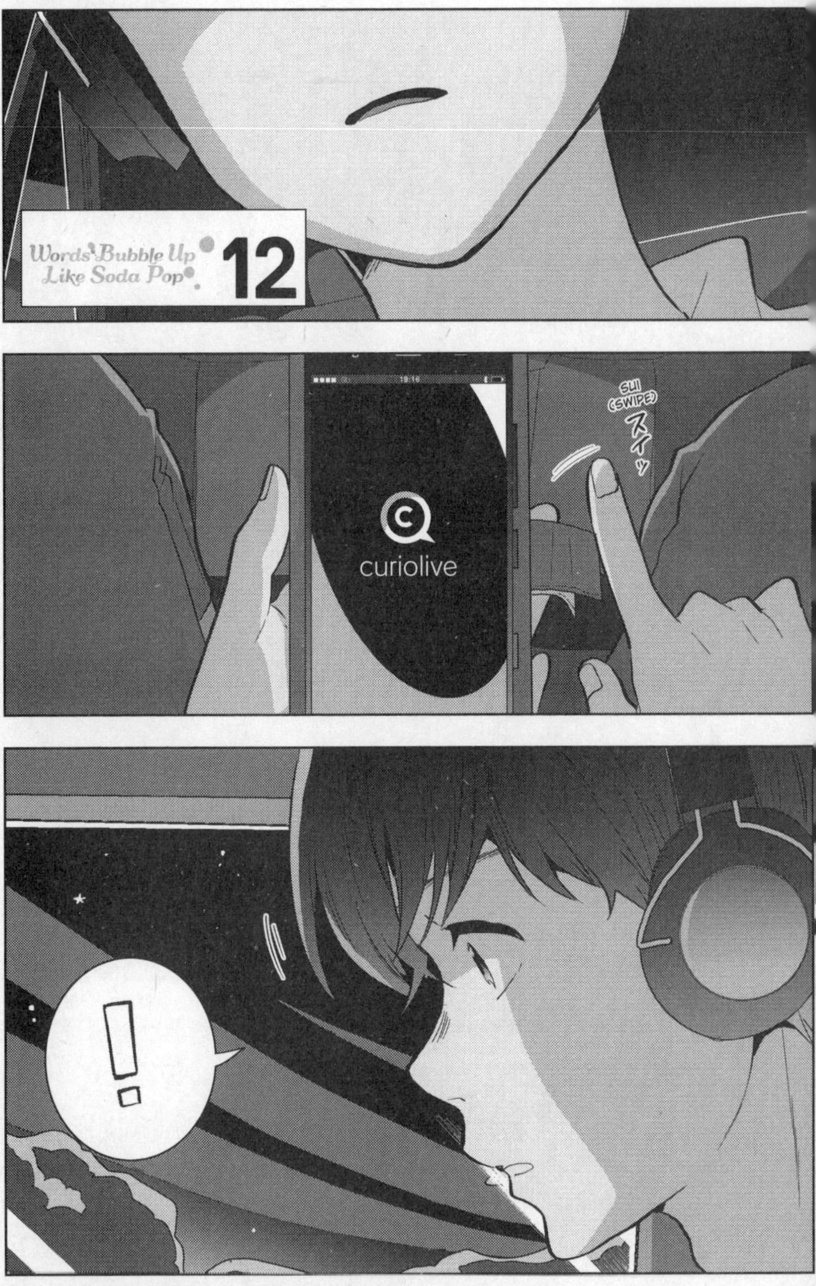
Words Bubble Up Like Soda Pop
12
19:16
curiolive
SUI (SWIPE)
スイッ
!!

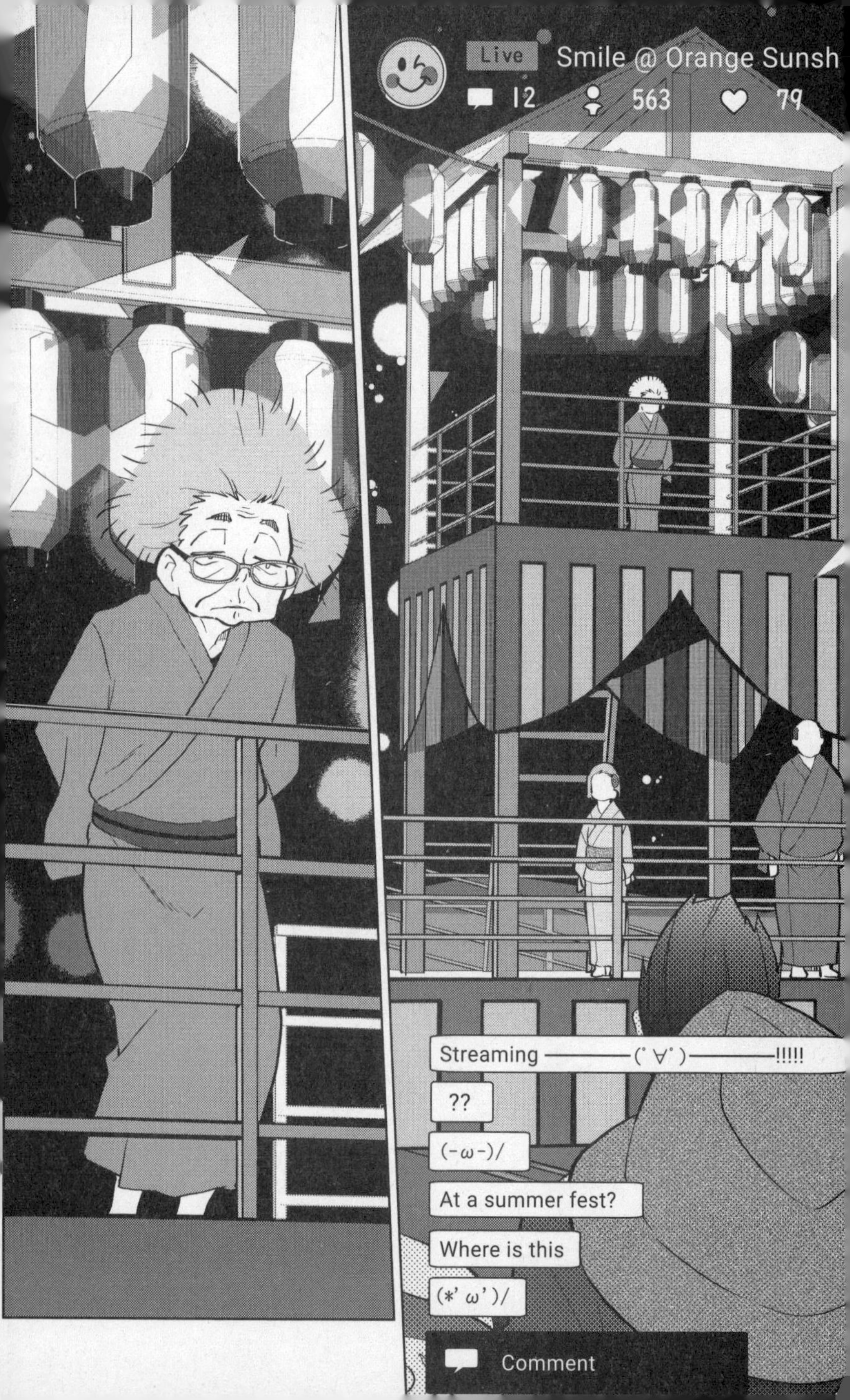
Live
Smile @ Orange Sunsh
12
563
79
Streaming ————(ﾟ∀ﾟ)————!!!!!
??
(-ω-)/
At a summer fest?
Where is this
(*'ω')/
Comment

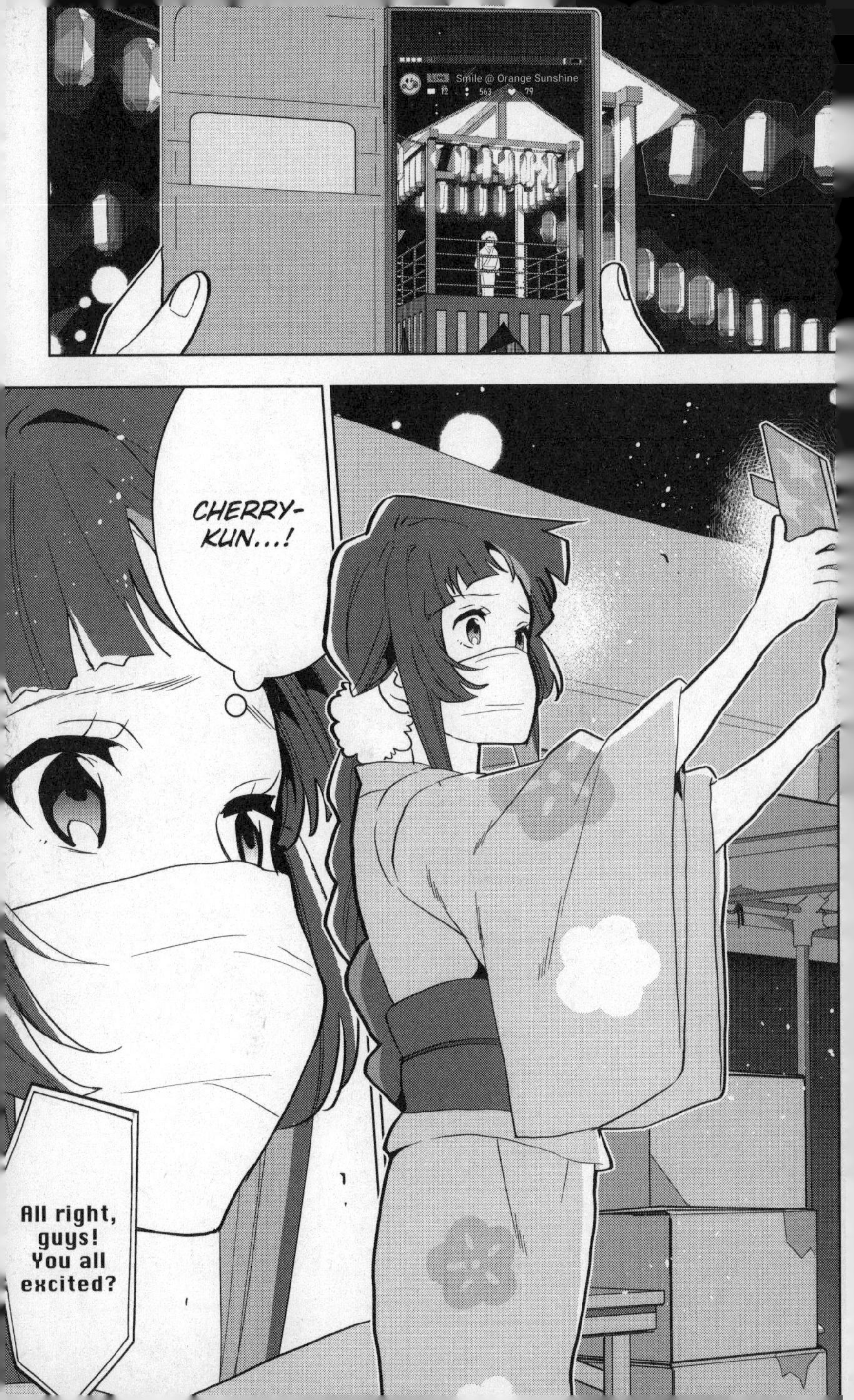
Smile @ Orange Sunshine
12 563 79
CHERRY-KUN...!
All right, guys! You all excited?

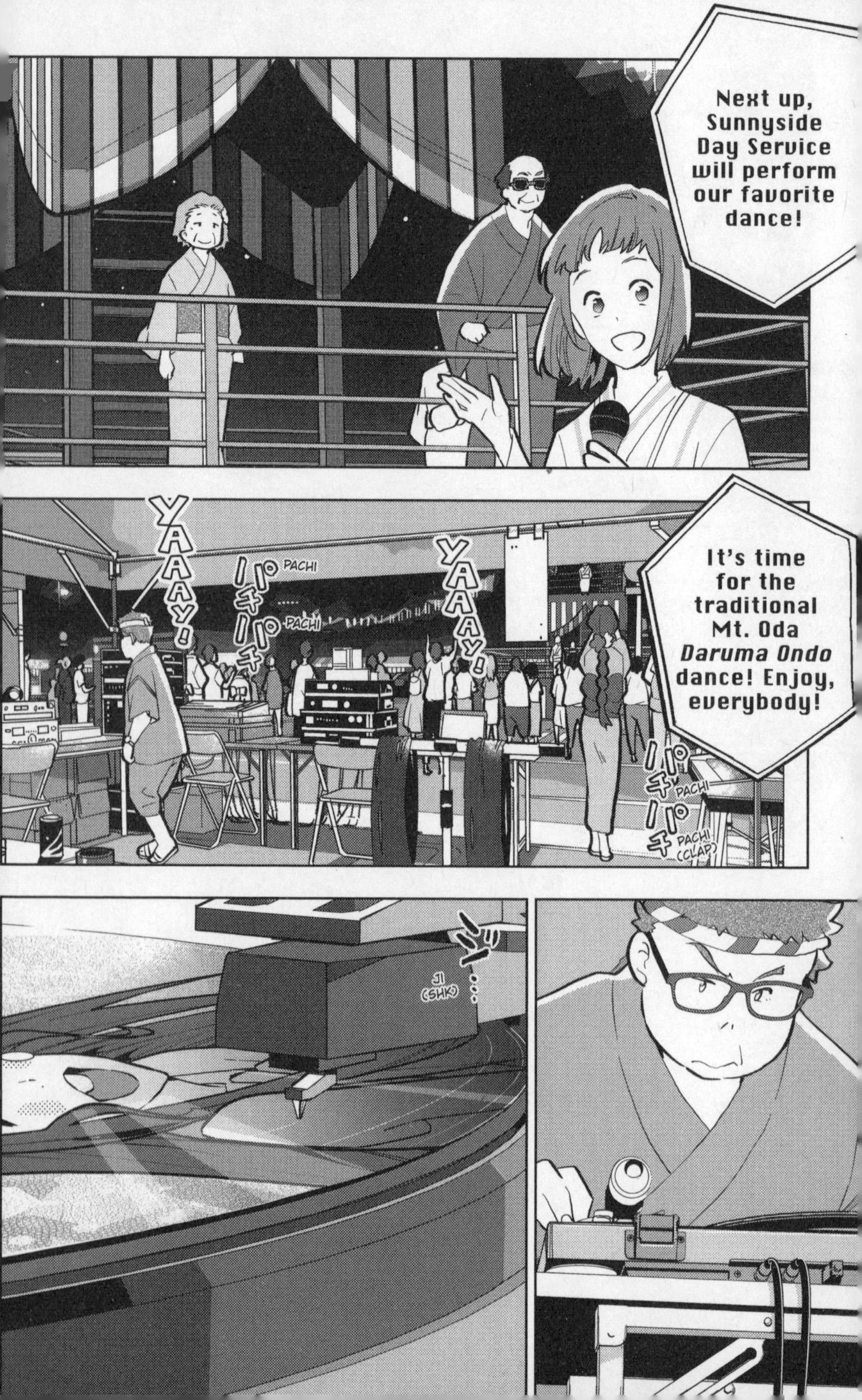

Next up, Sunnyside Day Service will perform our favorite dance!
It's time for the traditional Mt. Oda *Daruma Ondo* dance! Enjoy, everybody!
パチパチ
PACHI
PACHI (CLAP)
YAAAY!
パチパチ
PACHI
PACHI
YAAAY!
ジ…
JI (SHK)

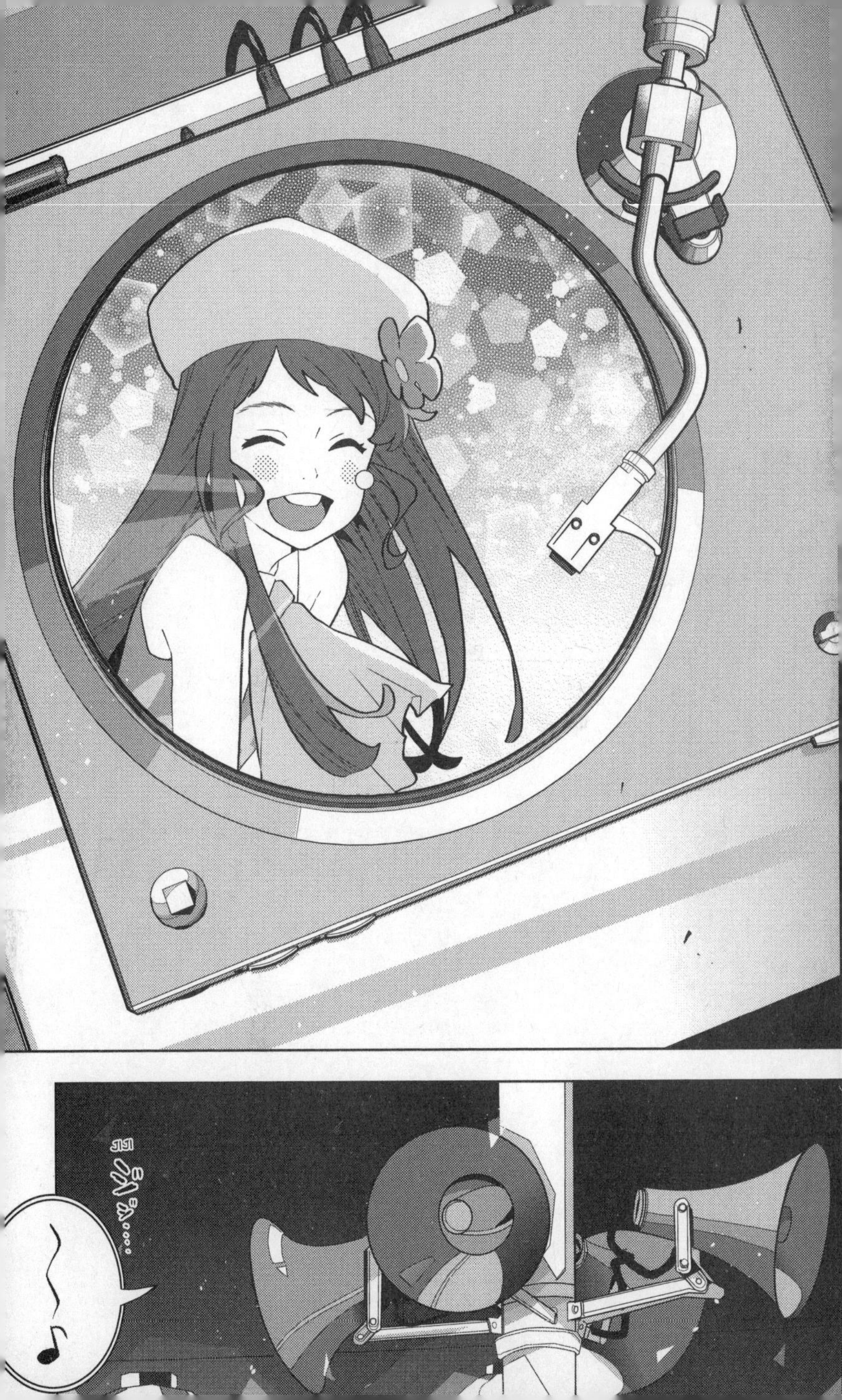
～♪

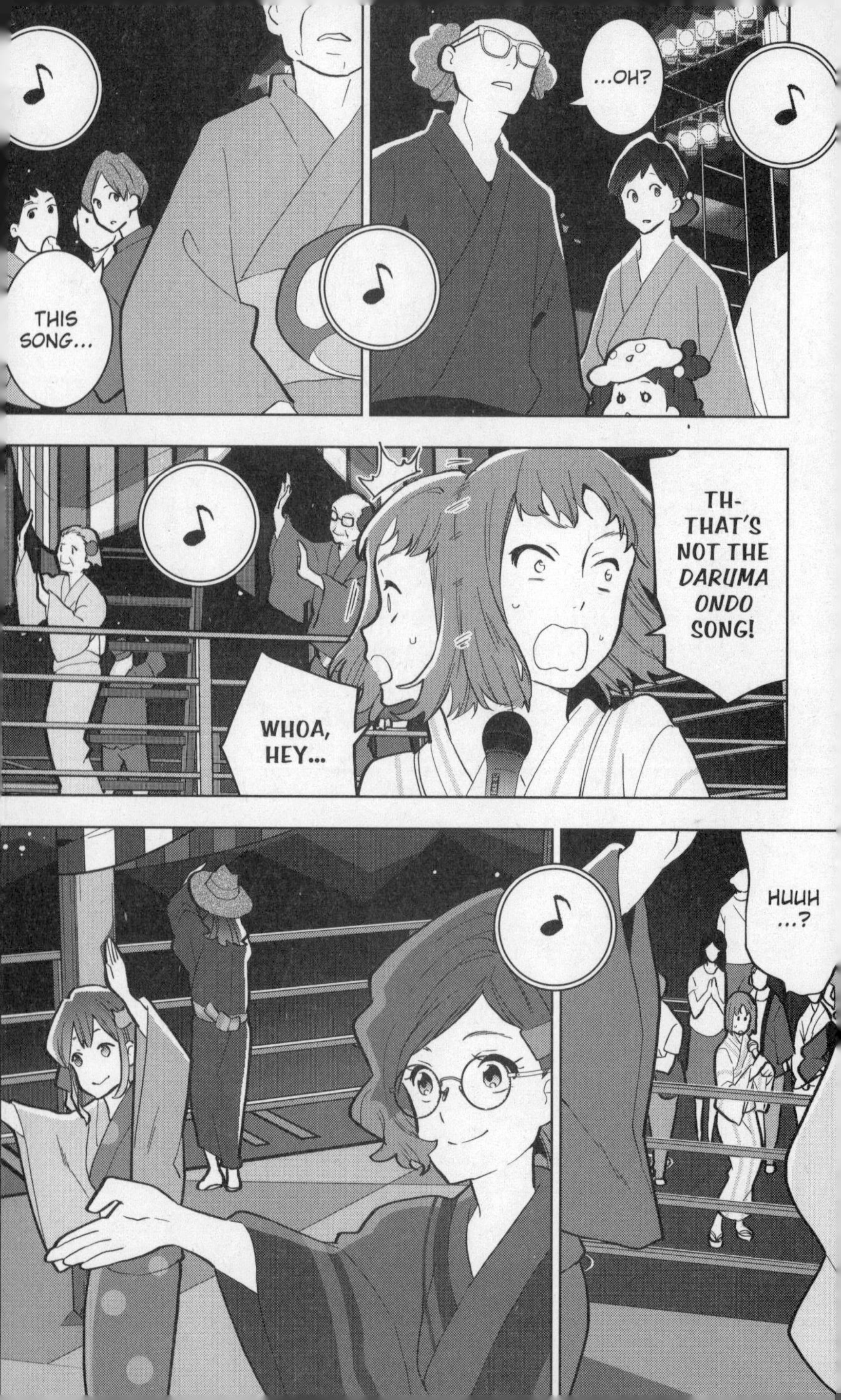
...OH?
THIS SONG...
TH- THAT'S NOT THE *DARUMA ONDO* SONG!
WHOA, HEY...
HUUH ...?

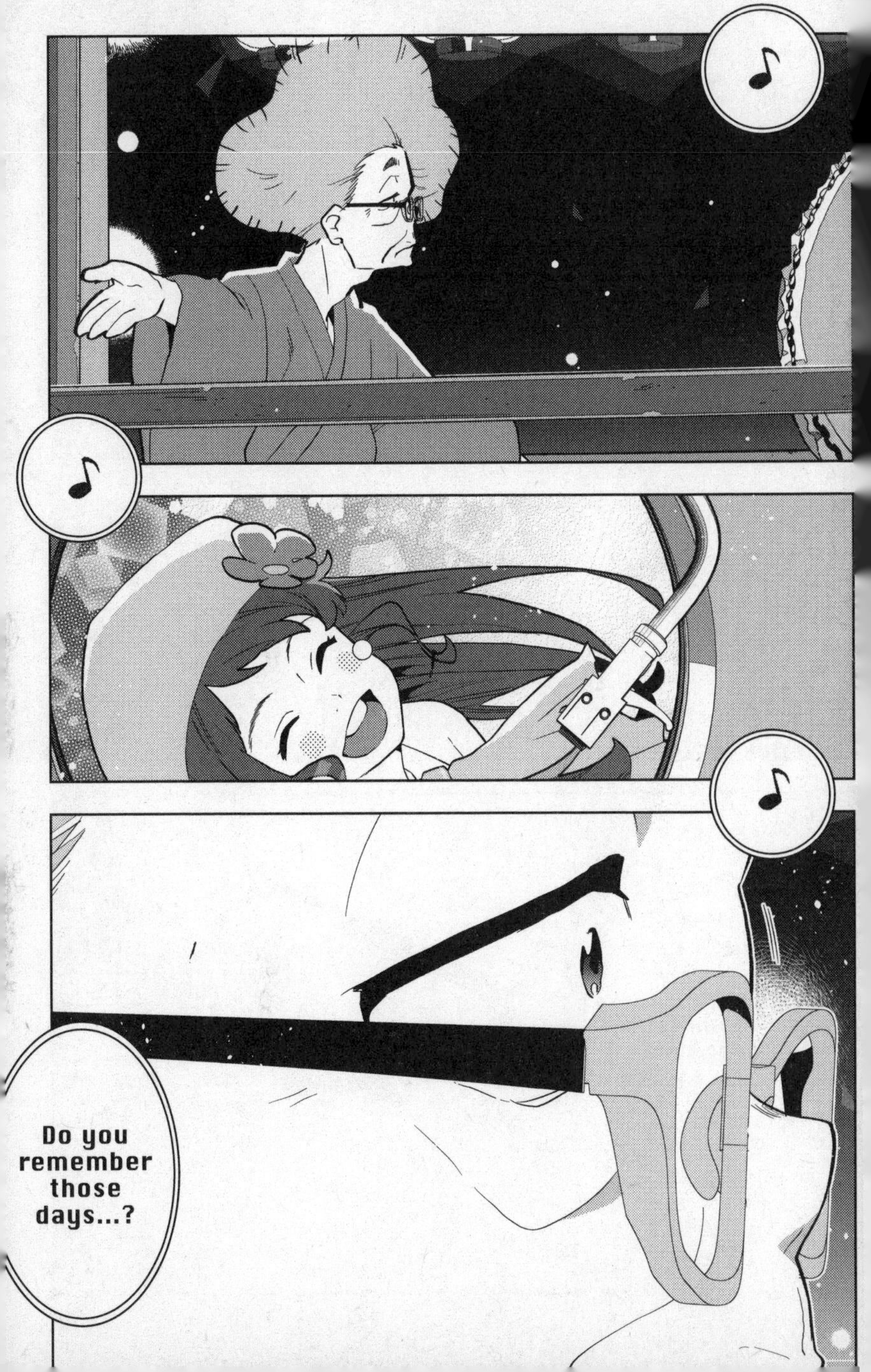
♪
♪
♪
Do you remember those days...?

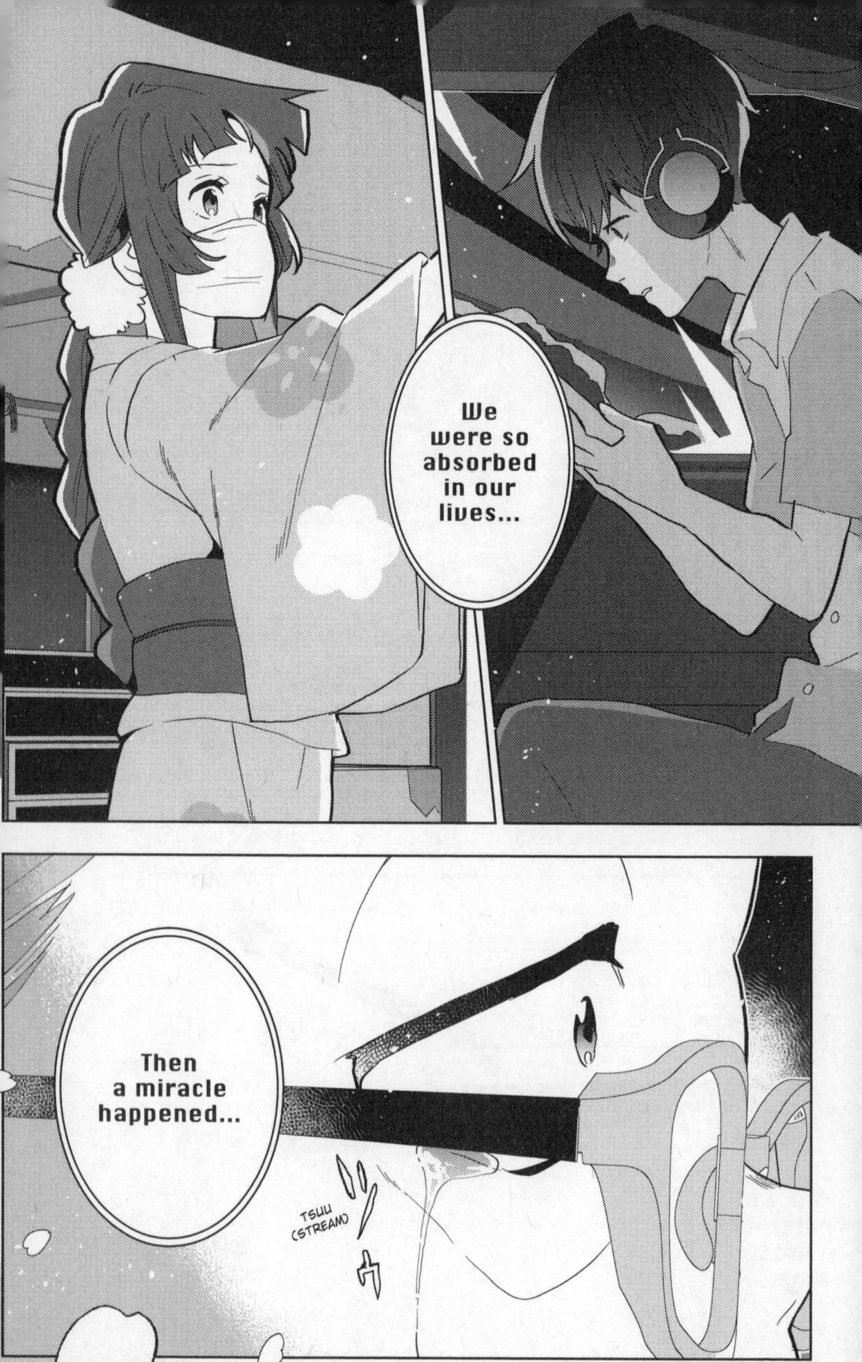
We were so absorbed in our lives...
Then a miracle happened...
TSUU (STREAM)

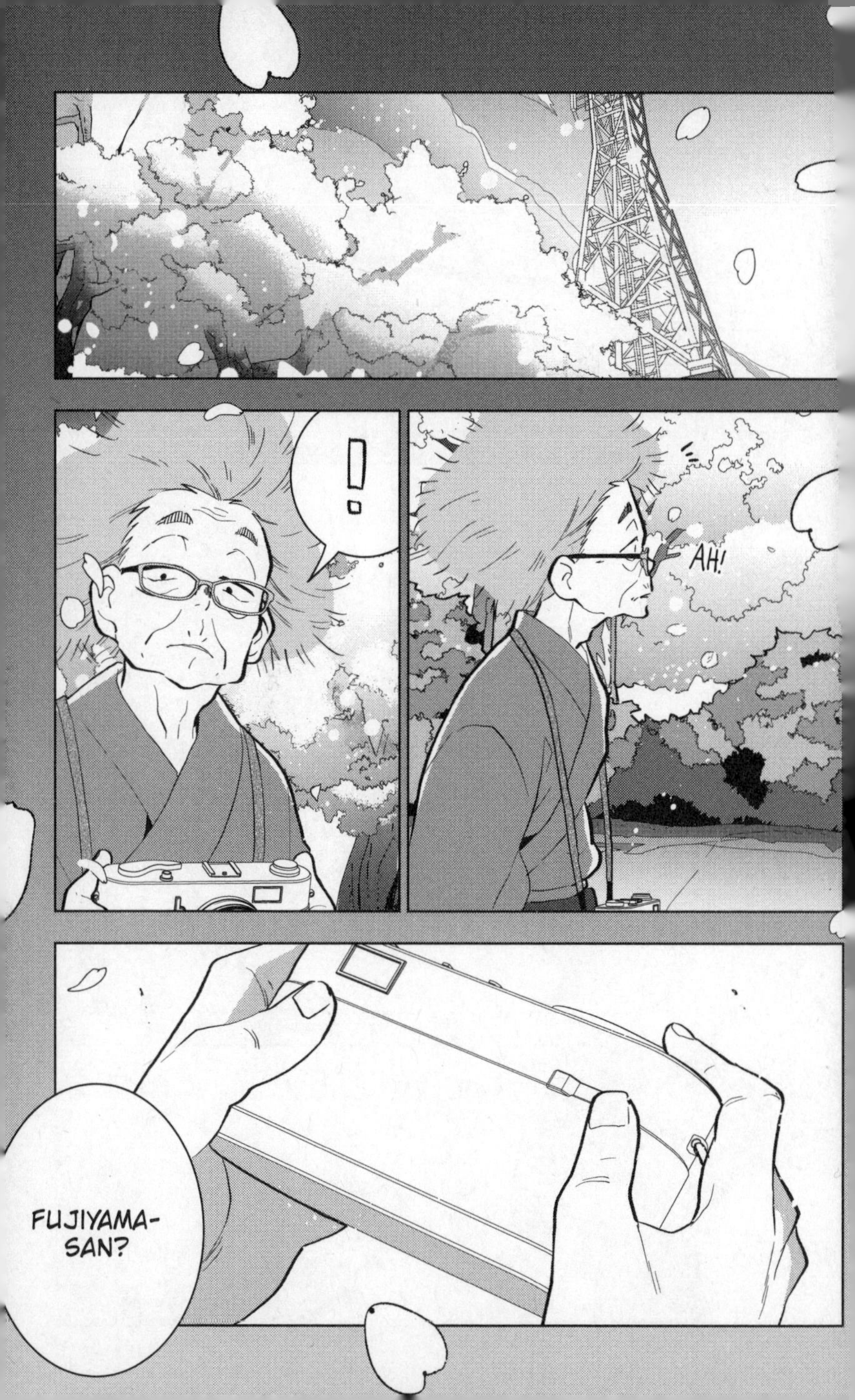
AH!
!
FUJIYAMA-SAN?

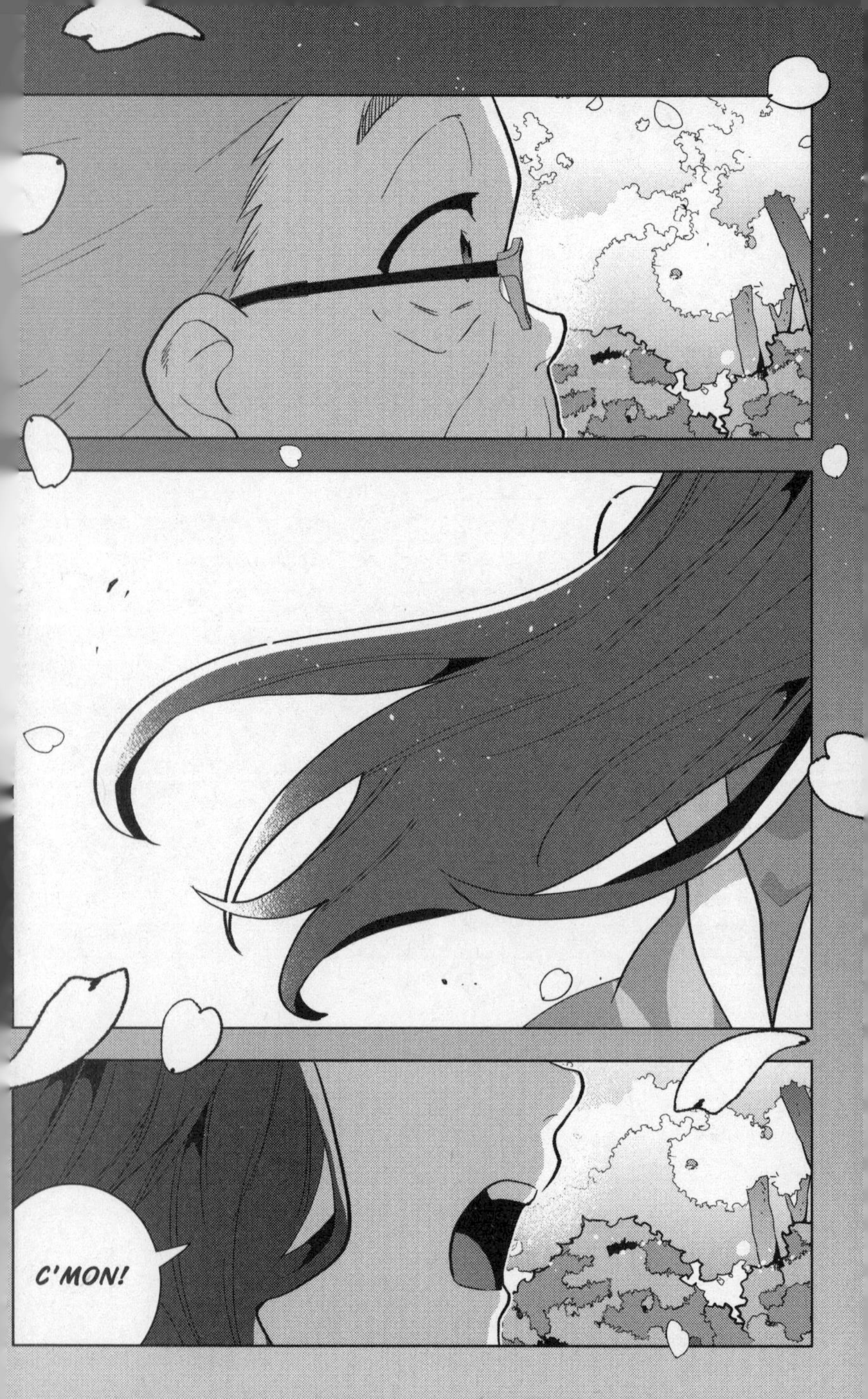
C'MON!

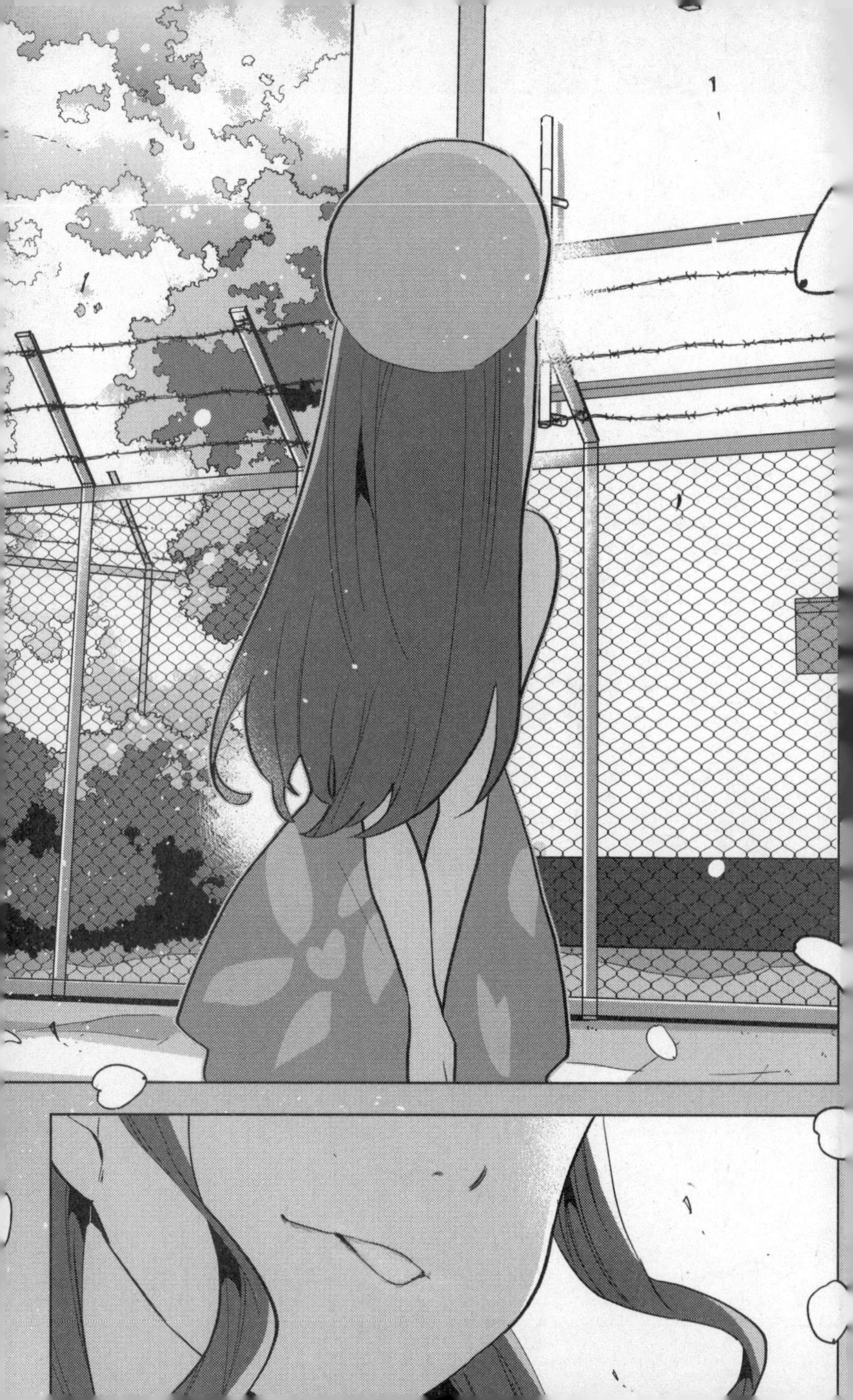

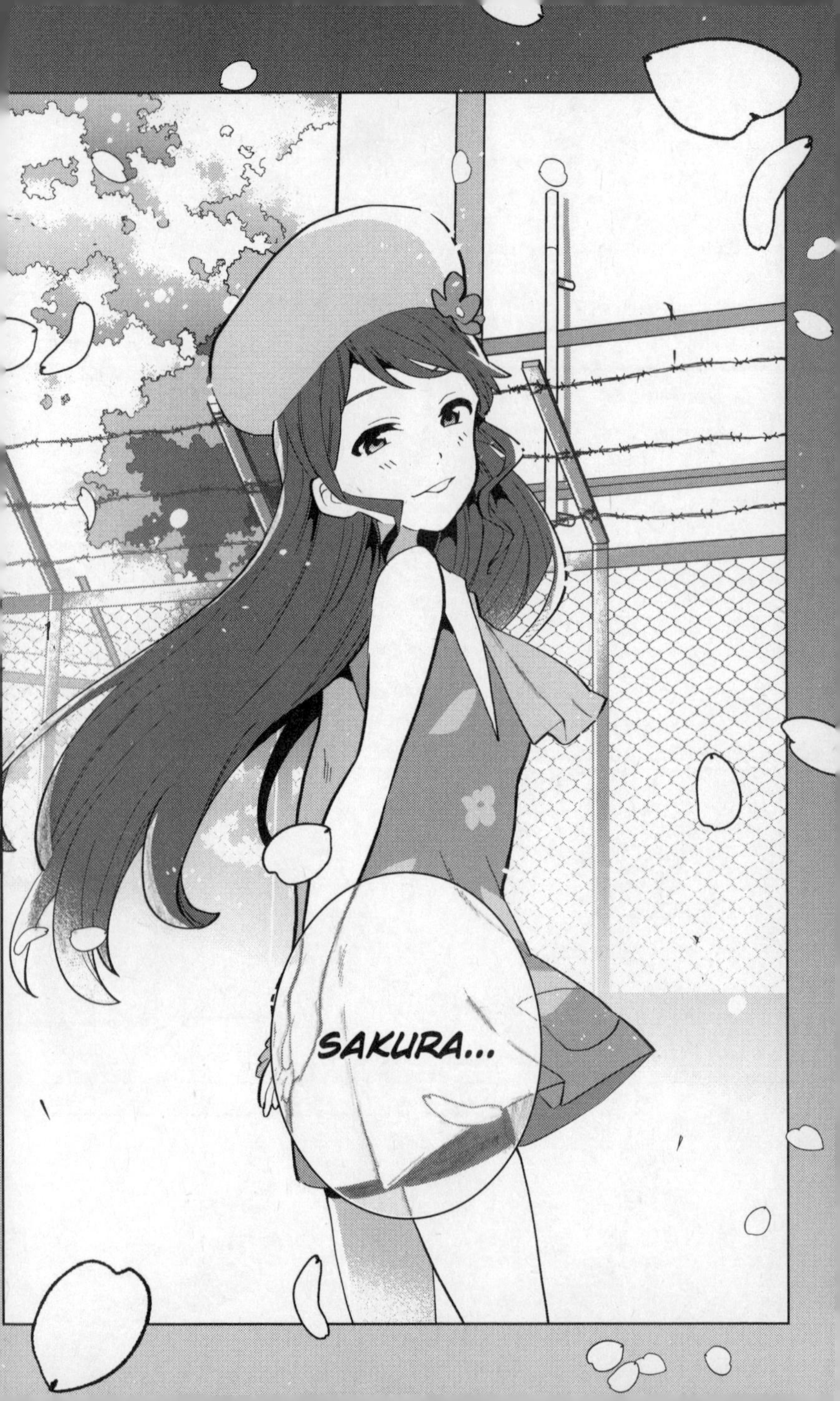
SAKURA...

Words Bubble Up
Like Soda Pop

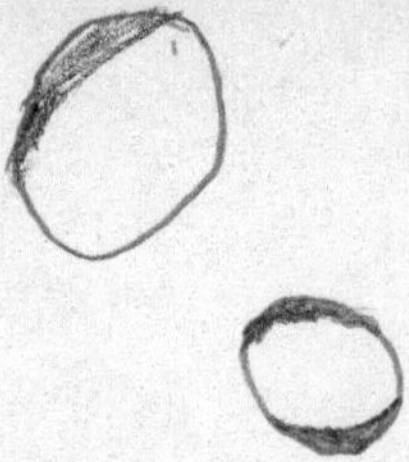

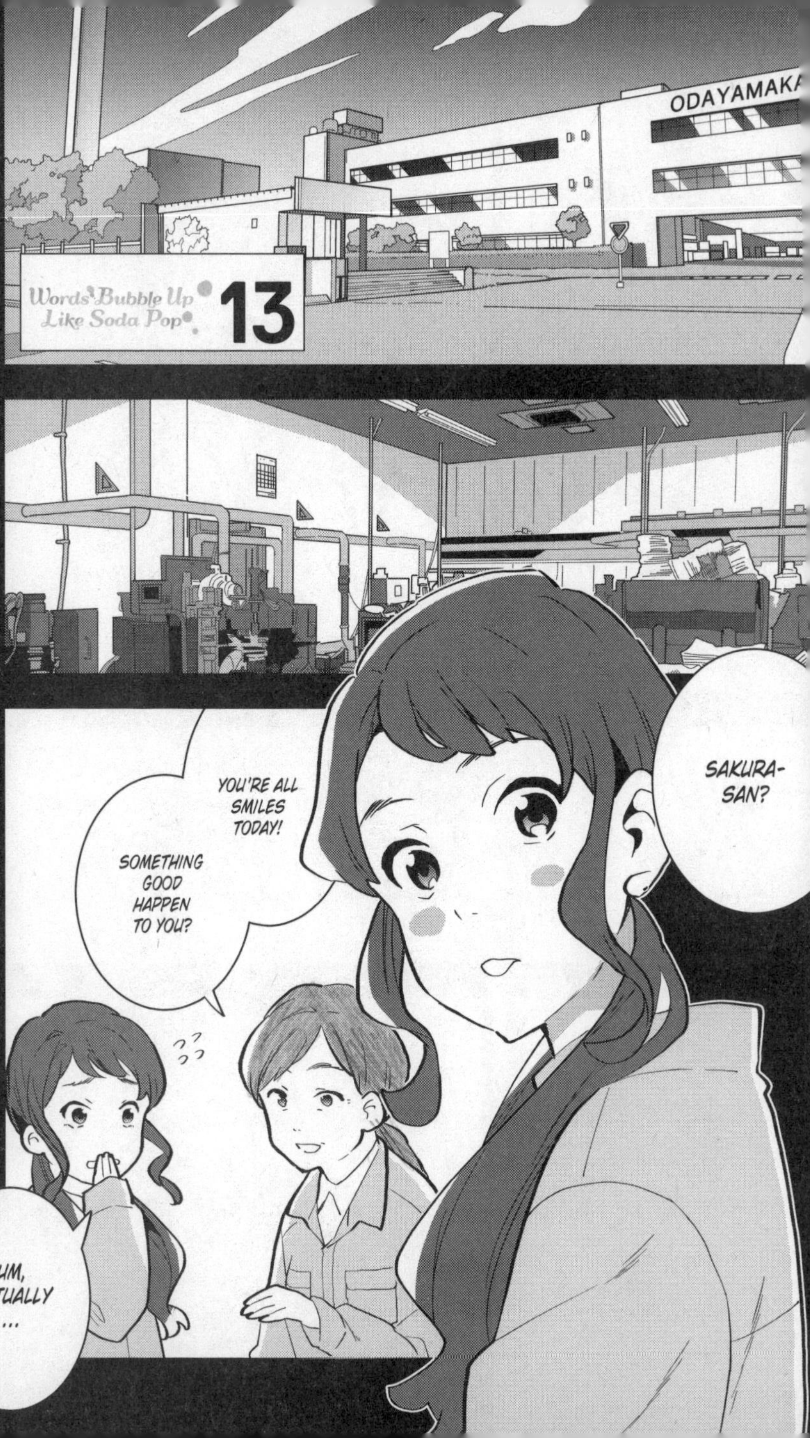
ODAYAMAKA
Words Bubble Up Like Soda Pop
13
SAKURA-SAN?
YOU'RE ALL SMILES TODAY!
SOMETHING GOOD HAPPEN TO YOU?
UM, ACTUALLY ...

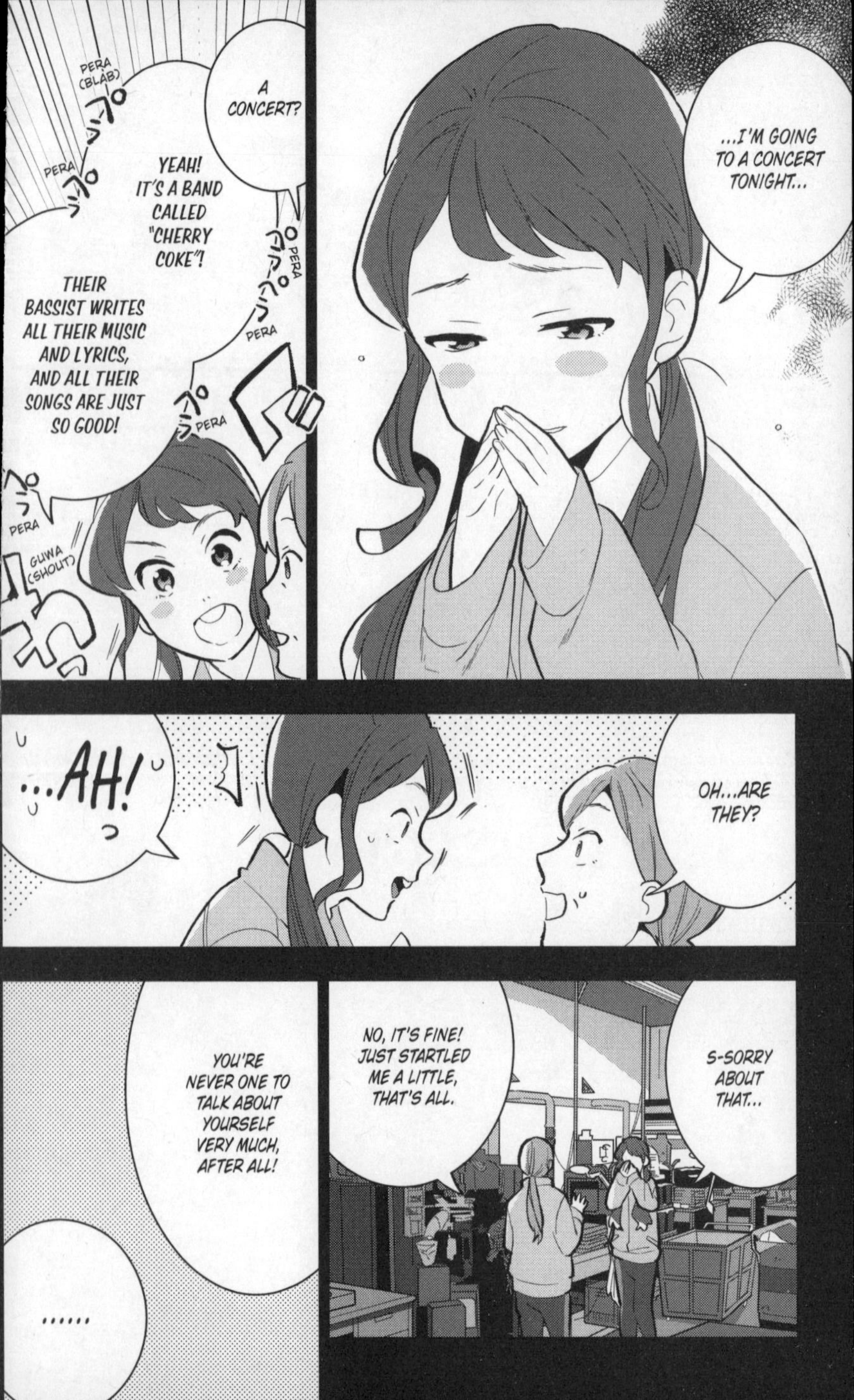
...I'M GOING TO A CONCERT TONIGHT...
A CONCERT?
PERA (BLAB)
PERA
YEAH! IT'S A BAND CALLED "CHERRY COKE"!
PERA
PERA
THEIR BASSIST WRITES ALL THEIR MUSIC AND LYRICS, AND ALL THEIR SONGS ARE JUST SO GOOD!
PERA
PERA
GUWA (SHOUT)
OH...ARE THEY?
...AH!
S-SORRY ABOUT THAT...
NO, IT'S FINE! JUST STARTLED ME A LITTLE, THAT'S ALL.
YOU'RE NEVER ONE TO TALK ABOUT YOURSELF VERY MUCH, AFTER ALL!
......

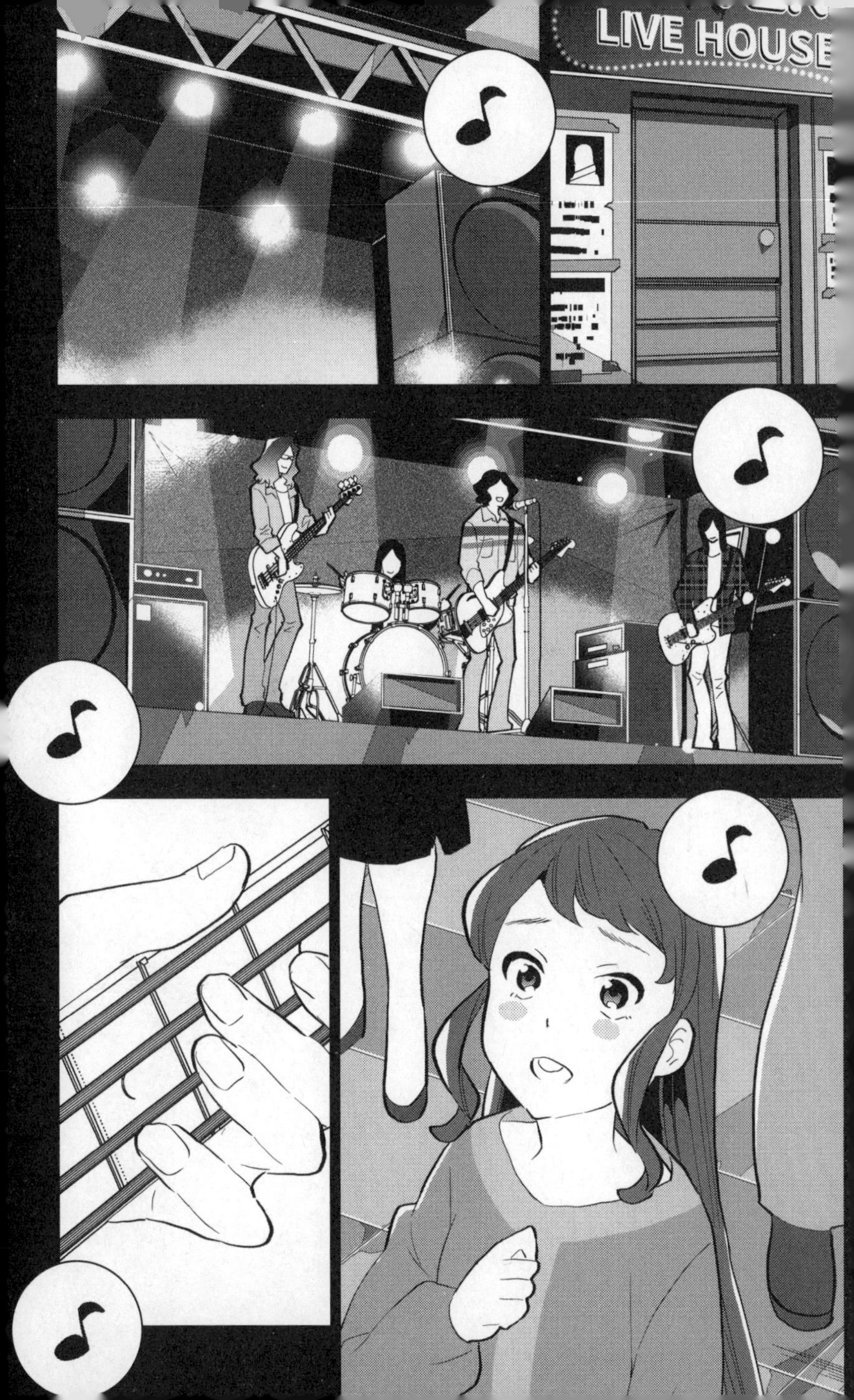
LIVE HOUSE

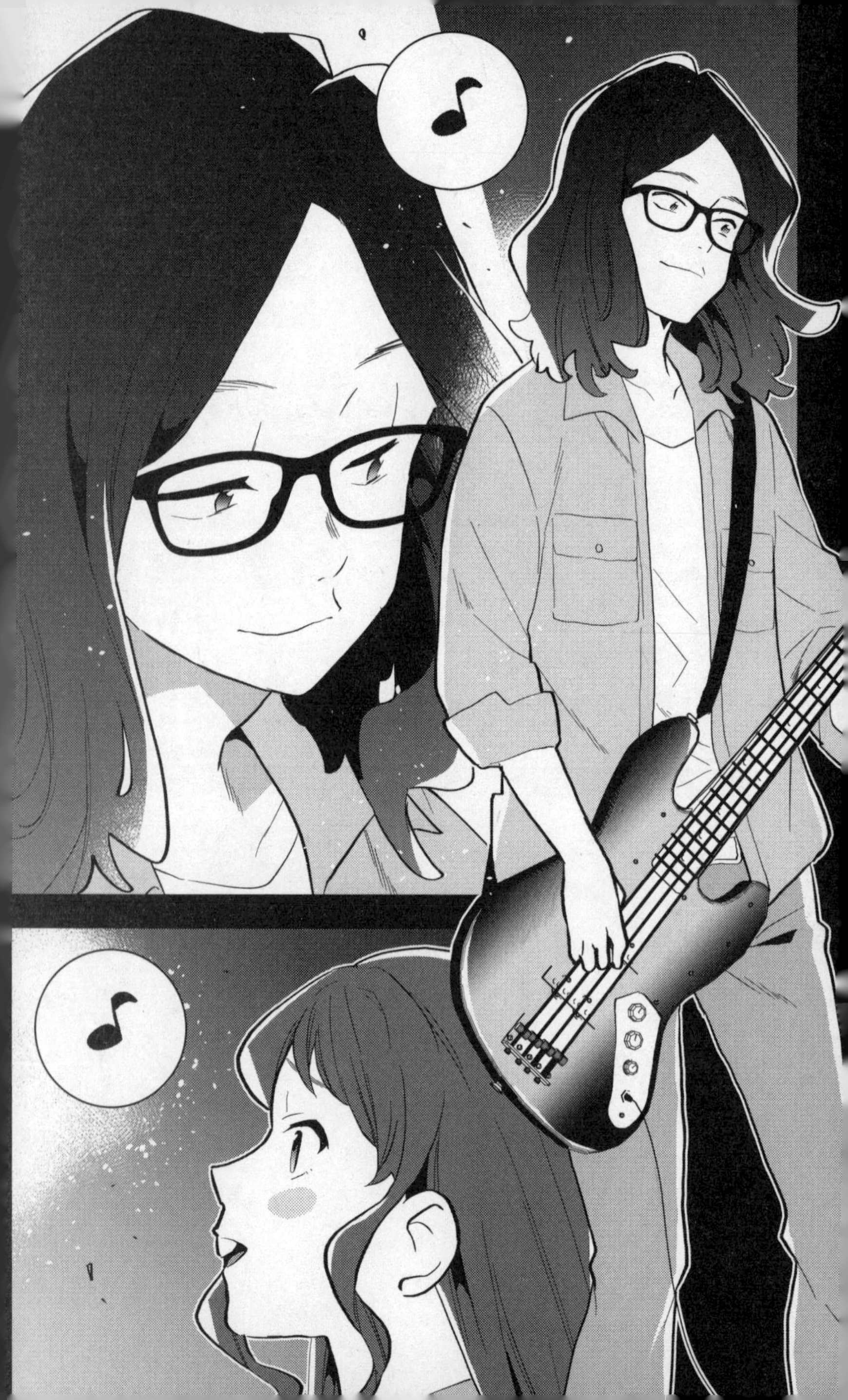

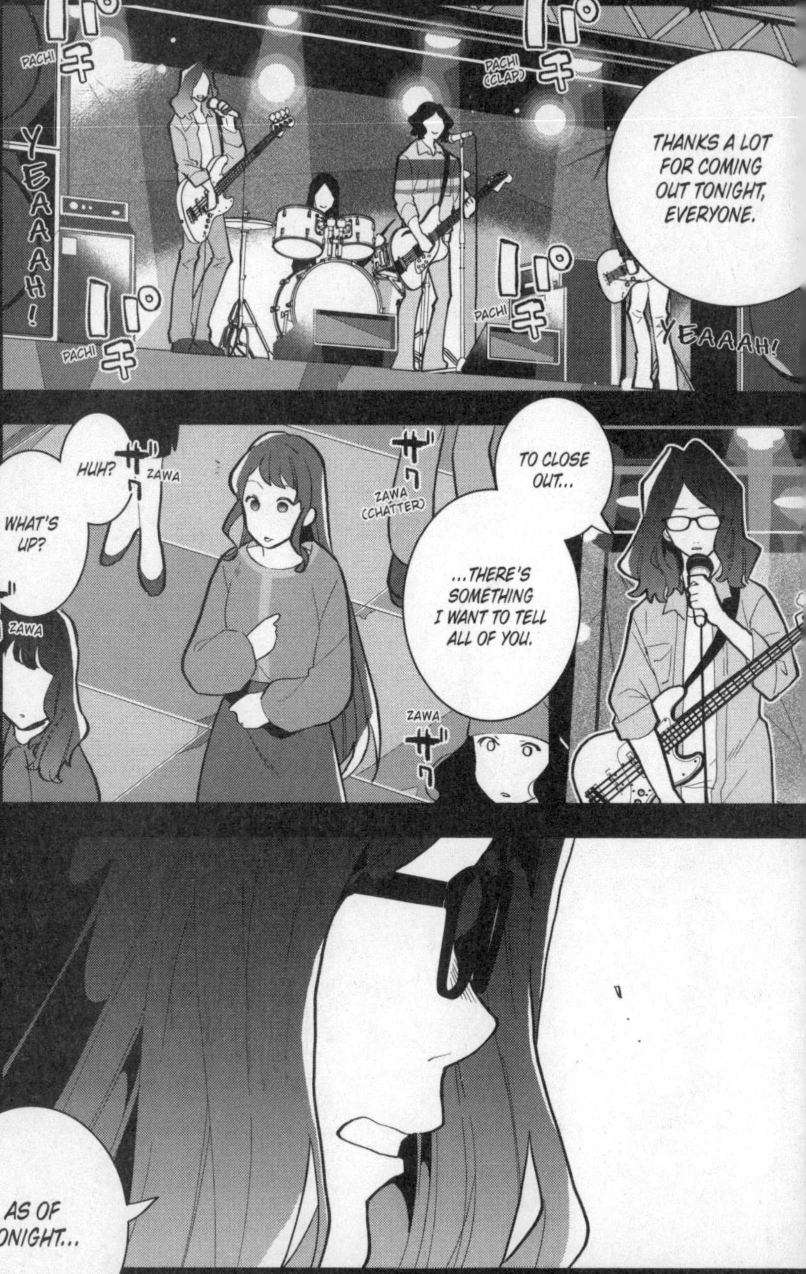
THANKS A LOT FOR COMING OUT TONIGHT, EVERYONE.
PACHI (CLAP)
PACHI
YEAAAAH!
PACHI
YEAAAH!
PACHI
TO CLOSE OUT...
...THERE'S SOMETHING I WANT TO TELL ALL OF YOU.
ZAWA (CHATTER)
ZAWA
HUH?
ZAWA
WHAT'S UP?
ZAWA
AS OF TONIGHT...

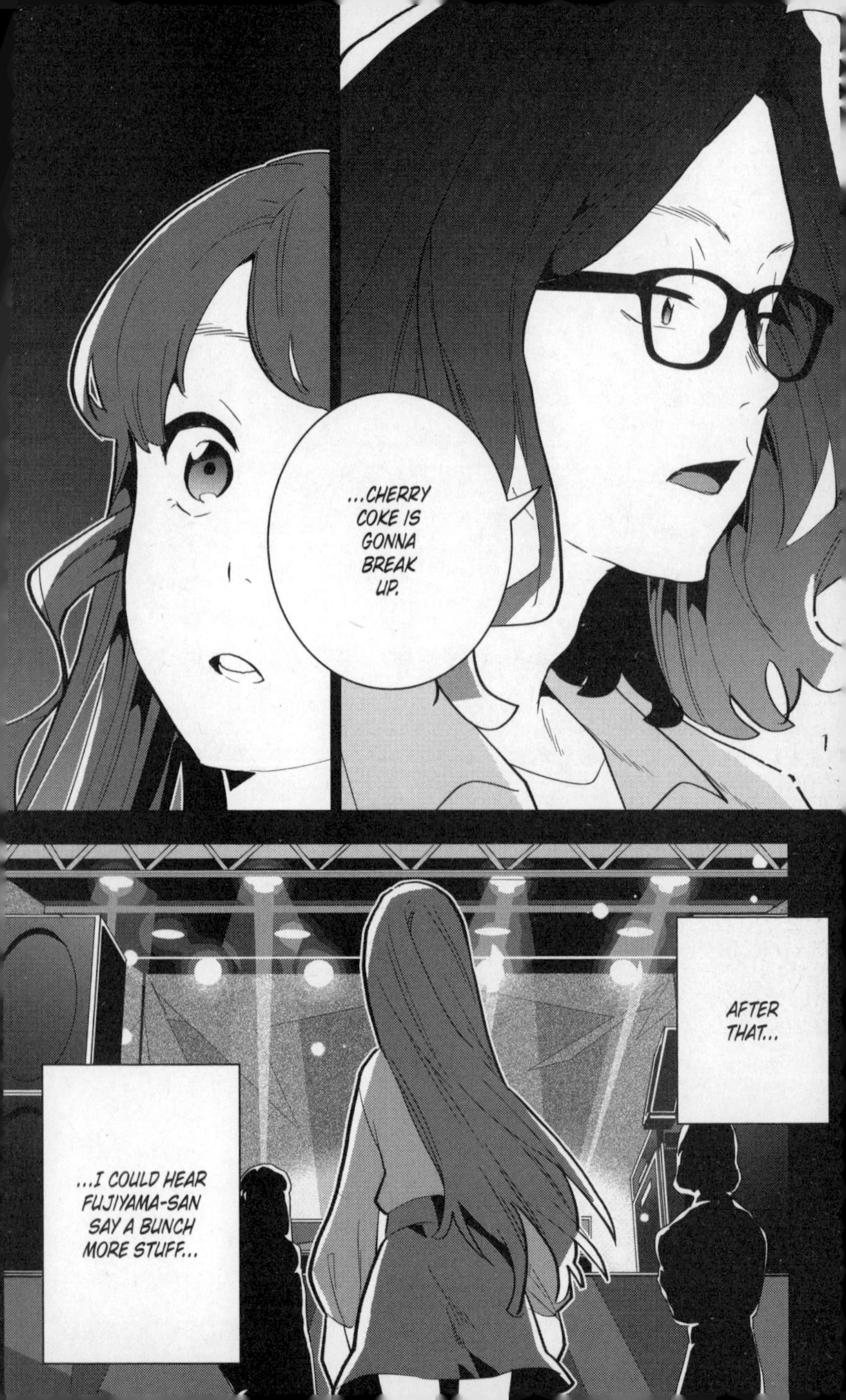
...CHERRY COKE IS GONNA BREAK UP.
AFTER THAT...
...I COULD HEAR FUJIYAMA-SAN SAY A BUNCH MORE STUFF...

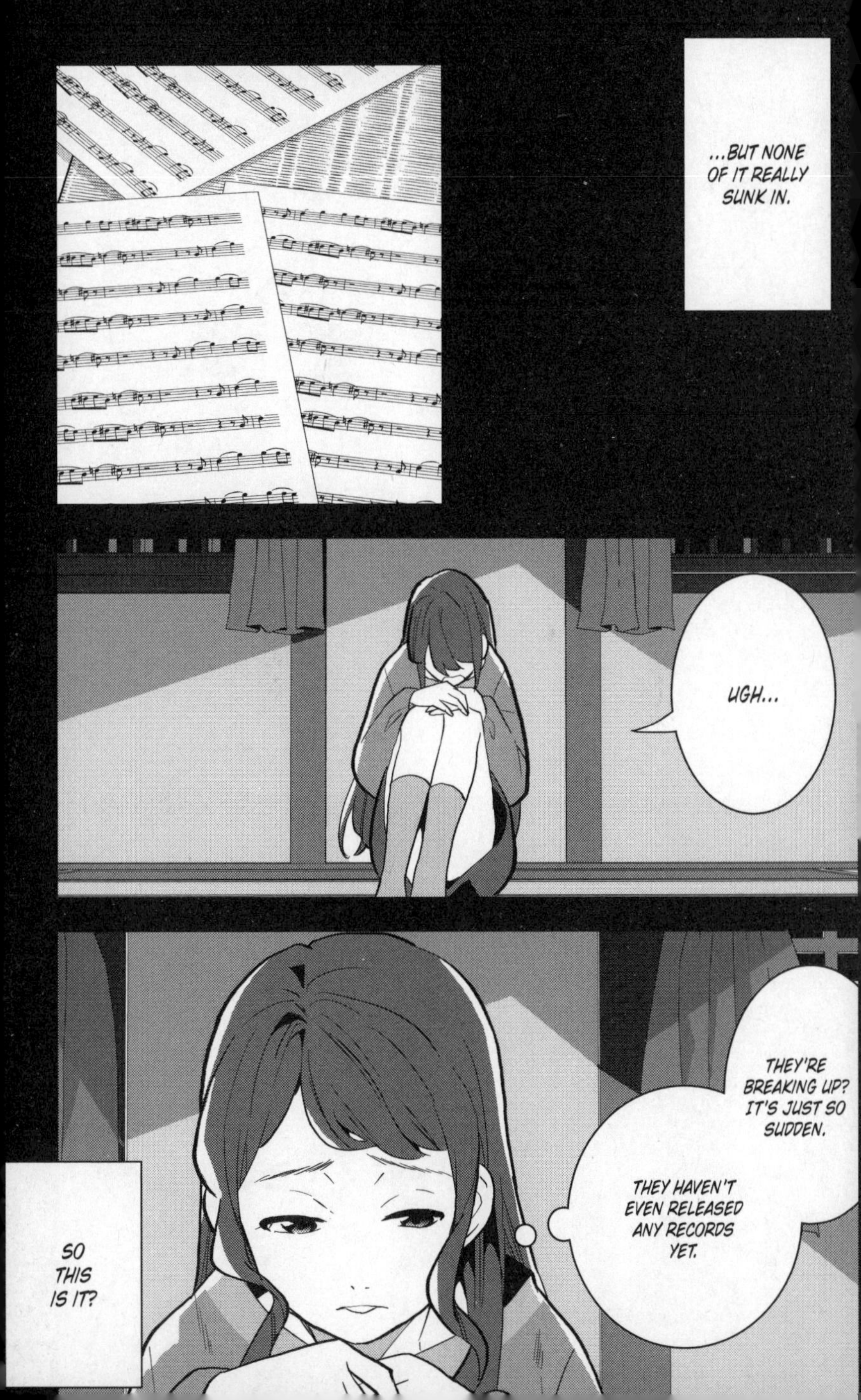
...BUT NONE OF IT REALLY SUNK IN.
UGH...
THEY'RE BREAKING UP? IT'S JUST SO SUDDEN.
THEY HAVEN'T EVEN RELEASED ANY RECORDS YET.
SO THIS IS IT?

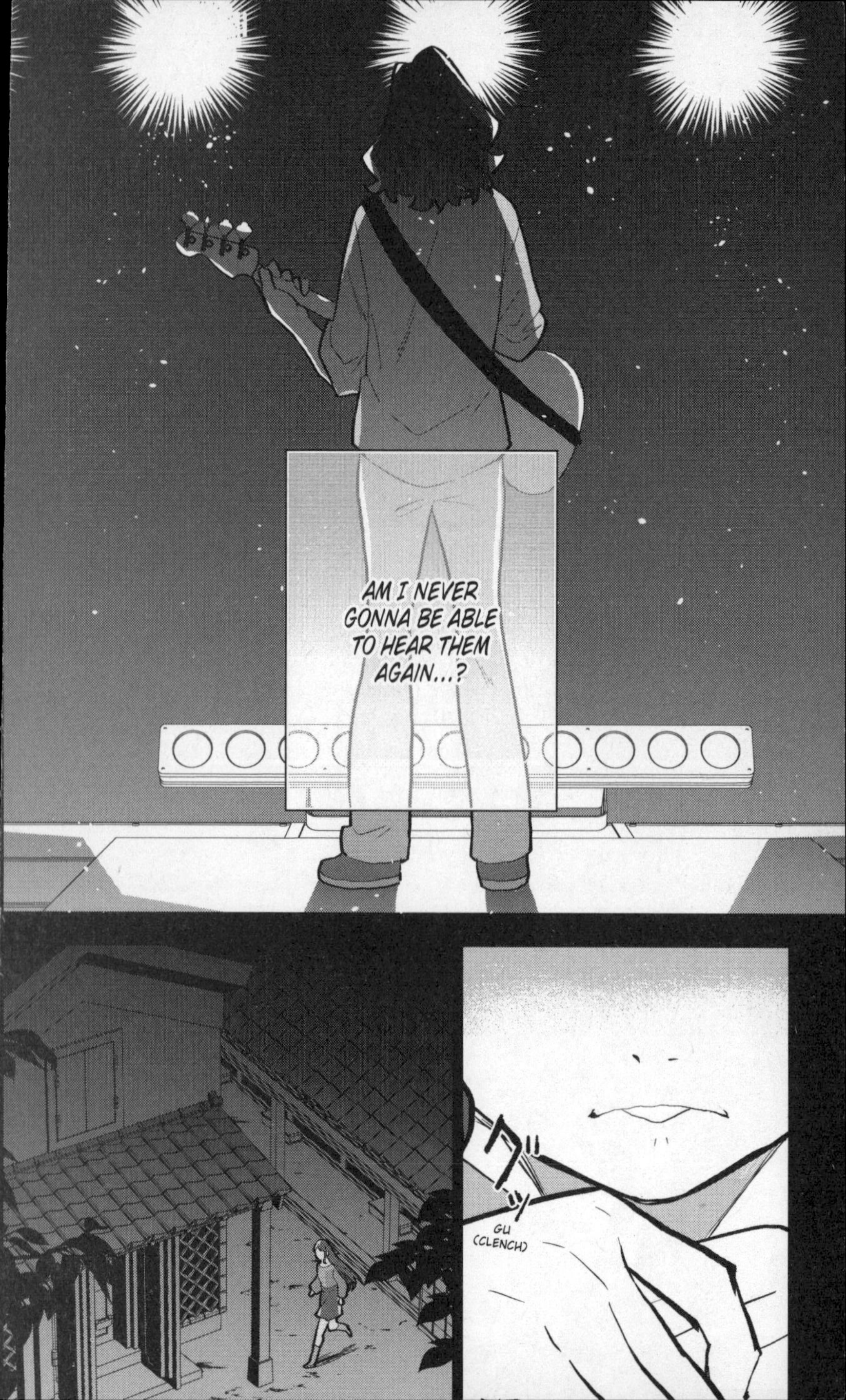
AM I NEVER GONNA BE ABLE TO HEAR THEM AGAIN...?
GU (CLENCH)

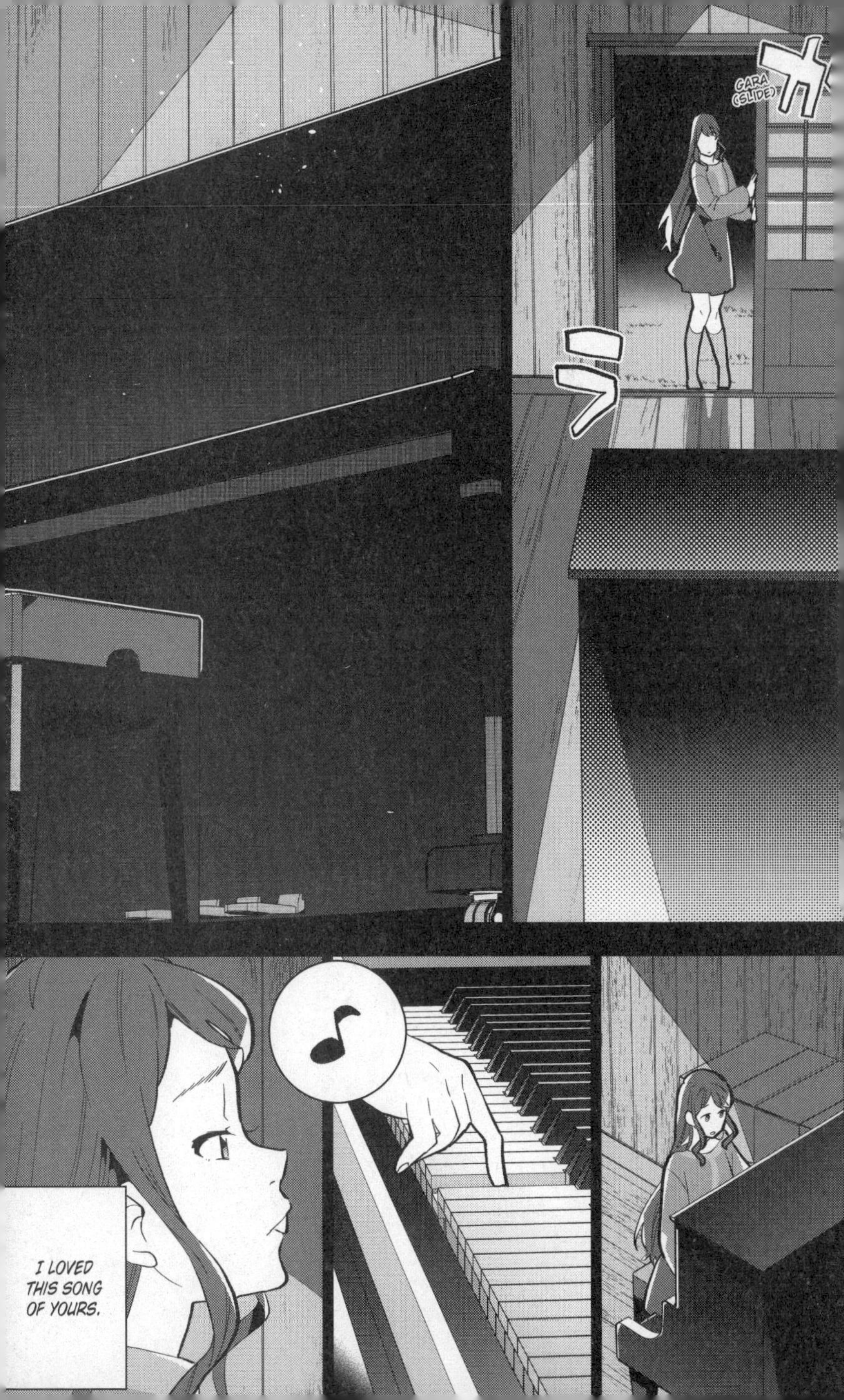
GARA (SLIDE)
I LOVED THIS SONG OF YOURS.

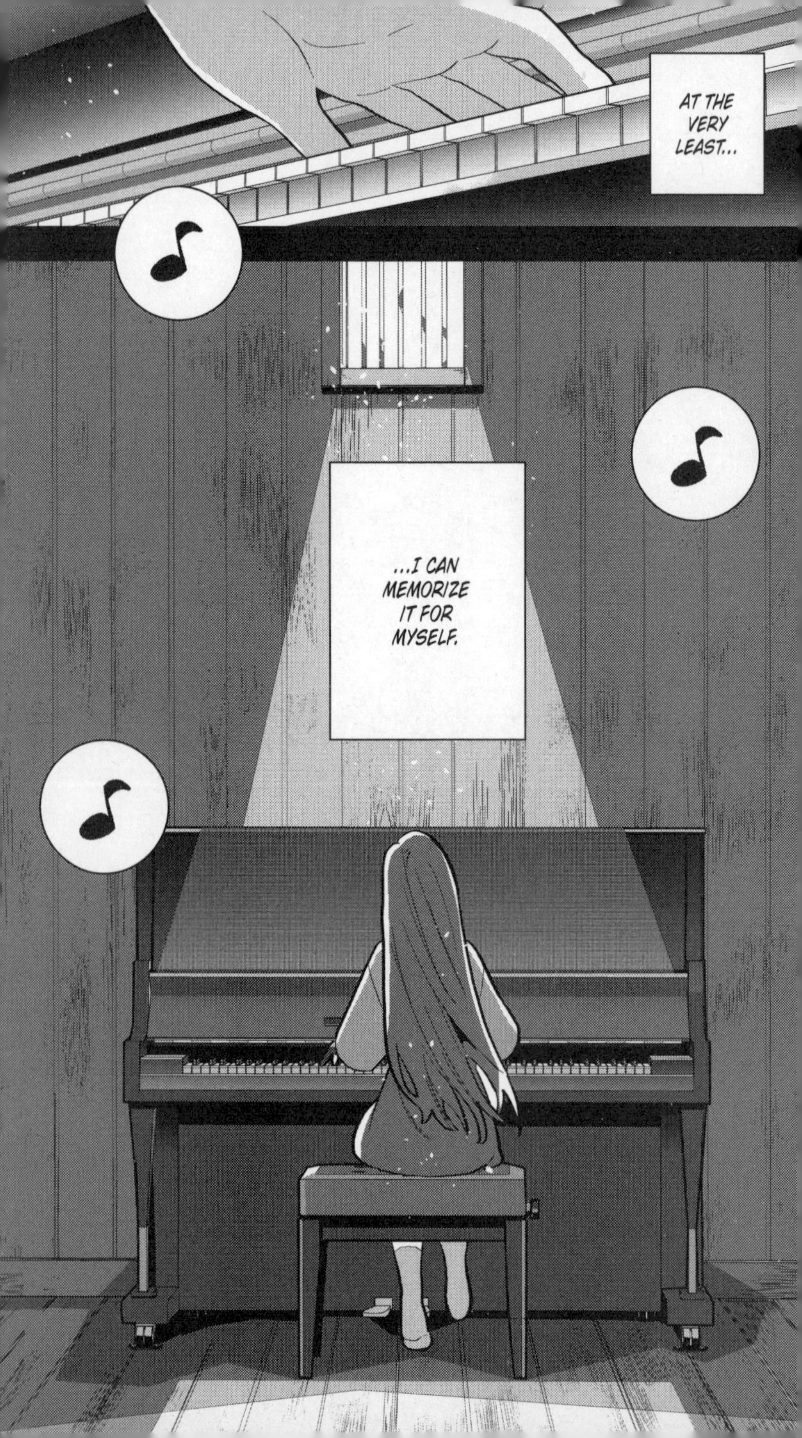
AT THE VERY LEAST...
...I CAN MEMORIZE IT FOR MYSELF.

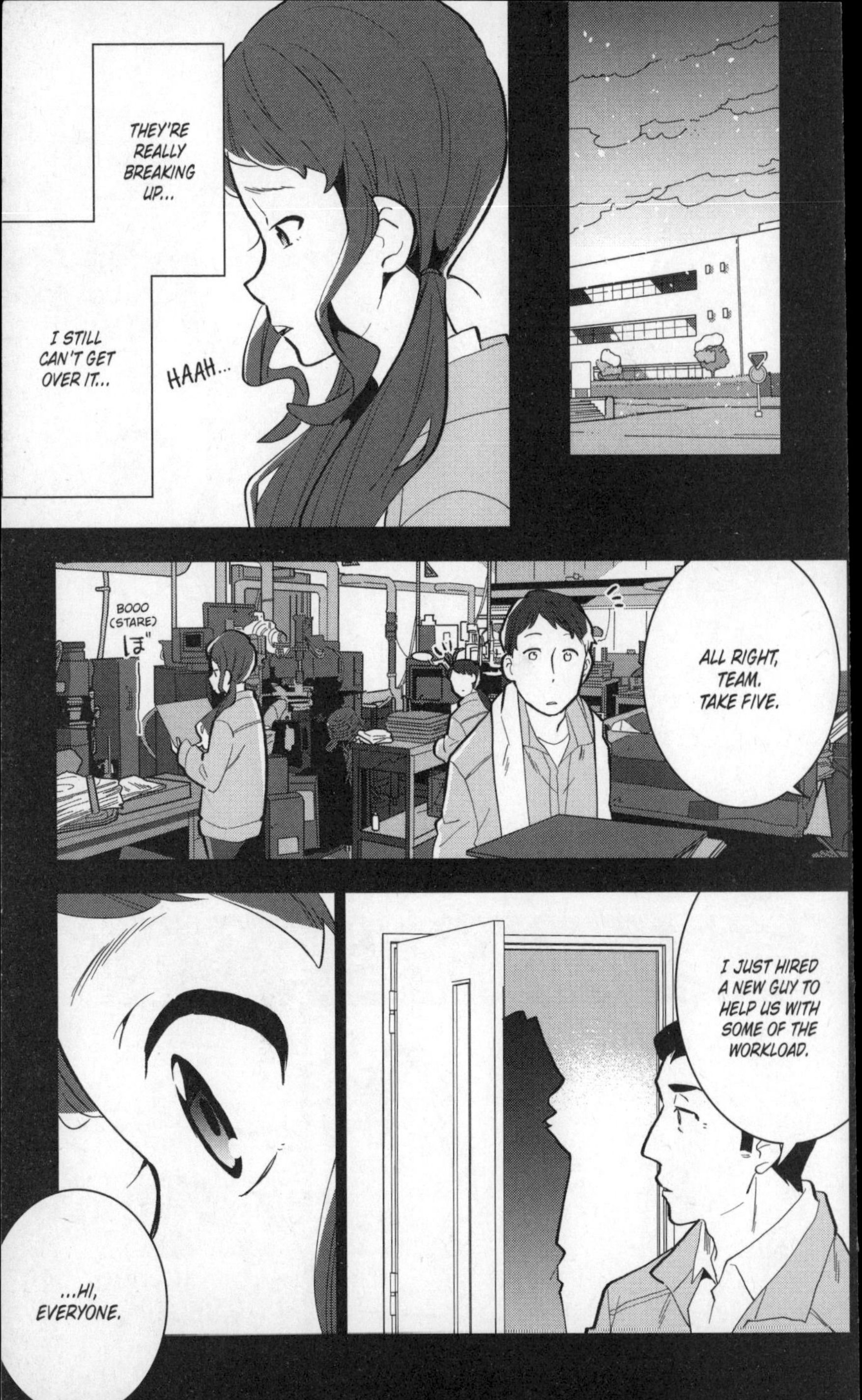
THEY'RE REALLY BREAKING UP...
HAAH...
I STILL CAN'T GET OVER IT...
ALL RIGHT, TEAM. TAKE FIVE.
BOOO (STARE)
ぼ
I JUST HIRED A NEW GUY TO HELP US WITH SOME OF THE WORKLOAD.
...HI, EVERYONE.

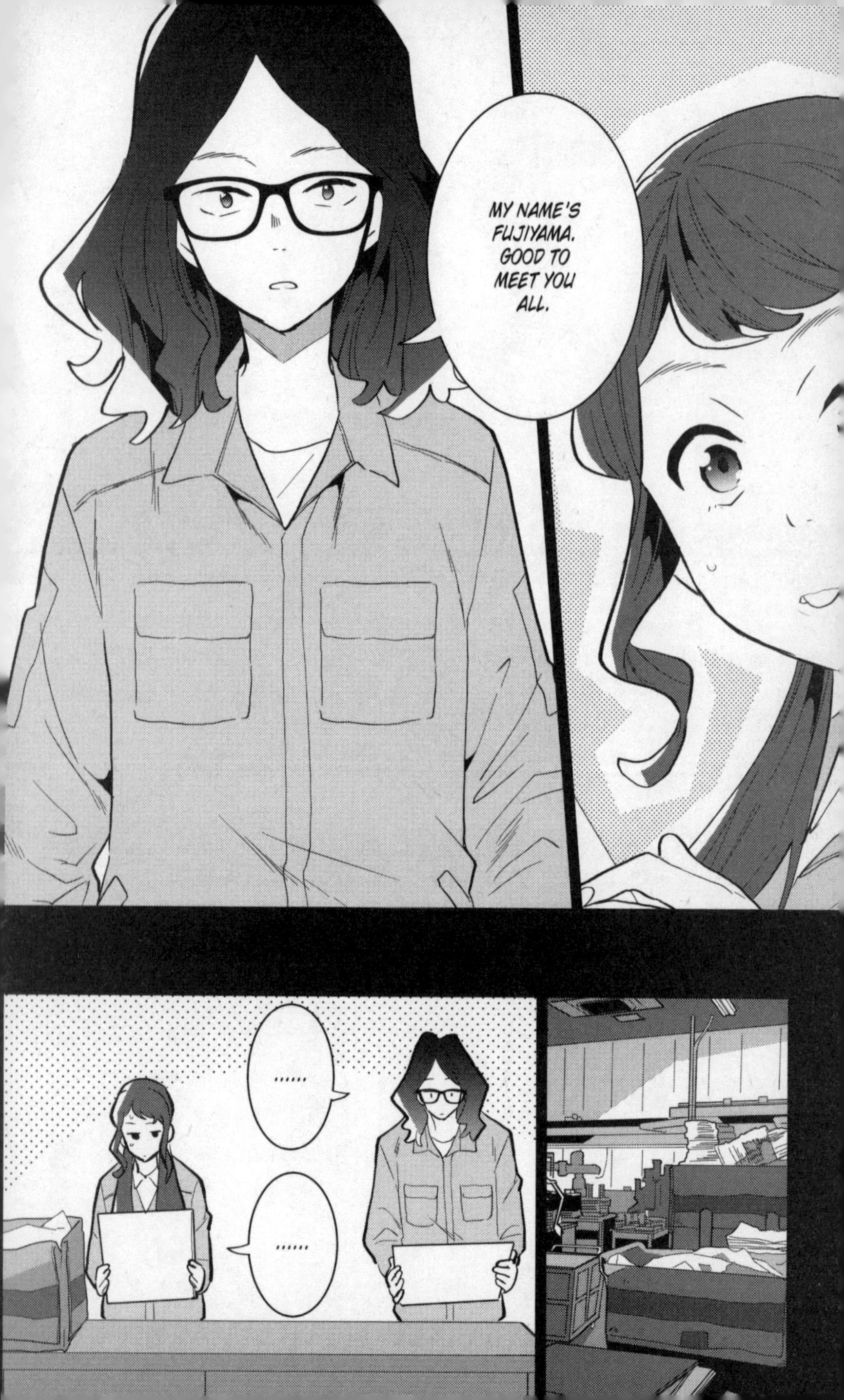
MY NAME'S FUJIYAMA. GOOD TO MEET YOU ALL.
......
......

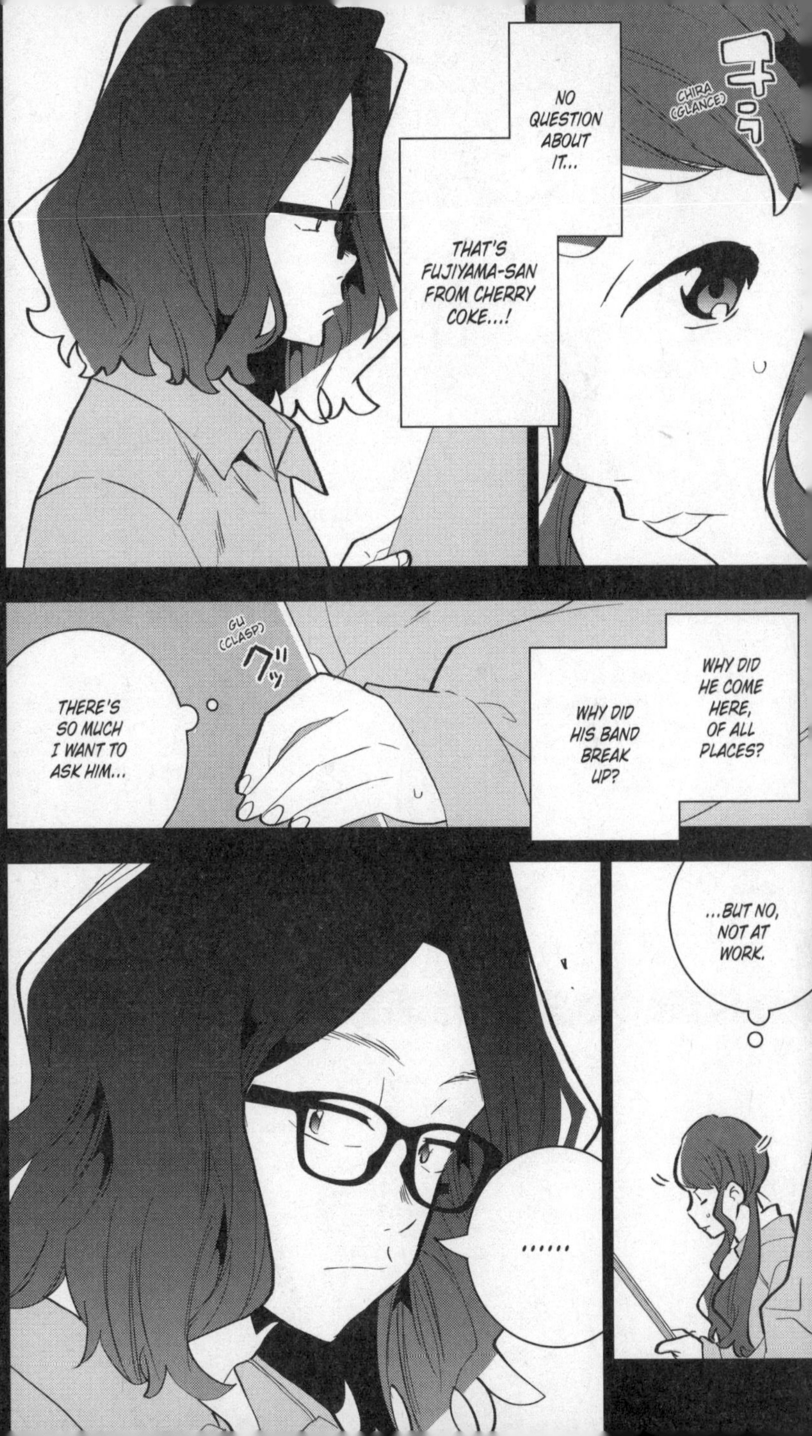
CHIRA (GLANCE)
NO QUESTION ABOUT IT...
THAT'S FUJIYAMA-SAN FROM CHERRY COKE...!
WHY DID HE COME HERE, OF ALL PLACES?
WHY DID HIS BAND BREAK UP?
GU (CLASP)
THERE'S SO MUCH I WANT TO ASK HIM...
...BUT NO, NOT AT WORK.
......

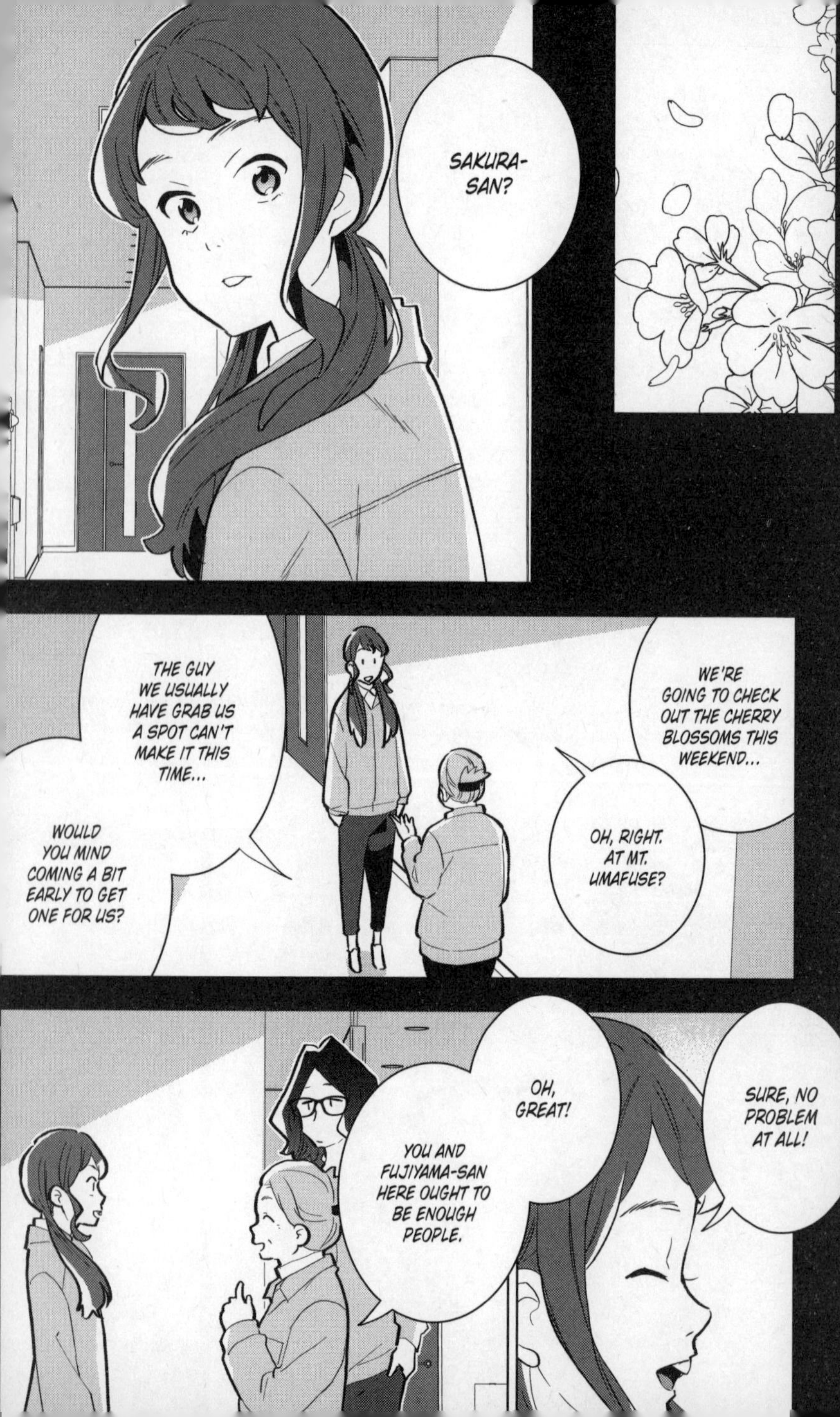
SAKURA-SAN?
WE'RE GOING TO CHECK OUT THE CHERRY BLOSSOMS THIS WEEKEND...
OH, RIGHT. AT MT. UMAFUSE?
THE GUY WE USUALLY HAVE GRAB US A SPOT CAN'T MAKE IT THIS TIME...
WOULD YOU MIND COMING A BIT EARLY TO GET ONE FOR US?
SURE, NO PROBLEM AT ALL!
OH, GREAT!
YOU AND FUJIYAMA-SAN HERE OUGHT TO BE ENOUGH PEOPLE.

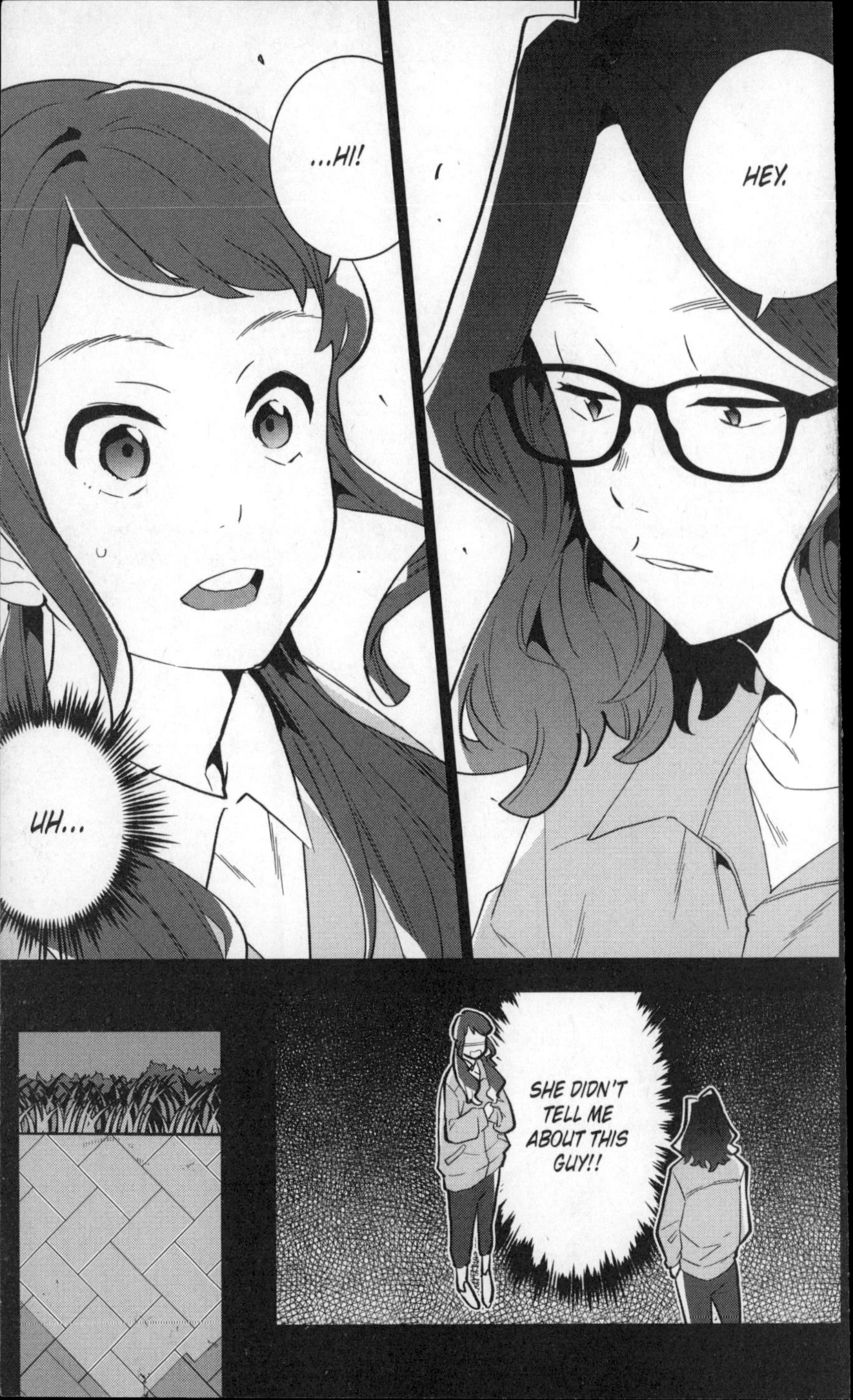
HEY.
...HI!
UH...
SHE DIDN'T TELL ME ABOUT THIS GUY!!

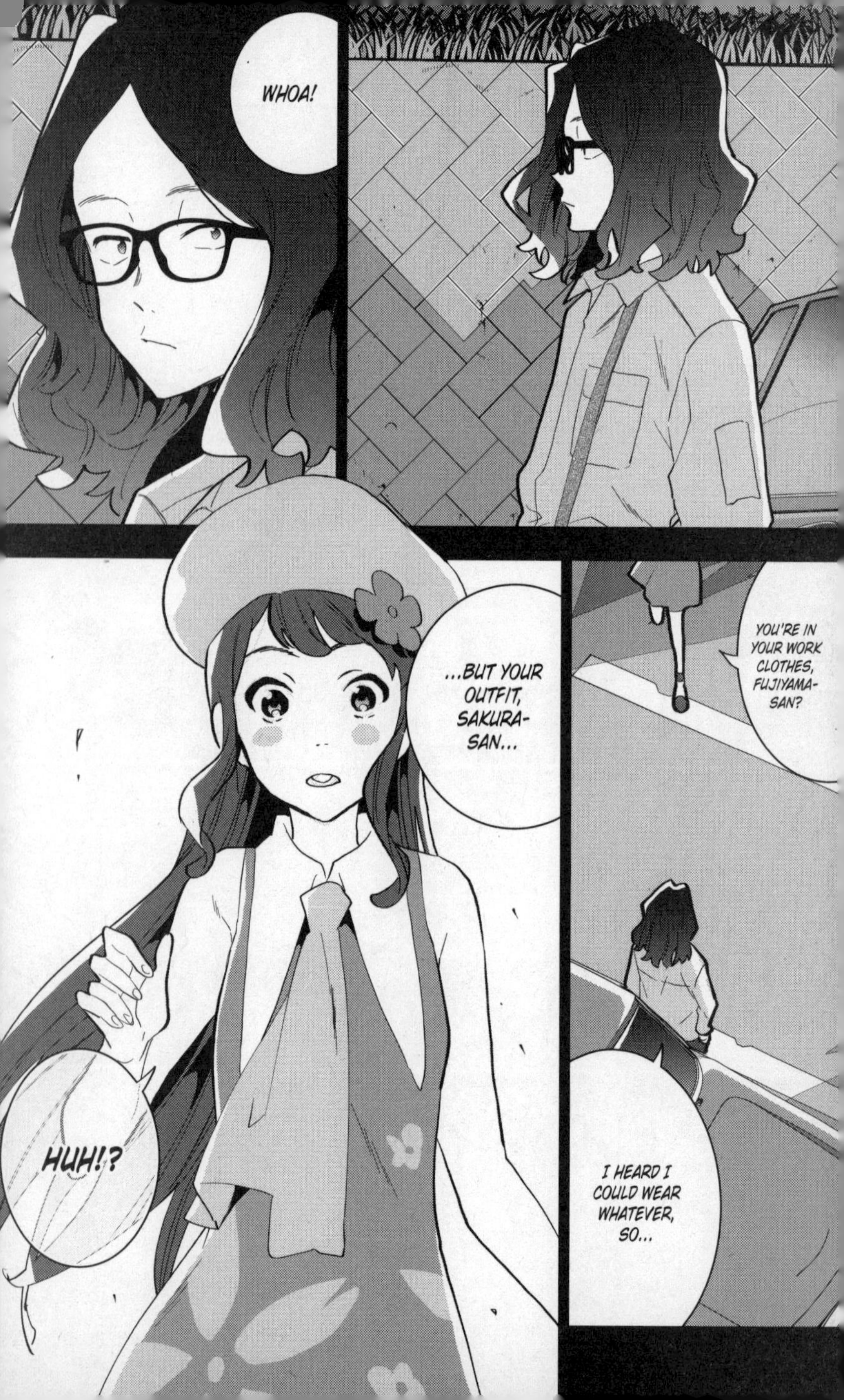
WHOA!
YOU'RE IN YOUR WORK CLOTHES, FUJIYAMA-SAN?
I HEARD I COULD WEAR WHATEVER, SO...
...BUT YOUR OUTFIT, SAKURA-SAN...
HUH!?

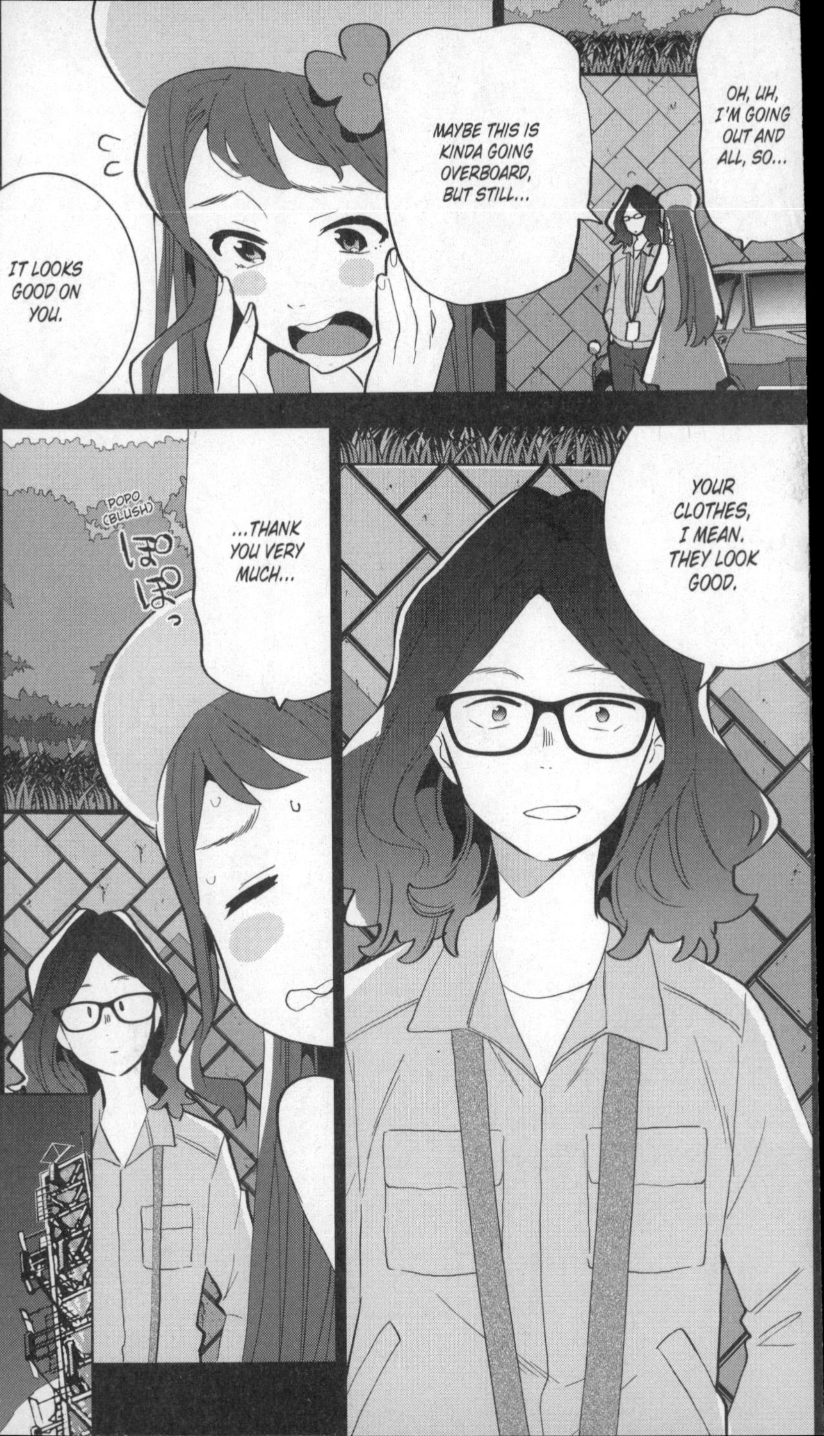
OH, UH, I'M GOING OUT AND ALL, SO...
MAYBE THIS IS KINDA GOING OVERBOARD, BUT STILL...
IT LOOKS GOOD ON YOU.
YOUR CLOTHES, I MEAN. THEY LOOK GOOD.
...THANK YOU VERY MUCH...
POPO (BLUSH)
ぽぽっ

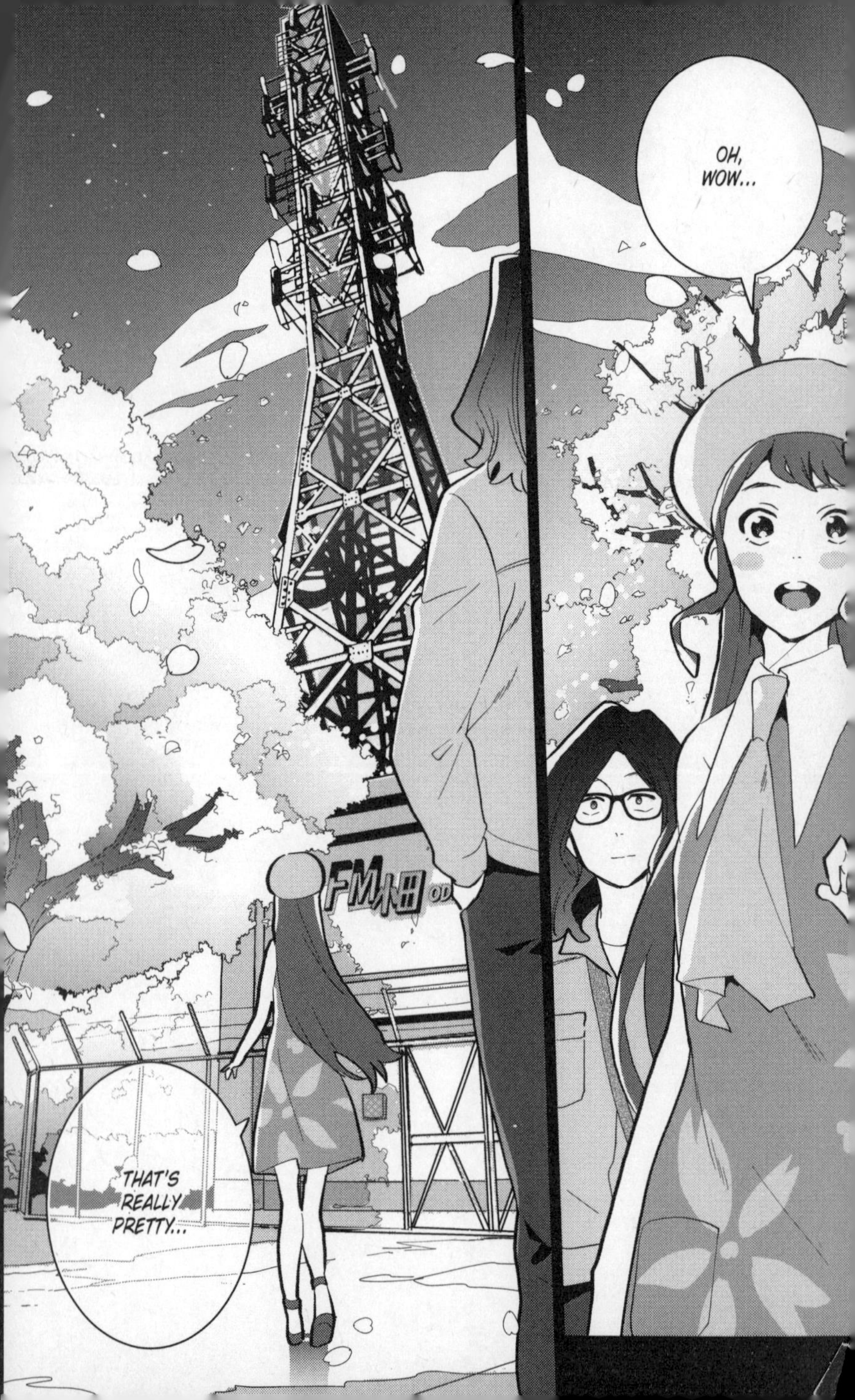
OH, WOW...
THAT'S REALLY PRETTY...

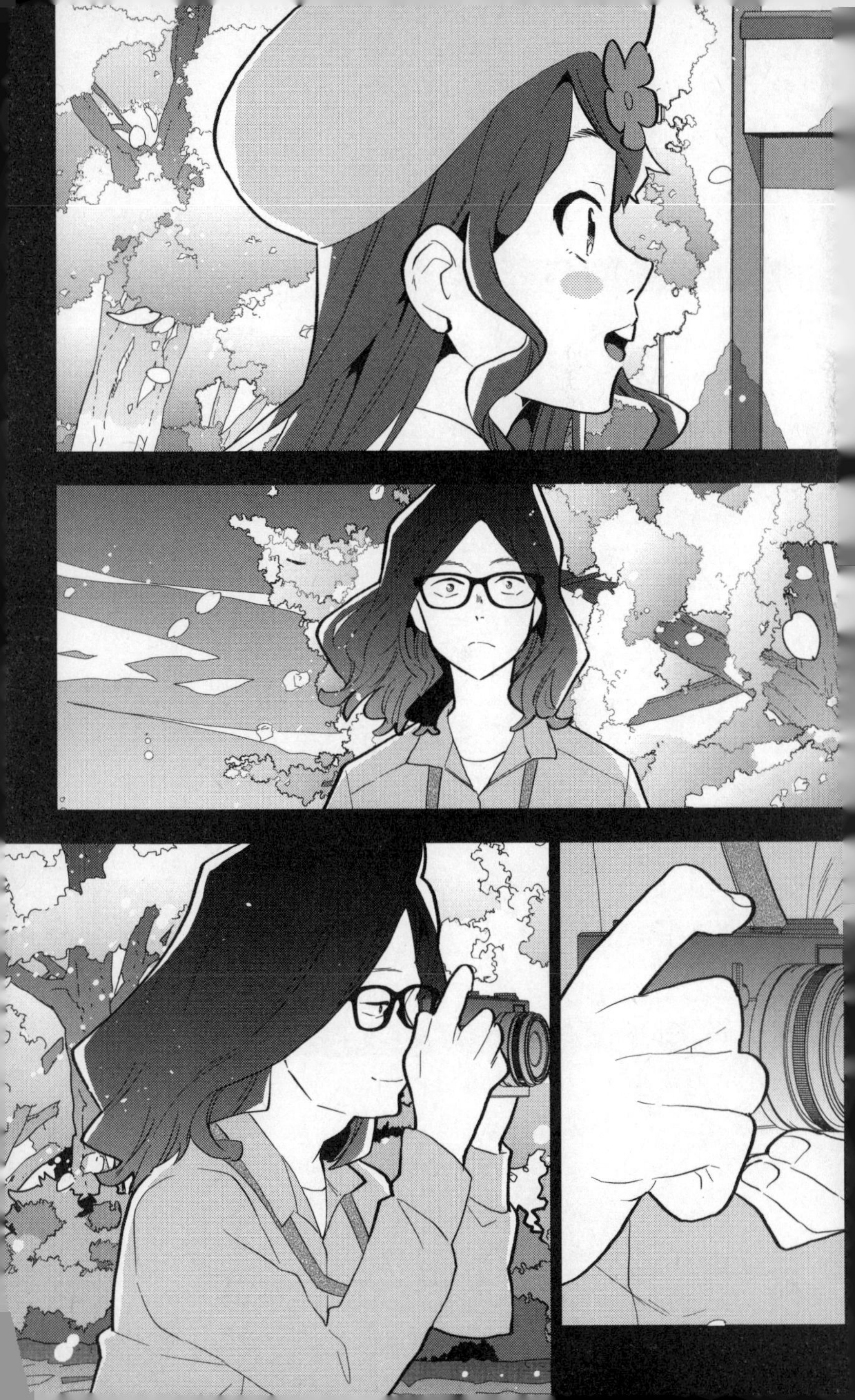

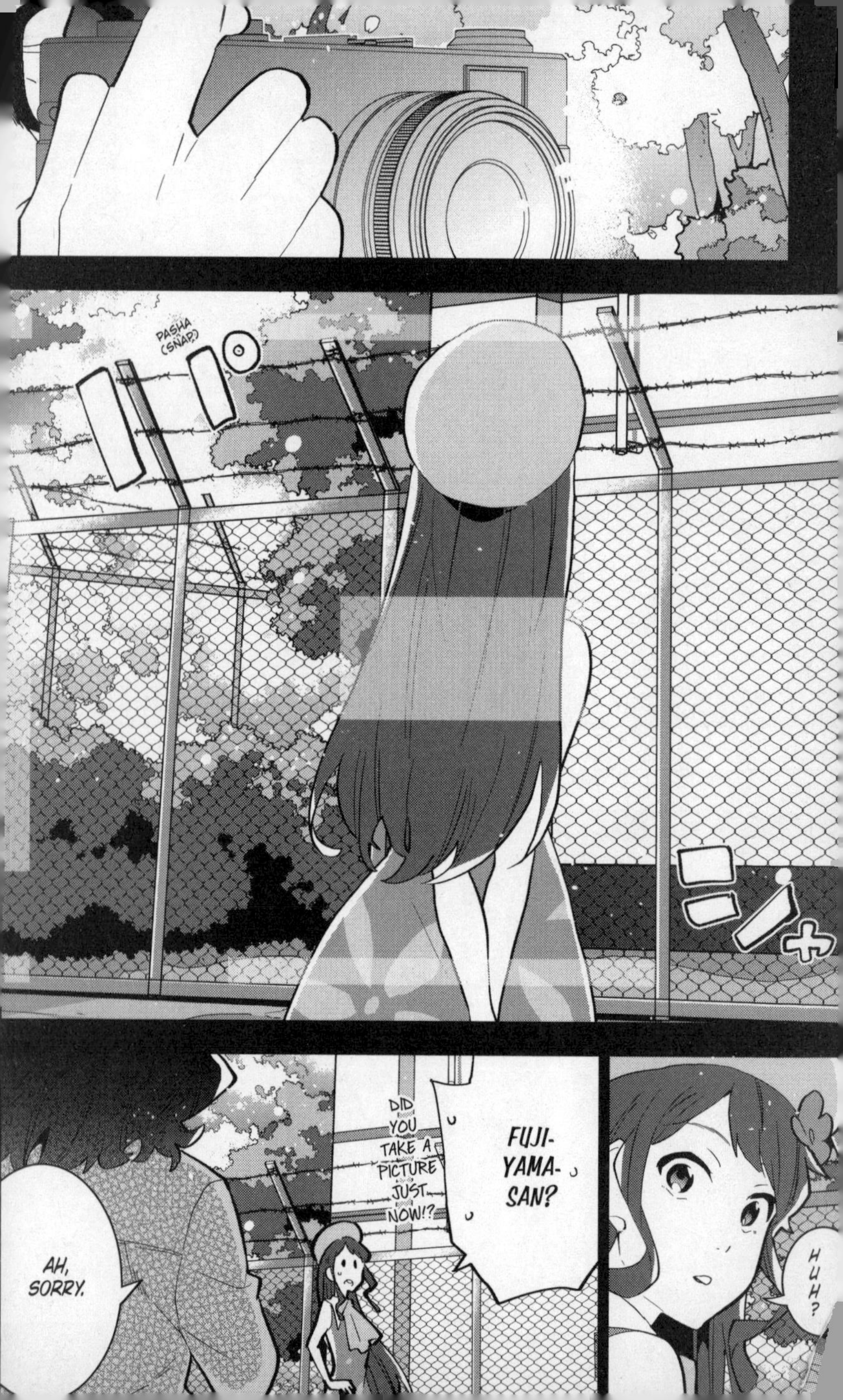
PASHA
(SNAP)
HUH?
FUJI-
YAMA-
SAN?
DID YOU TAKE A PICTURE JUST NOW!?
AH, SORRY.

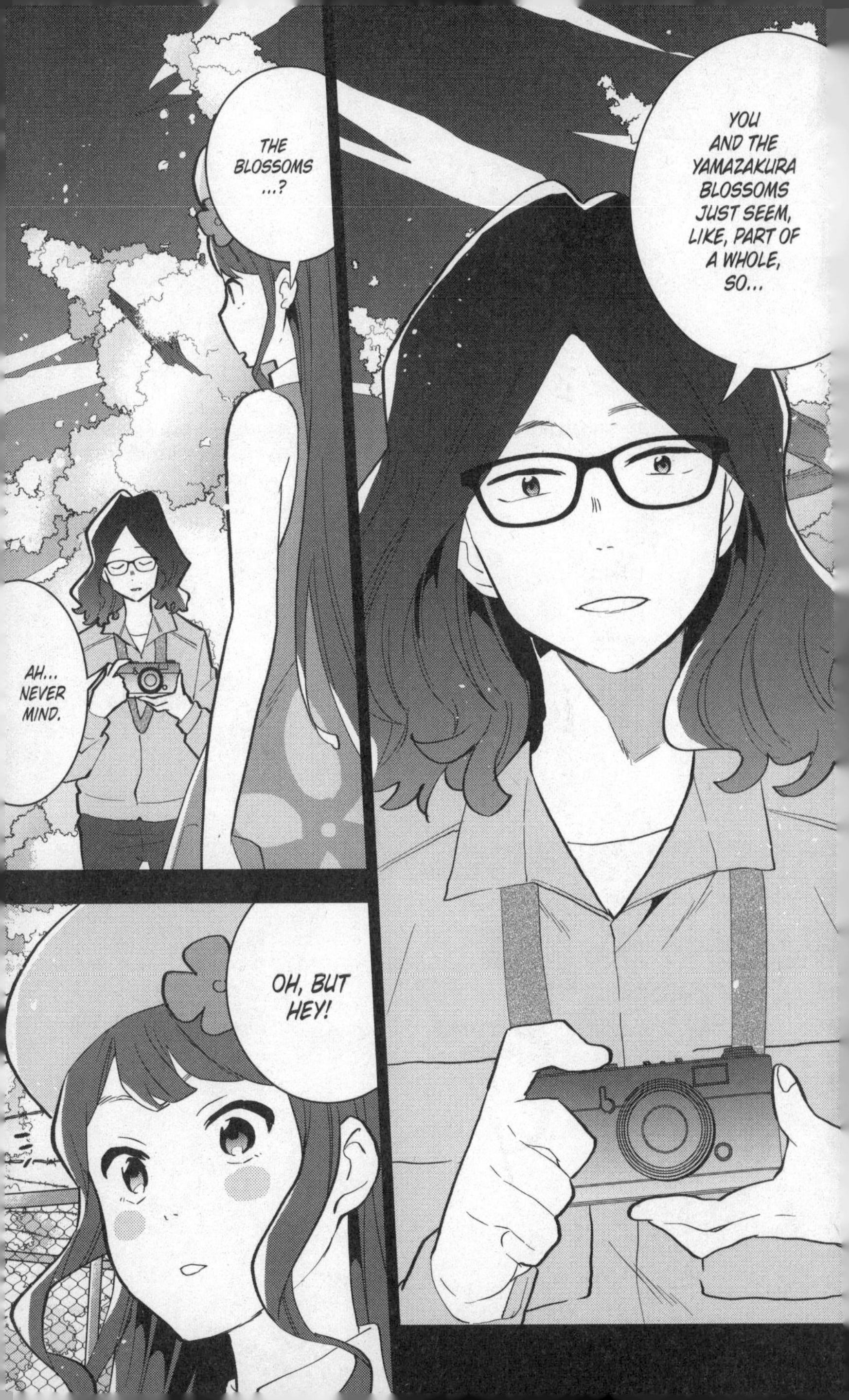
YOU AND THE YAMAZAKURA BLOSSOMS JUST SEEM, LIKE, PART OF A WHOLE, SO...
THE BLOSSOMS ...?
AH... NEVER MIND.
OH, BUT HEY!

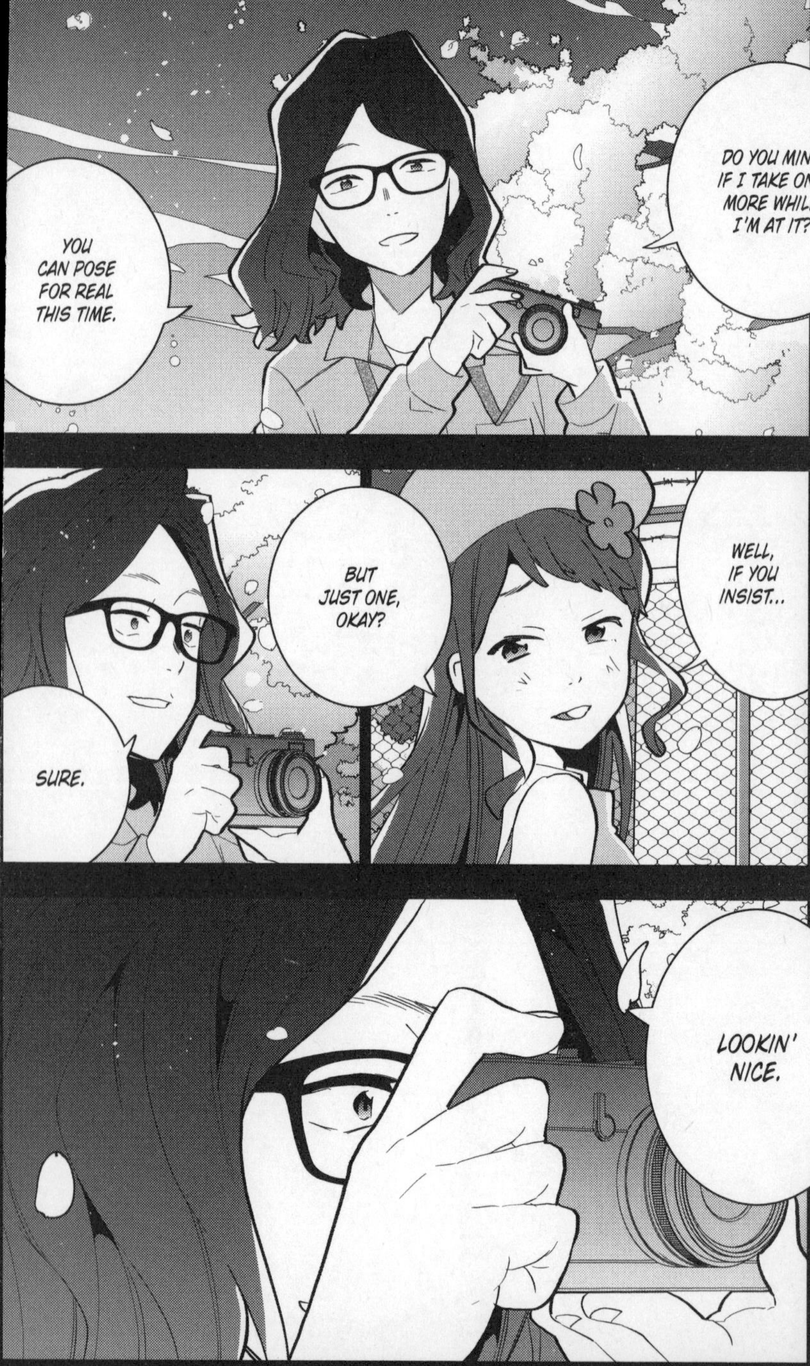
DO YOU MIND IF I TAKE ONE MORE WHILE I'M AT IT?
YOU CAN POSE FOR REAL THIS TIME.
WELL, IF YOU INSIST...
BUT JUST ONE, OKAY?
SURE.
LOOKIN' NICE.

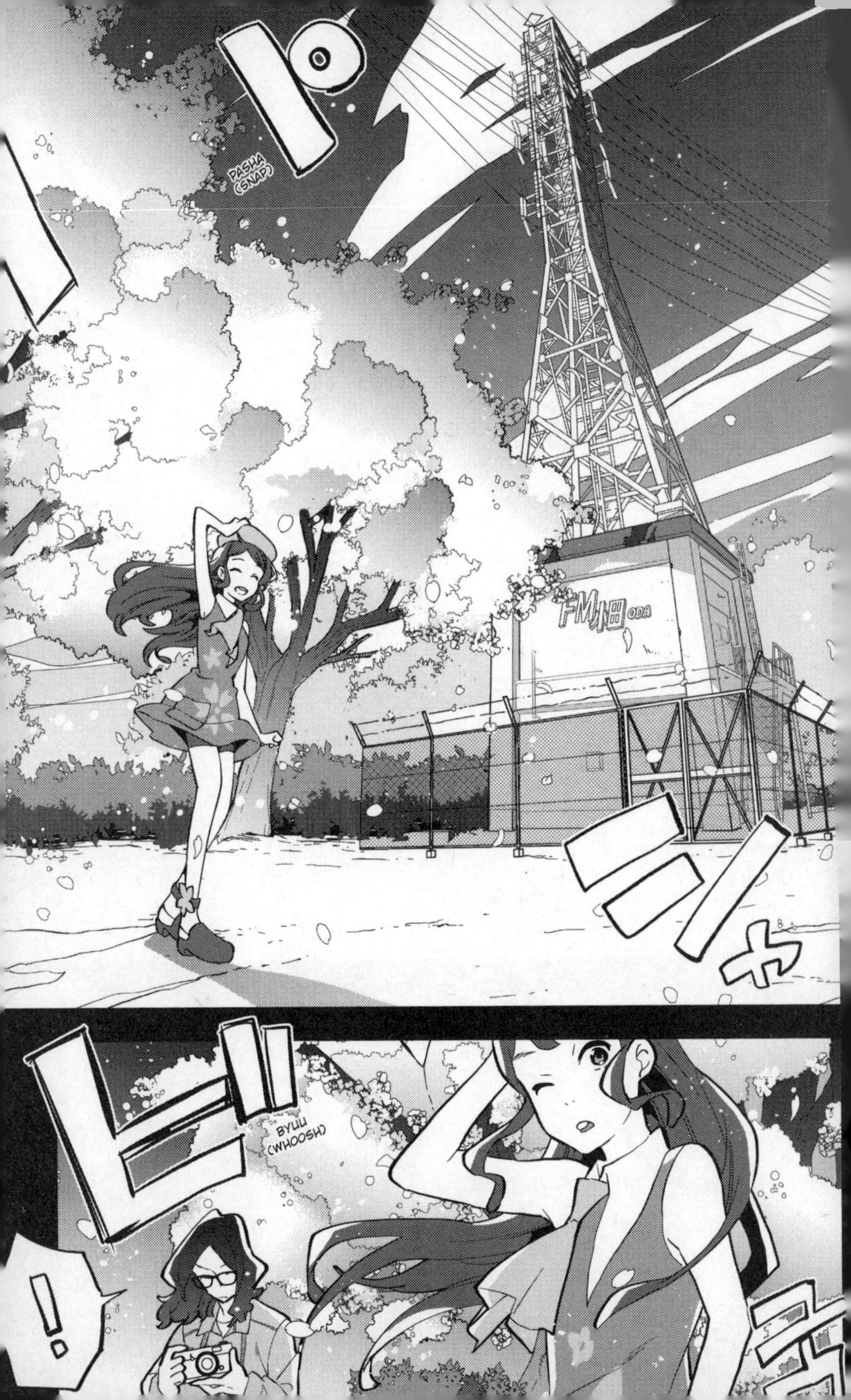
PASHA (SNAP)
FM ODA
BYUU (WHOOSH)
!

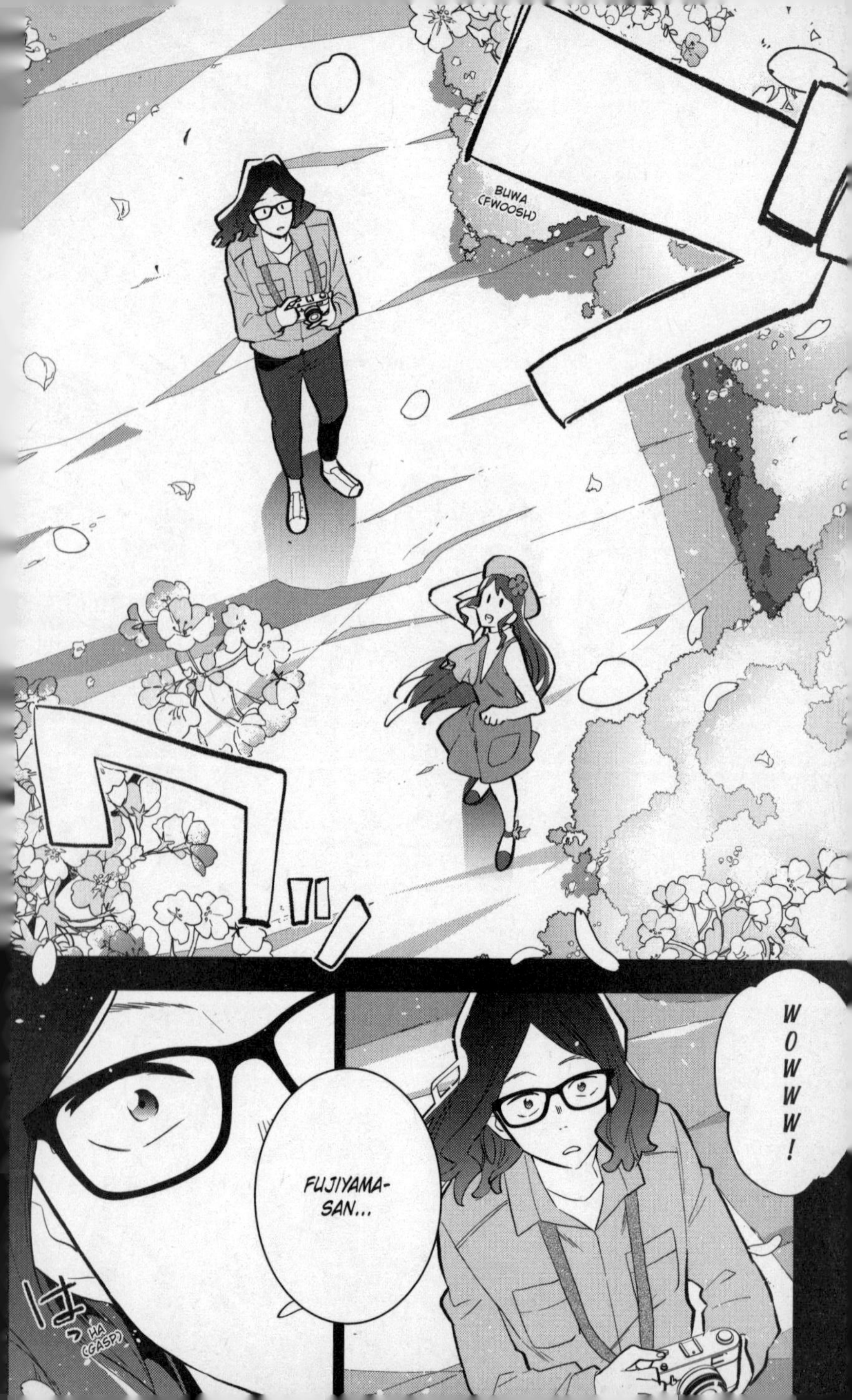
BUWA (FWOOSH)
WOWWW!
FUJIYAMA-SAN...
HA (GASP)

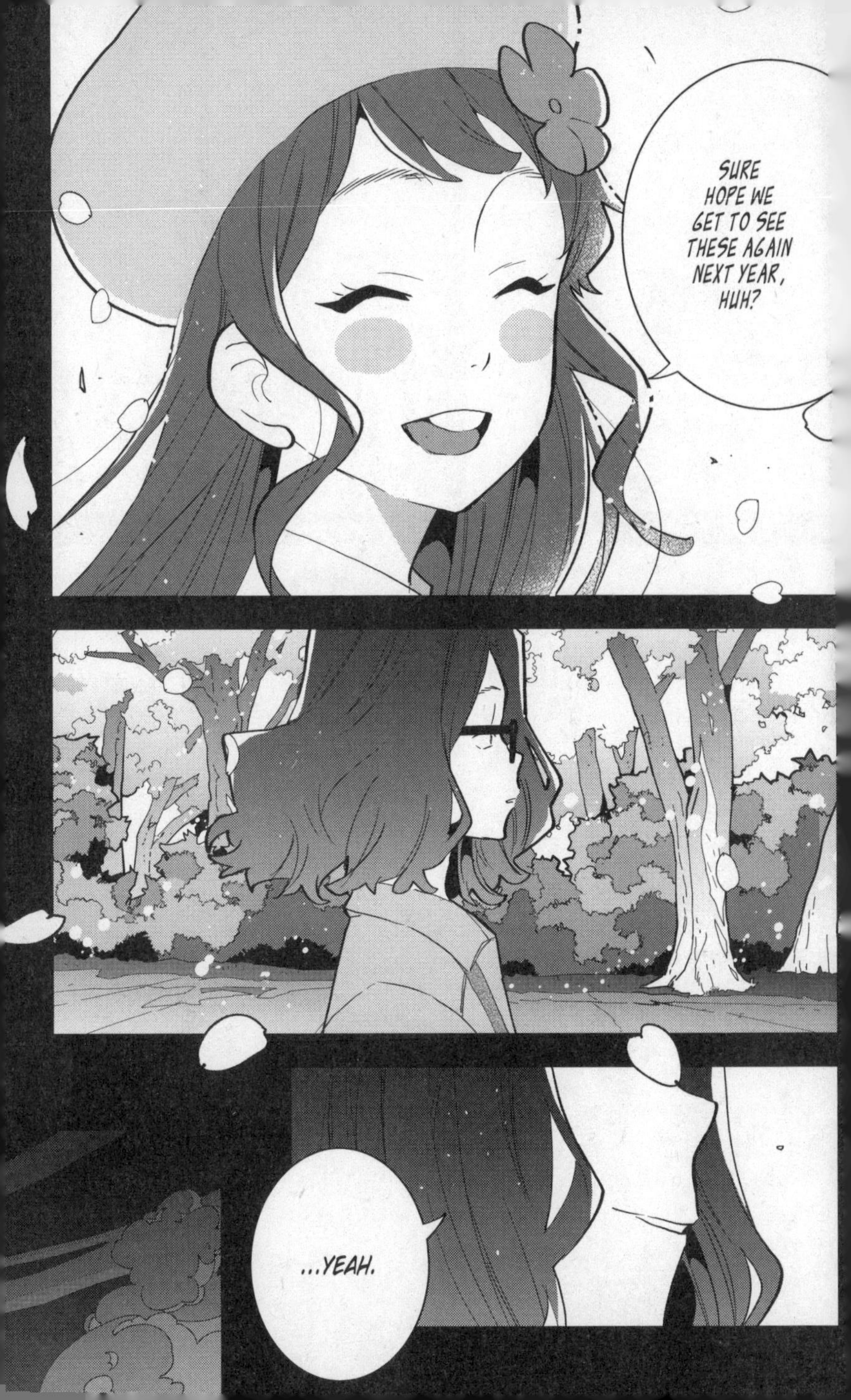
SURE HOPE WE GET TO SEE THESE AGAIN NEXT YEAR, HUH?
...YEAH.

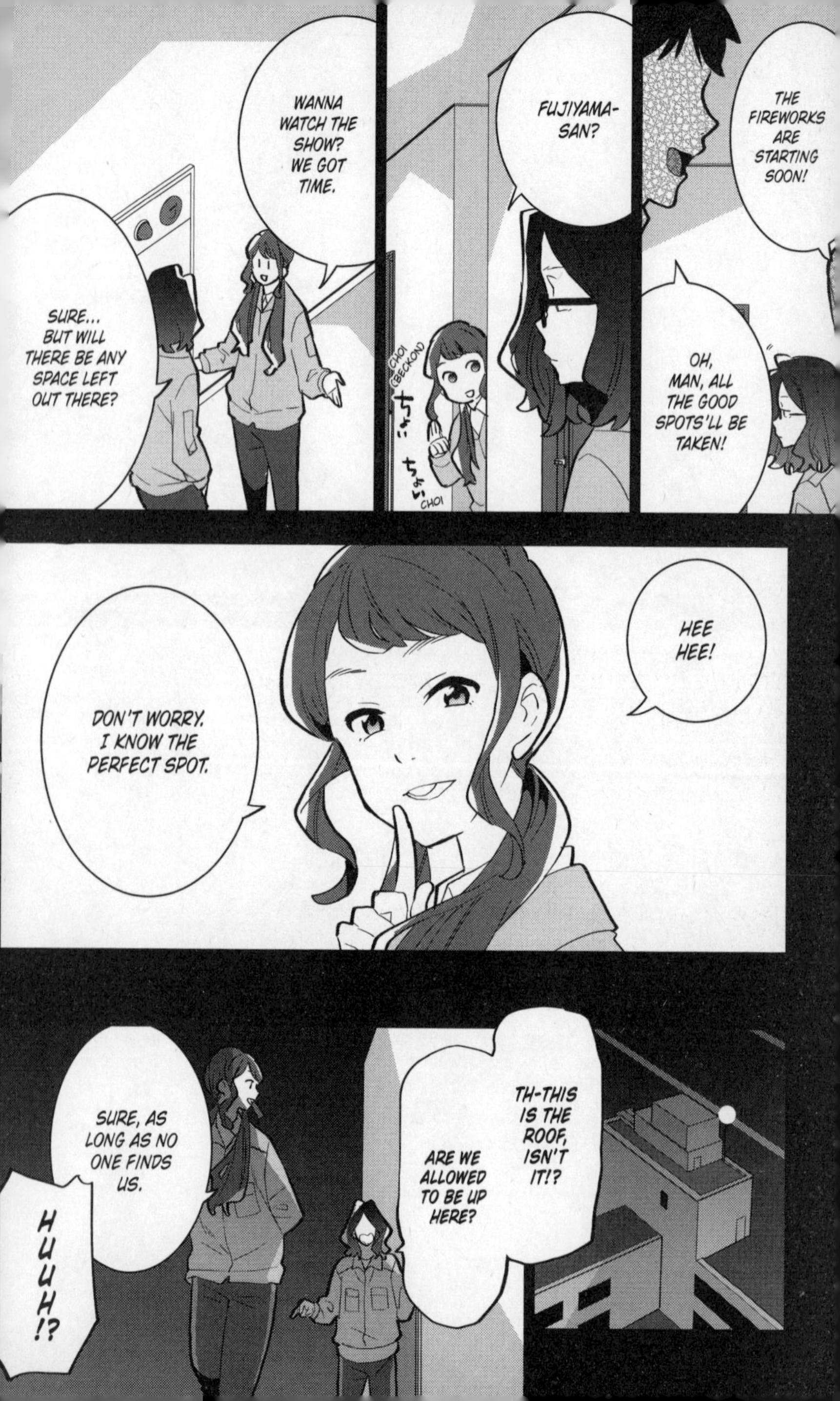
THE FIREWORKS ARE STARTING SOON!
OH, MAN, ALL THE GOOD SPOTS'LL BE TAKEN!
FUJIYAMA-SAN?
ちょい CHOI (BECKON)
ちょい CHOI
WANNA WATCH THE SHOW? WE GOT TIME.
SURE... BUT WILL THERE BE ANY SPACE LEFT OUT THERE?
HEE HEE!
DON'T WORRY. I KNOW THE PERFECT SPOT.
TH-THIS IS THE ROOF, ISN'T IT!?
ARE WE ALLOWED TO BE UP HERE?
SURE, AS LONG AS NO ONE FINDS US.
HUUUH!?

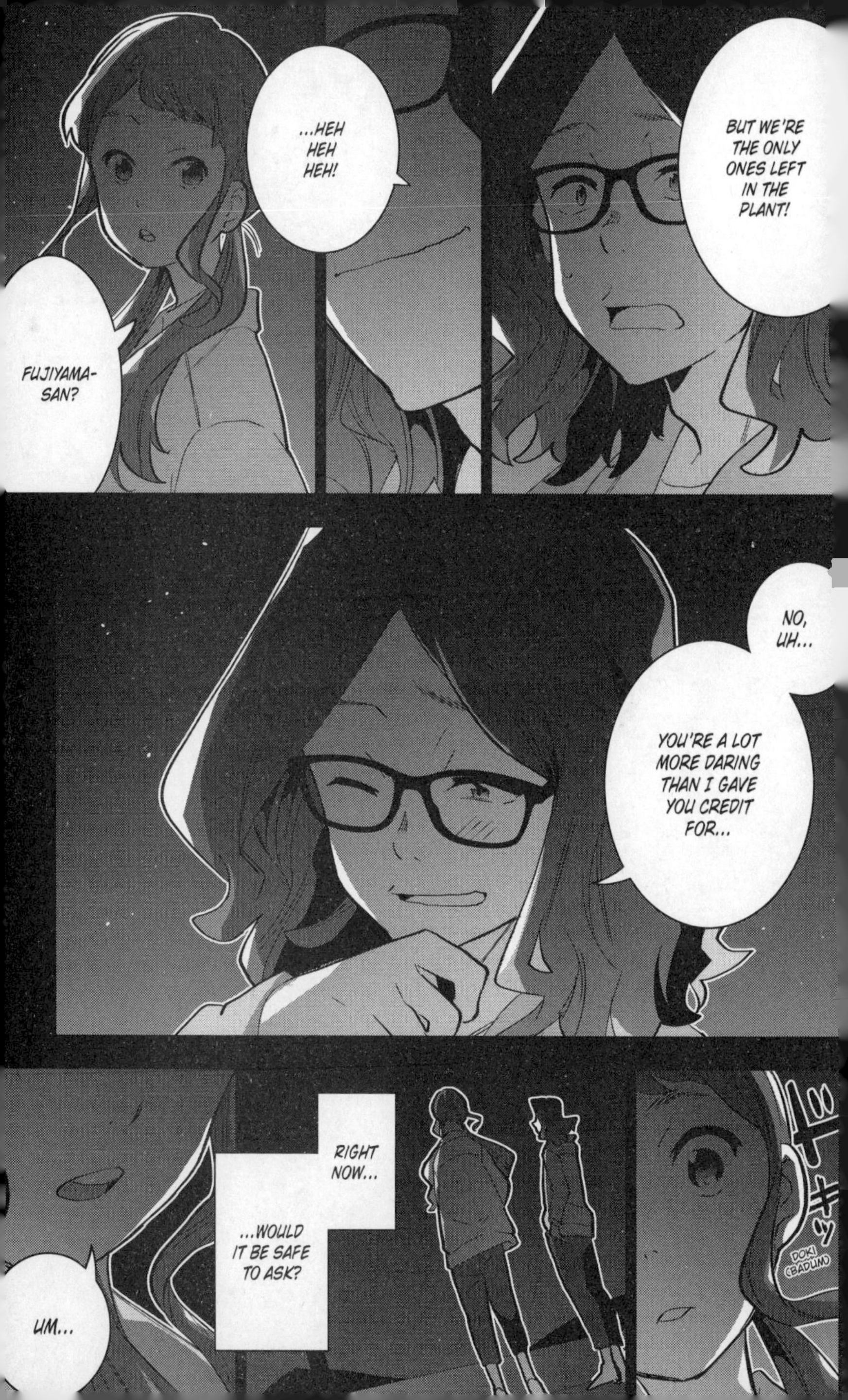
BUT WE'RE THE ONLY ONES LEFT IN THE PLANT!
...HEH HEH HEH!
FUJIYAMA-SAN?
NO, UH...
YOU'RE A LOT MORE DARING THAN I GAVE YOU CREDIT FOR...
DOKI (BADUM)
RIGHT NOW...
...WOULD IT BE SAFE TO ASK?
UM...

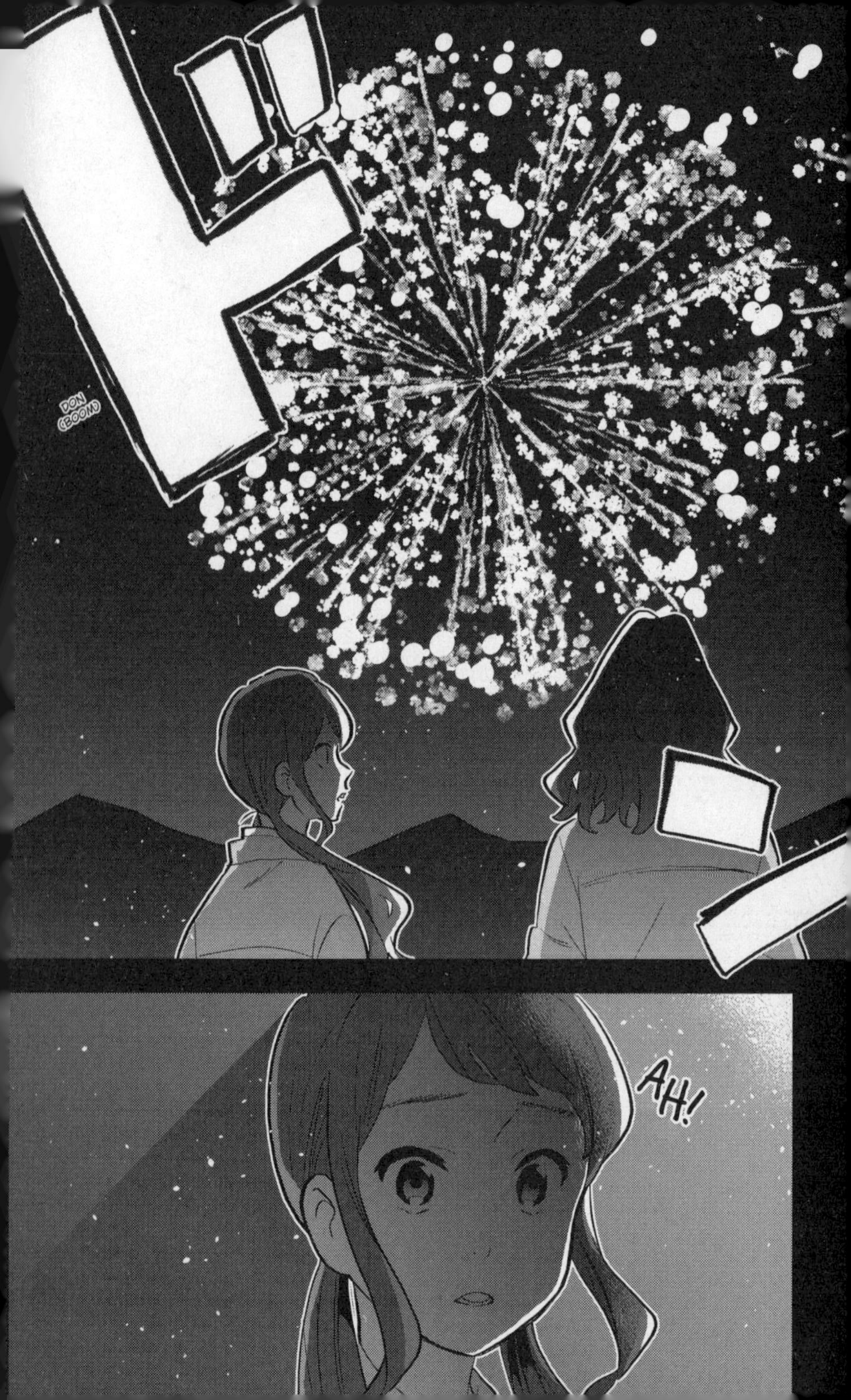
DON
(BOOM)
AH!

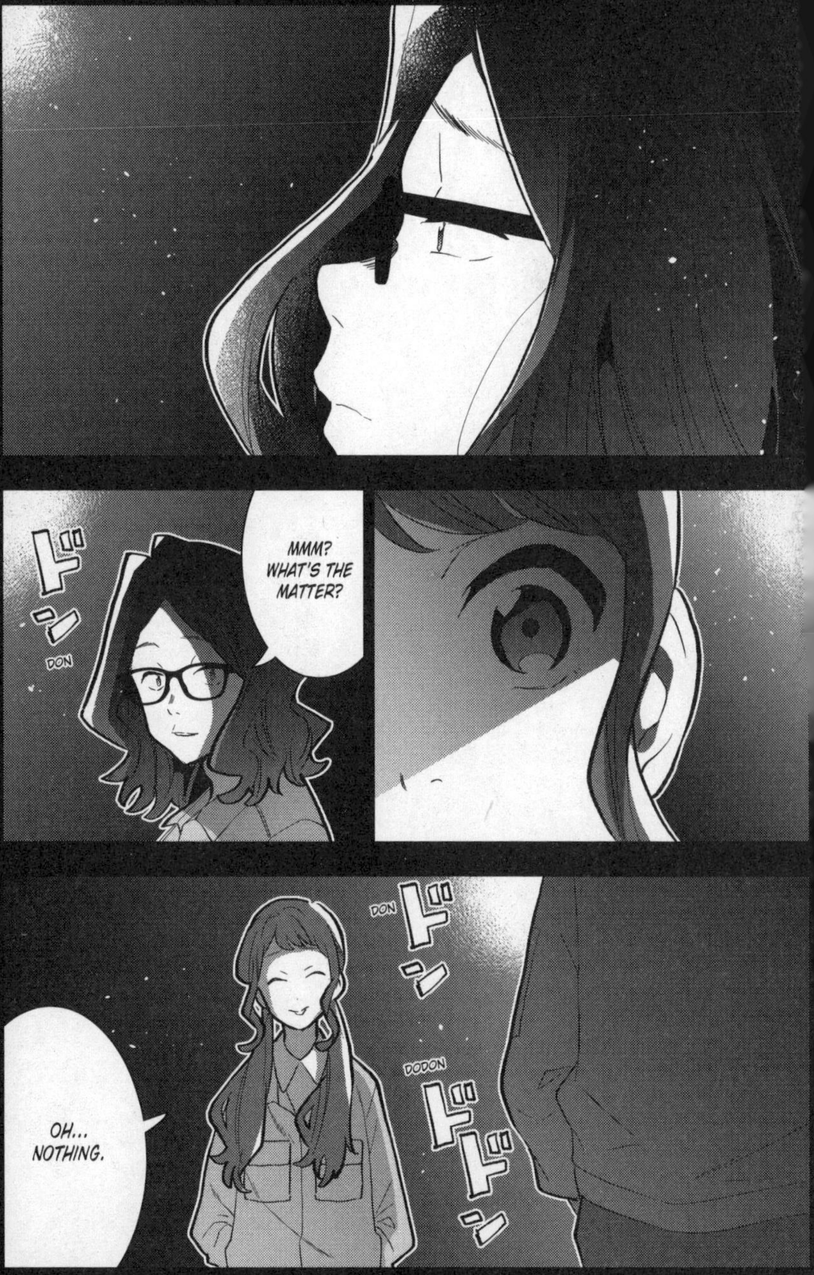
MMM? WHAT'S THE MATTER?
ドン
DON
ドン
DON
ドドン
DODON
OH... NOTHING.

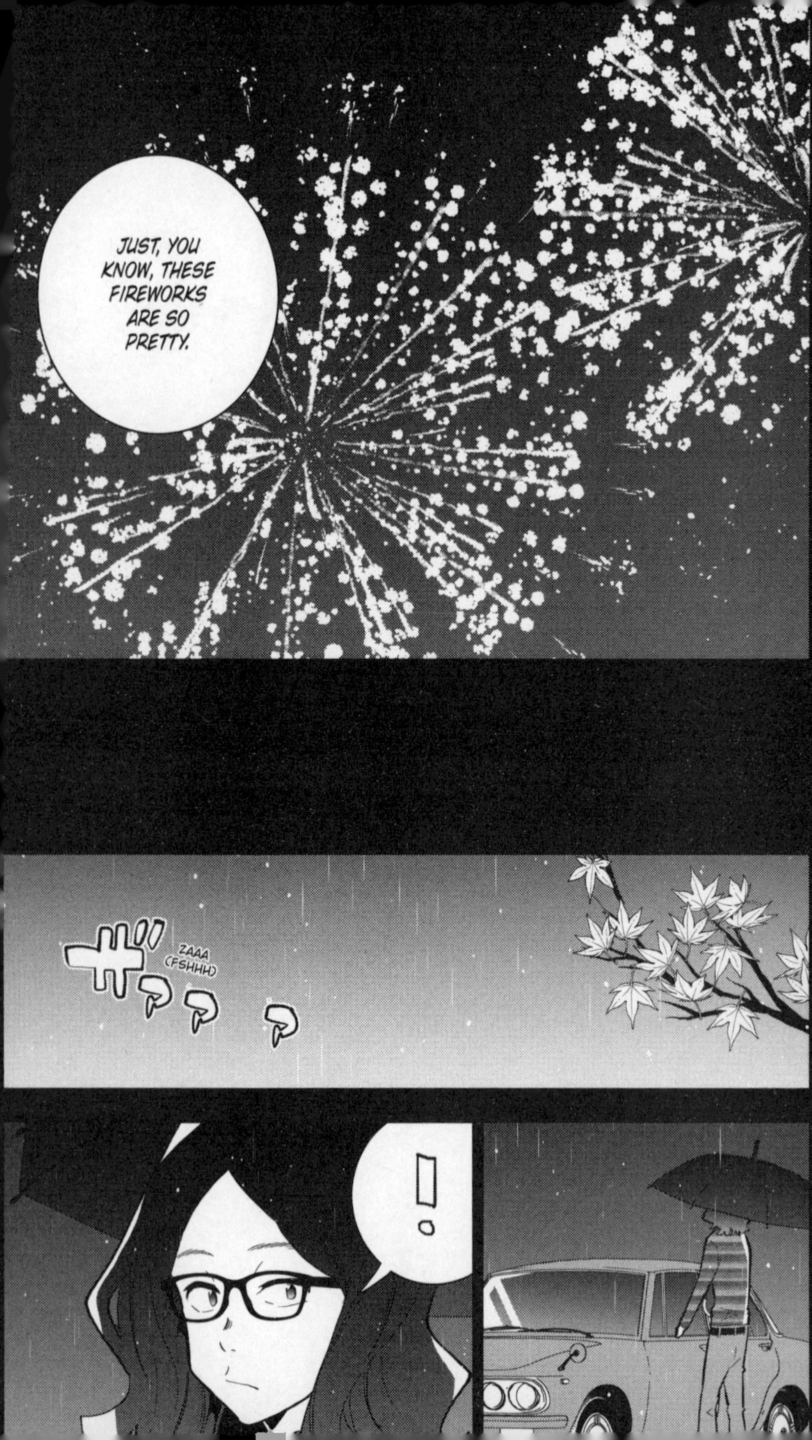
JUST, YOU KNOW, THESE FIREWORKS ARE SO PRETTY.
ZAAA (FSHHH)
!

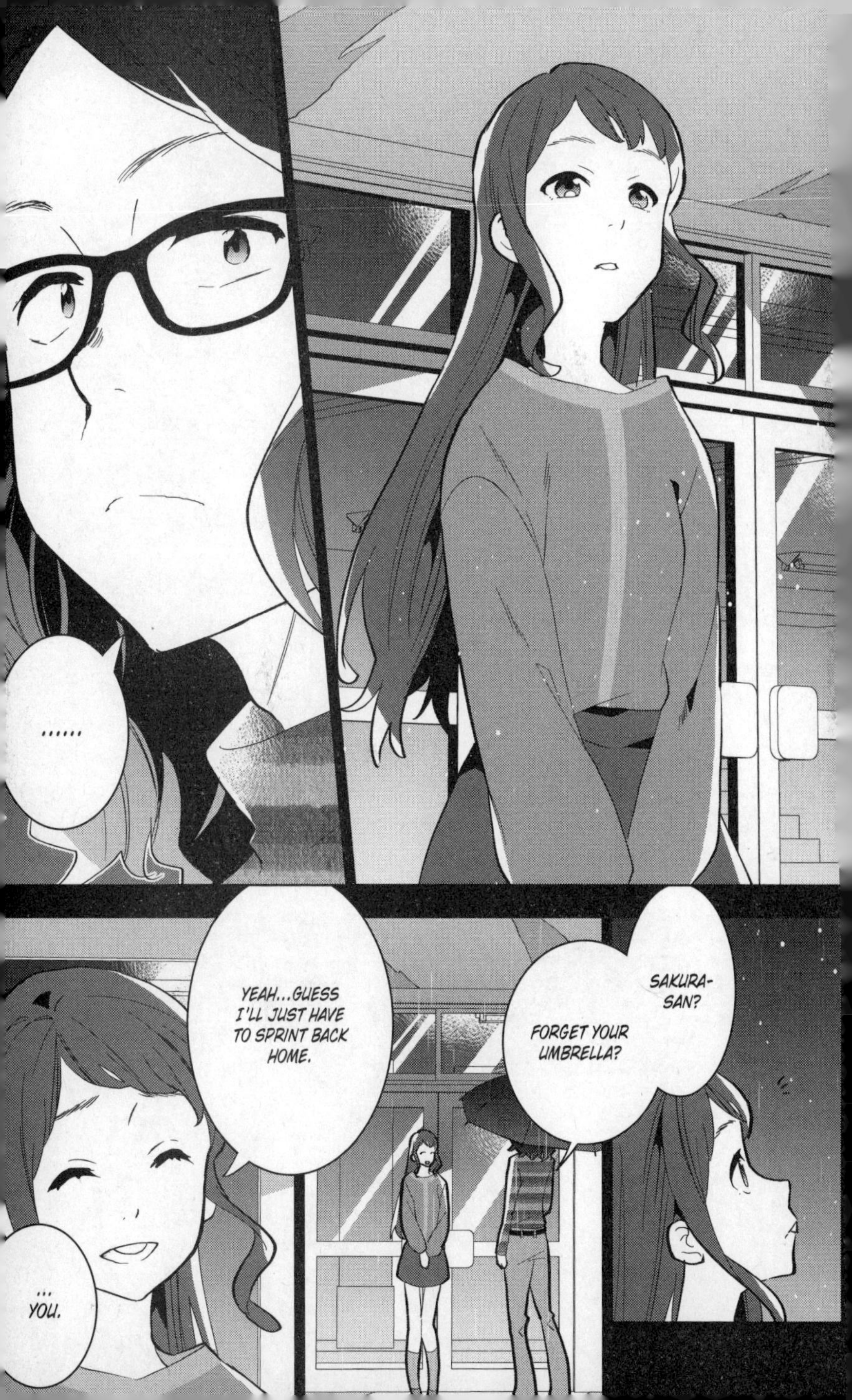
......
SAKURA-SAN?
FORGET YOUR UMBRELLA?
YEAH...GUESS I'LL JUST HAVE TO SPRINT BACK HOME.
... YOU.

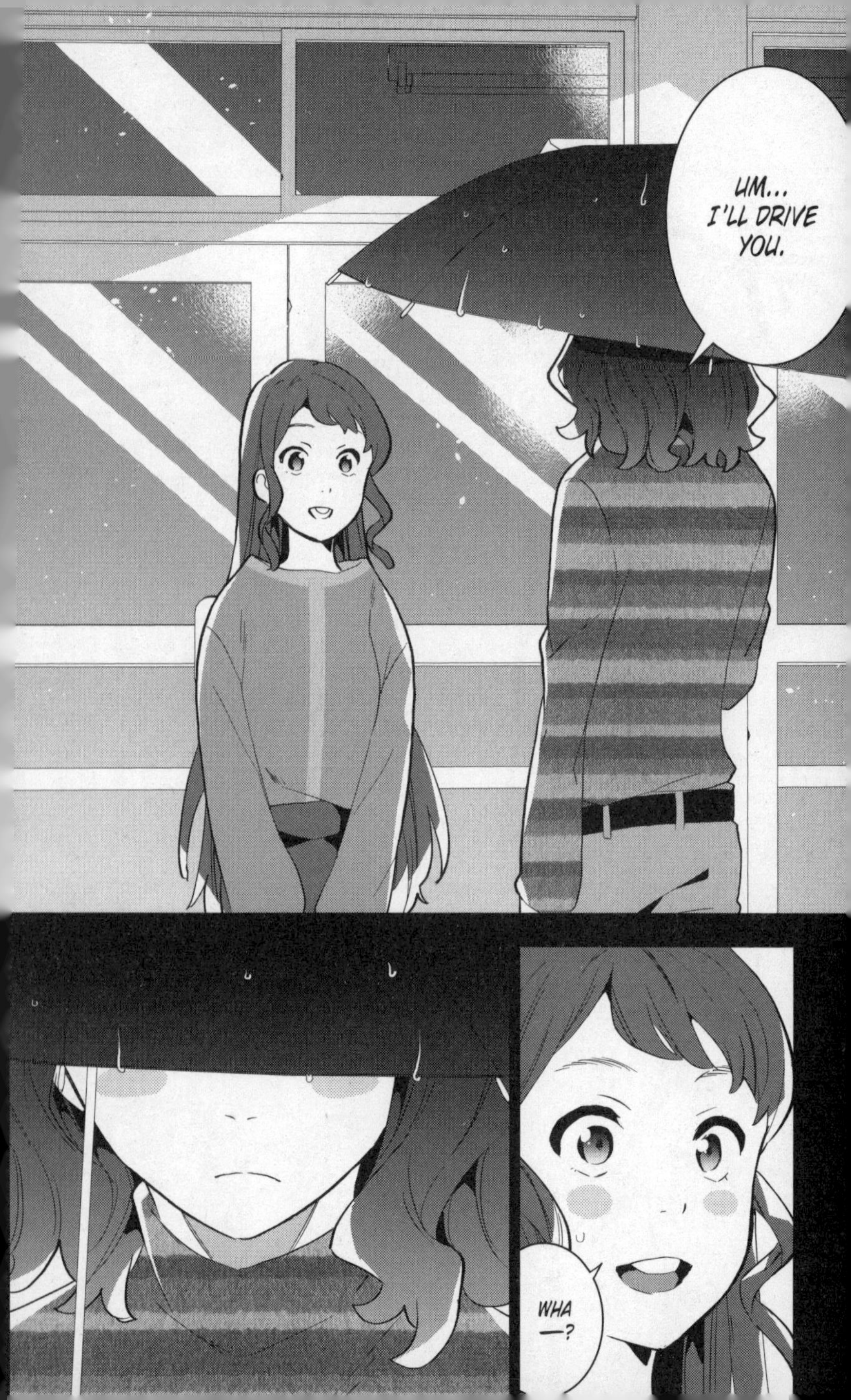
UM... I'LL DRIVE YOU.
WHA —?

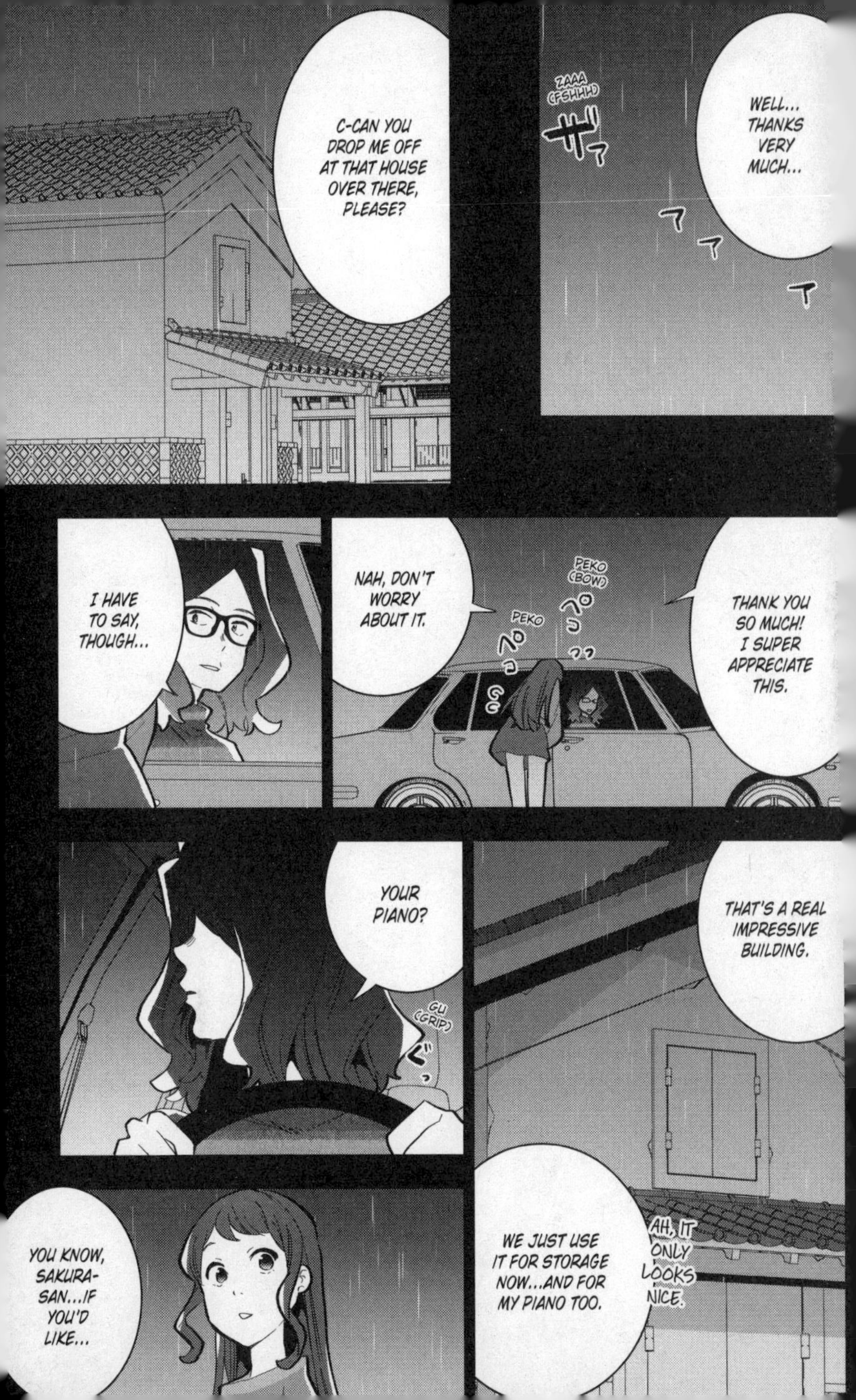
ZAAA (FSHHH)
WELL... THANKS VERY MUCH...
C-CAN YOU DROP ME OFF AT THAT HOUSE OVER THERE, PLEASE?
THANK YOU SO MUCH! I SUPER APPRECIATE THIS.
PEKO (BOW)
PEKO
NAH, DON'T WORRY ABOUT IT.
I HAVE TO SAY, THOUGH...
THAT'S A REAL IMPRESSIVE BUILDING.
AH, IT ONLY LOOKS NICE.
WE JUST USE IT FOR STORAGE NOW...AND FOR MY PIANO TOO.
YOUR PIANO?
GU (GRIP)
YOU KNOW, SAKURA-SAN...IF YOU'D LIKE...

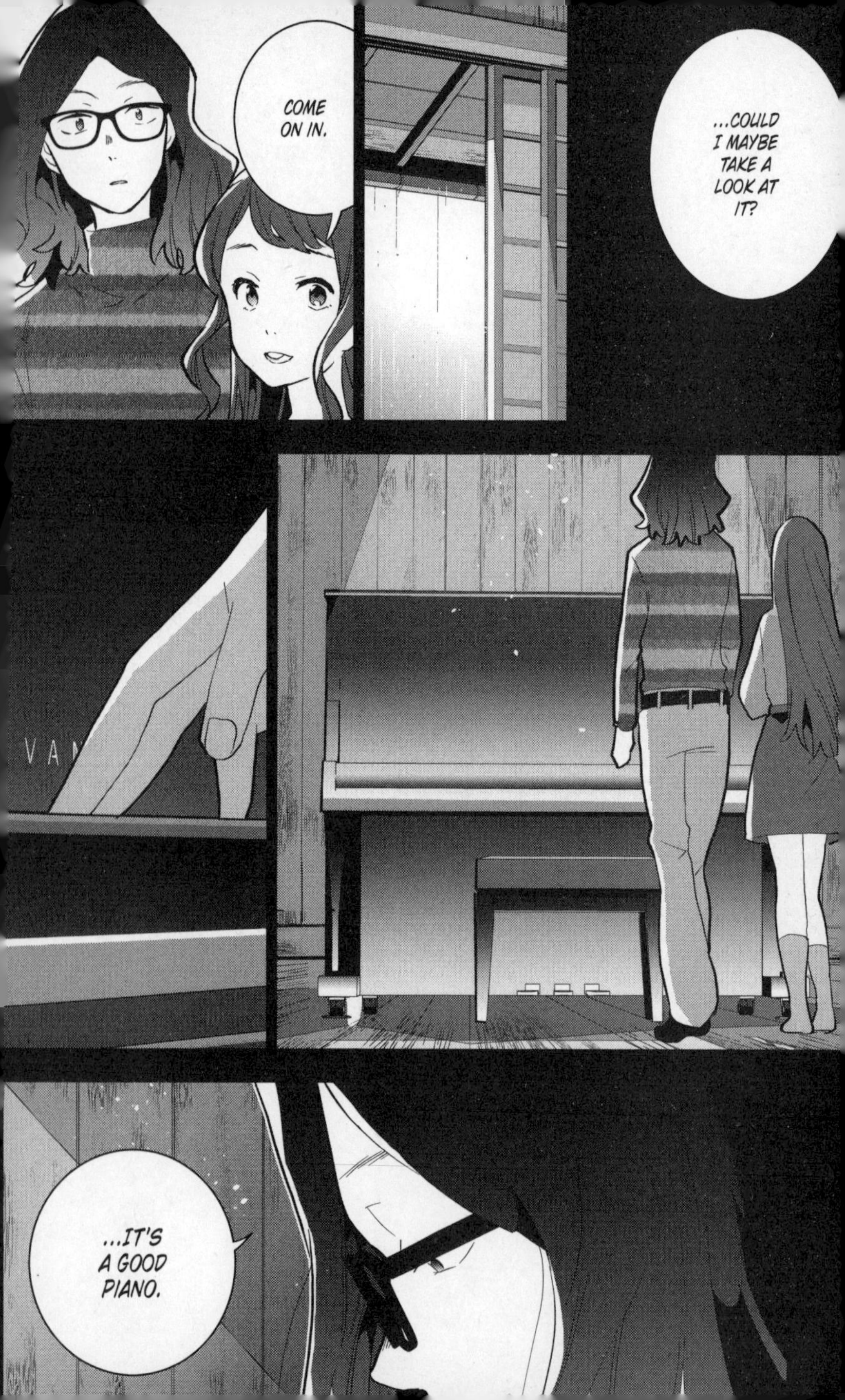
...COULD I MAYBE TAKE A LOOK AT IT?
COME ON IN.
...IT'S A GOOD PIANO.

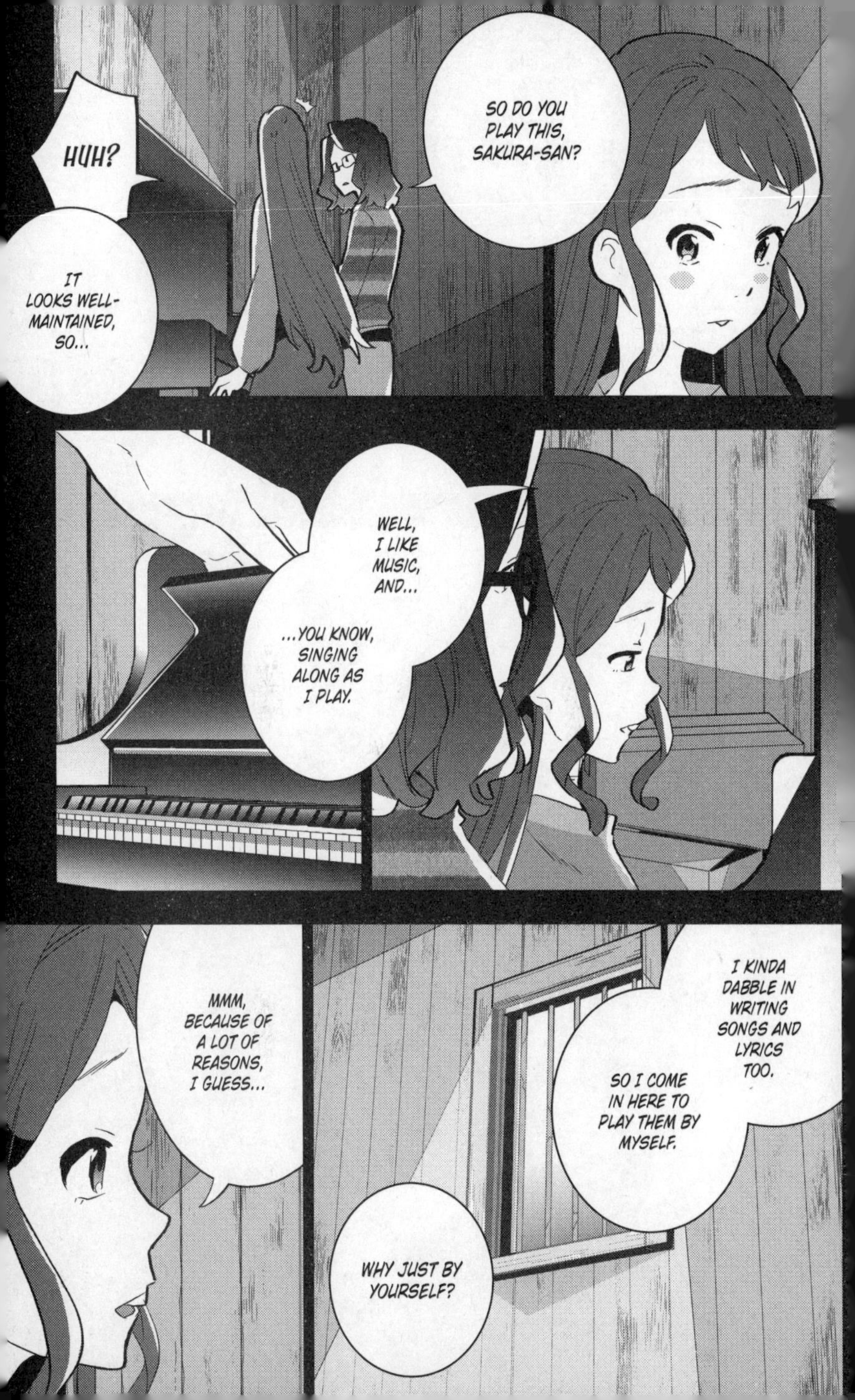
SO DO YOU PLAY THIS, SAKURA-SAN?
HUH?
IT LOOKS WELL-MAINTAINED, SO...
WELL, I LIKE MUSIC, AND...
...YOU KNOW, SINGING ALONG AS I PLAY.
I KINDA DABBLE IN WRITING SONGS AND LYRICS TOO.
SO I COME IN HERE TO PLAY THEM BY MYSELF.
WHY JUST BY YOURSELF?
MMM, BECAUSE OF A LOT OF REASONS, I GUESS...

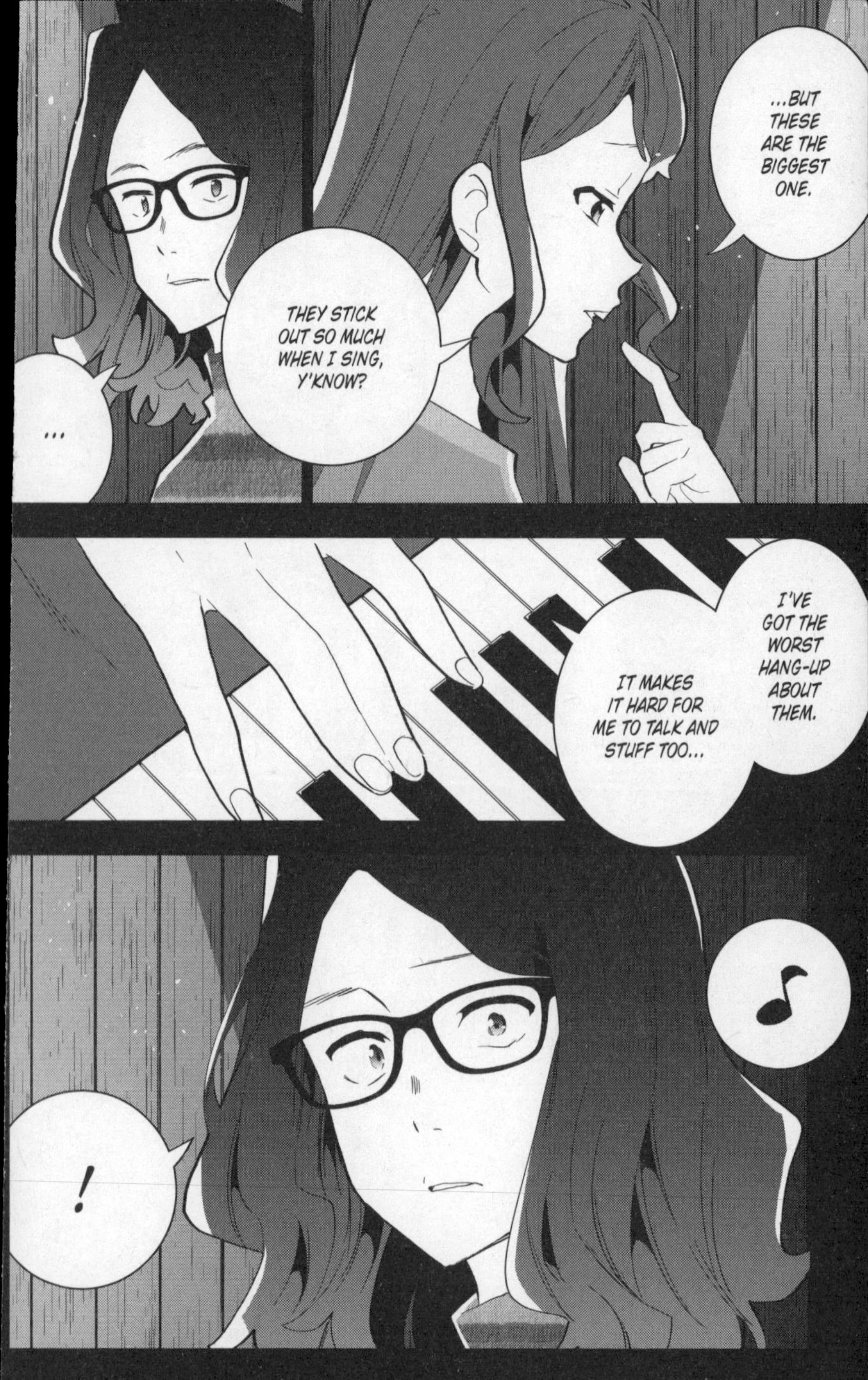
...BUT THESE ARE THE BIGGEST ONE.
THEY STICK OUT SO MUCH WHEN I SING, Y'KNOW?
...
I'VE GOT THE WORST HANG-UP ABOUT THEM.
IT MAKES IT HARD FOR ME TO TALK AND STUFF TOO...
♪
!

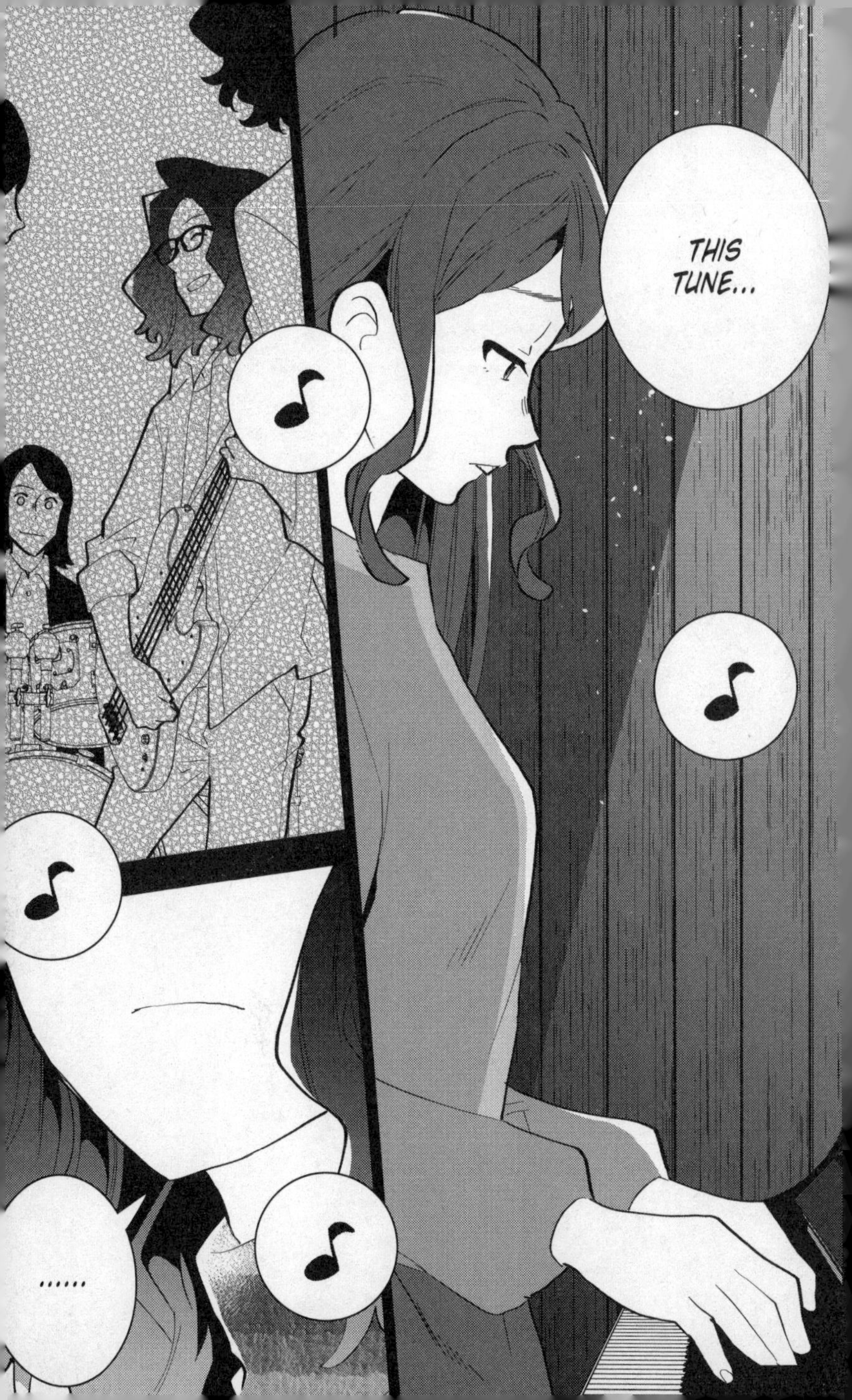
THIS TUNE...
♪
♪
♪
♪
......
♪

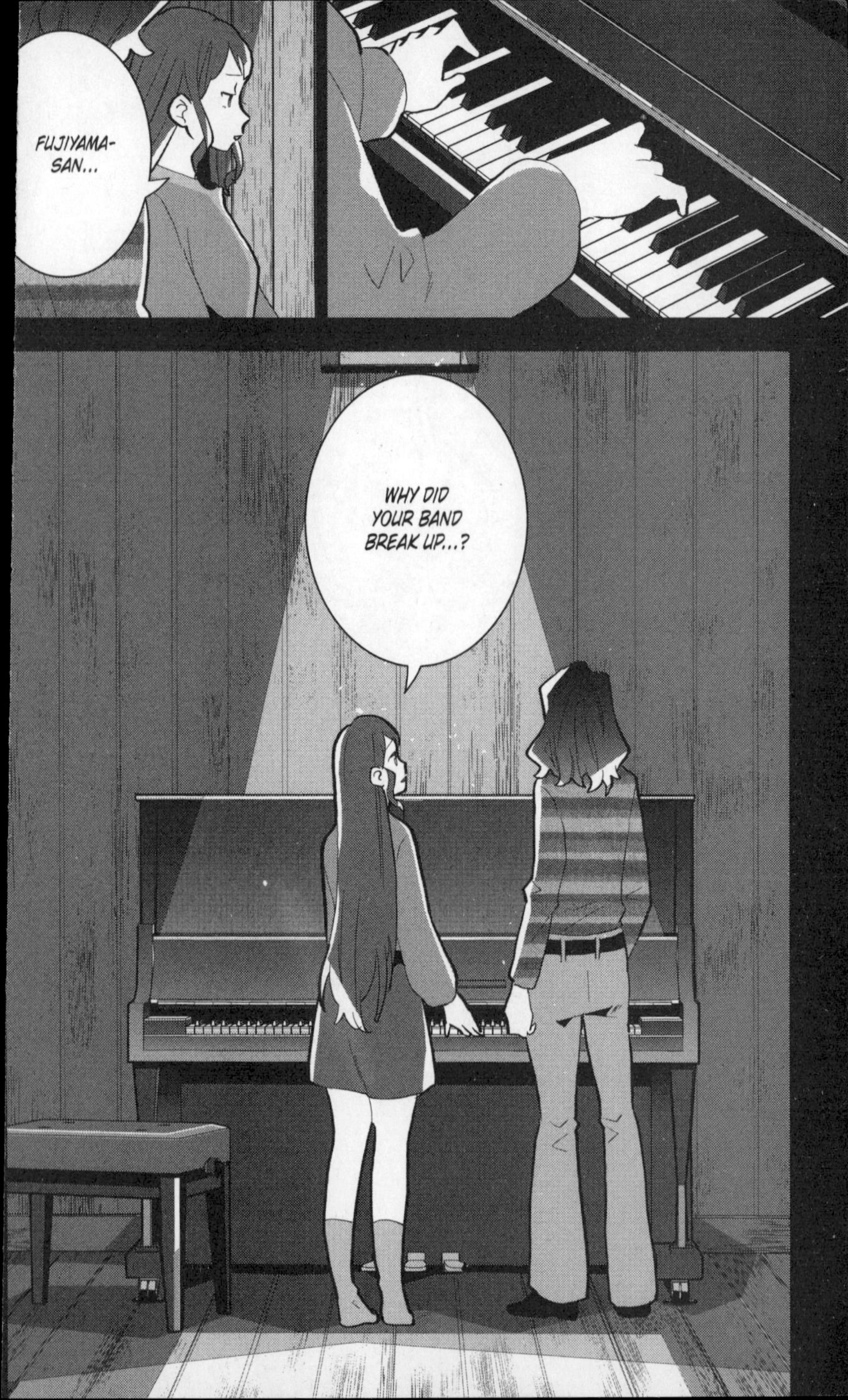
FUJIYAMA-SAN...
WHY DID YOUR BAND BREAK UP...?

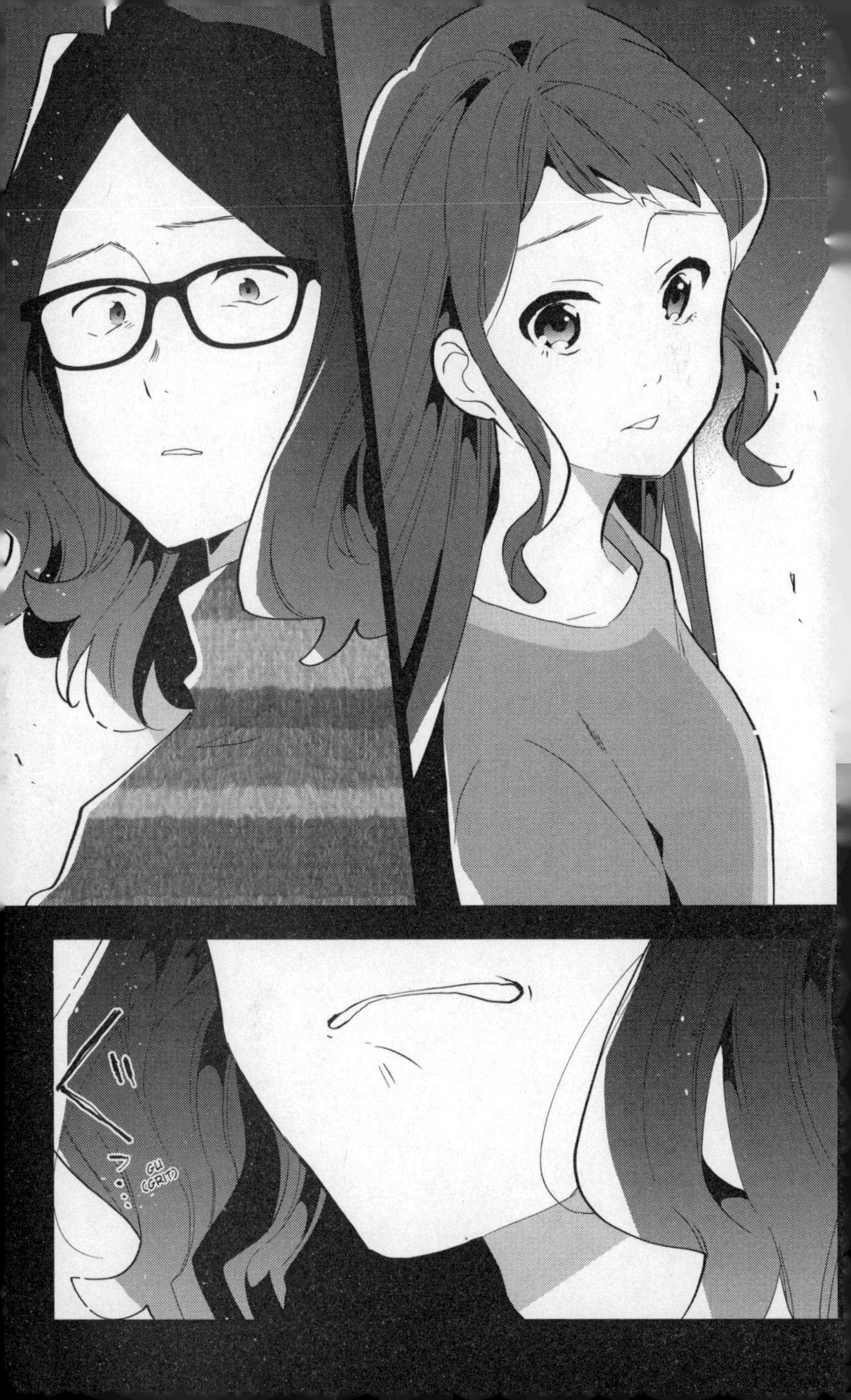
ぐっ…
GU
(GRIT)

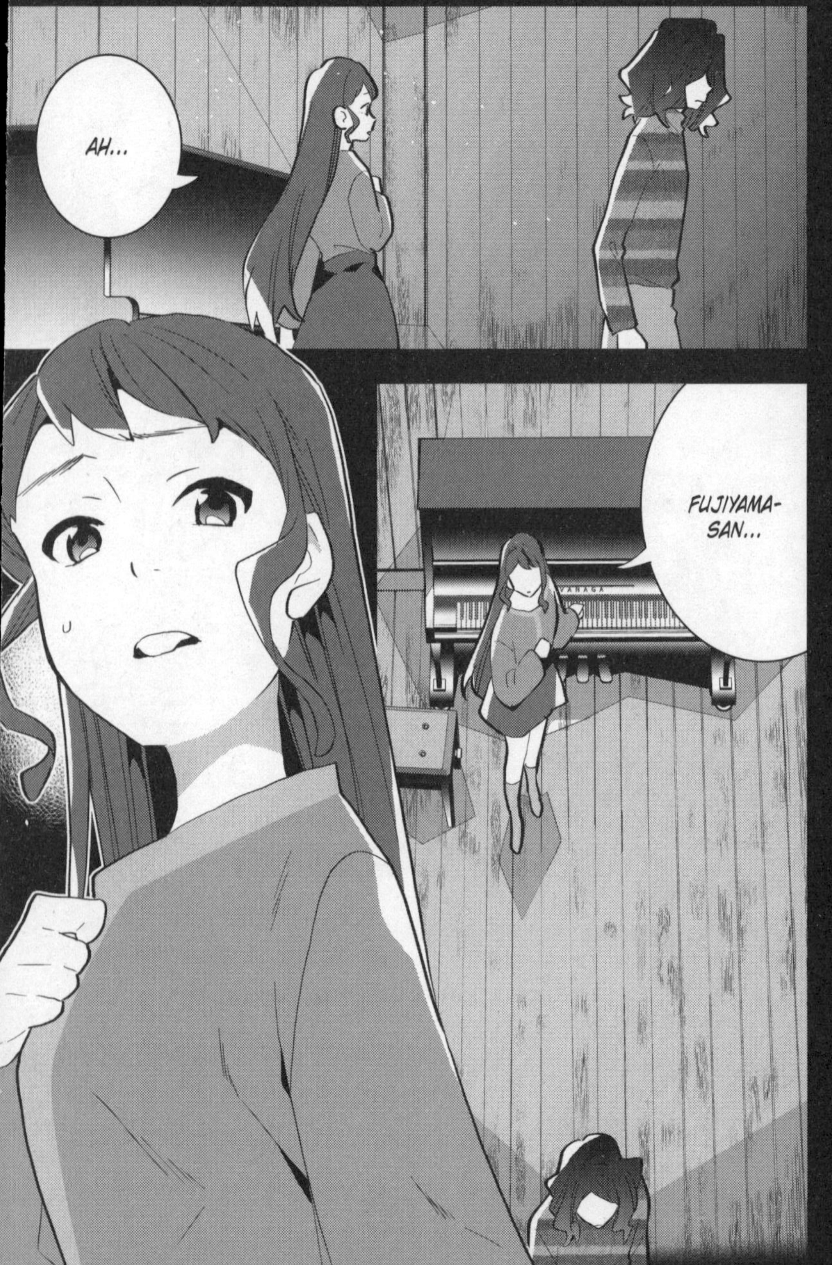
AH...
FUJIYAMA-SAN...

Words Bubble Up
Like Soda Pop

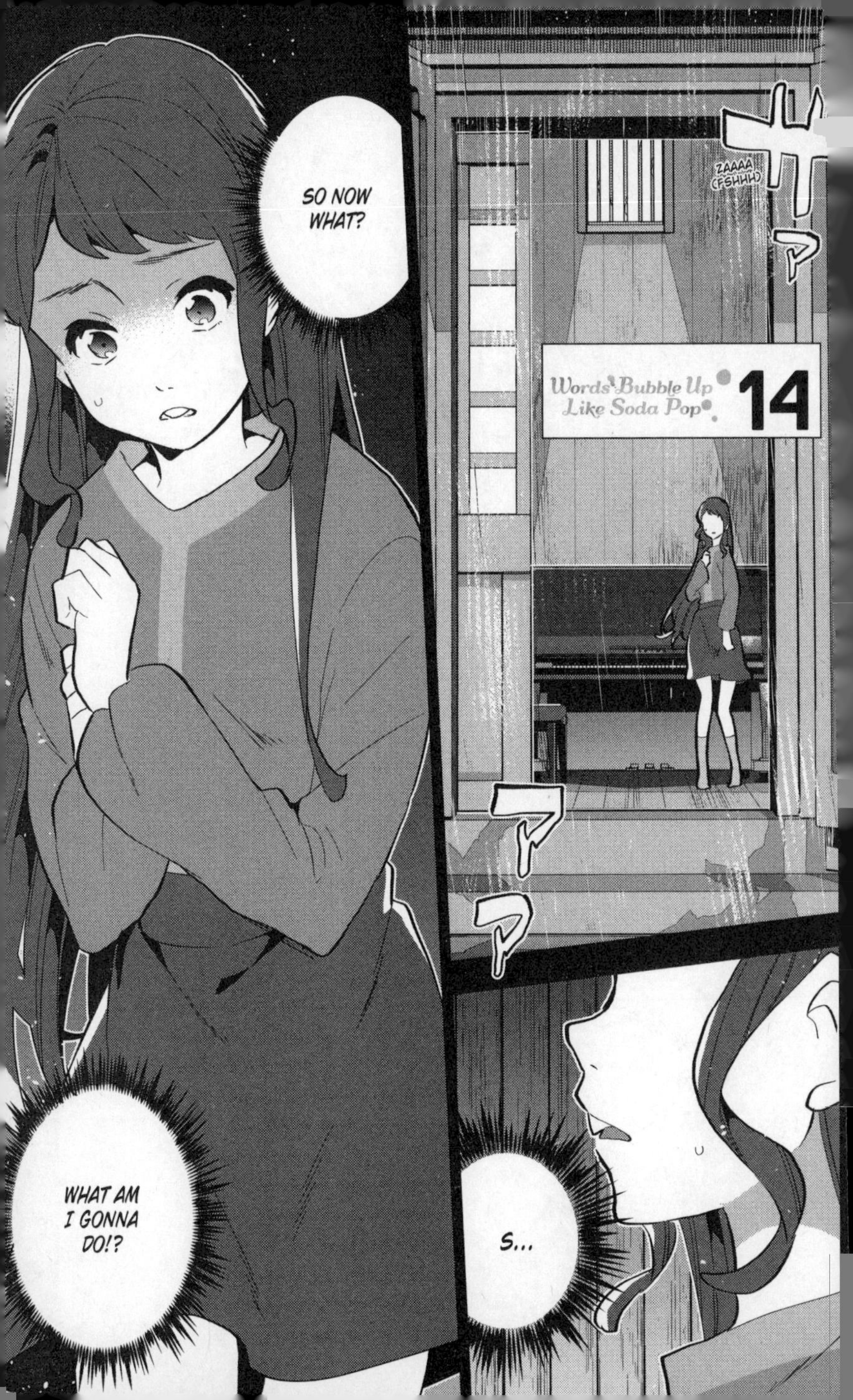
ZAAAA (FSHHH)
Words Bubble Up Like Soda Pop 14
S...
SO NOW WHAT?
WHAT AM I GONNA DO!?

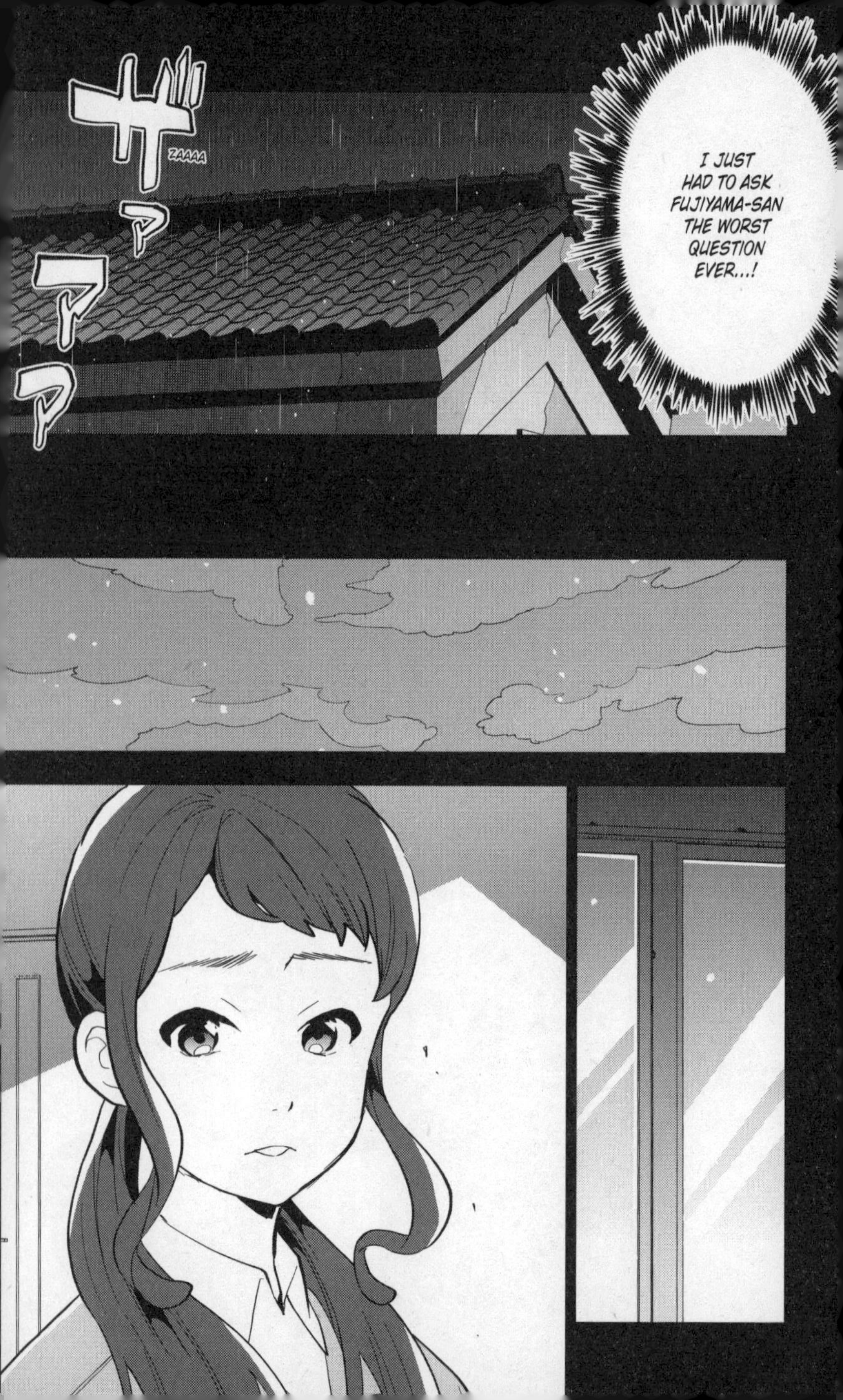
I JUST HAD TO ASK FUJIYAMA-SAN THE WORST QUESTION EVER...!
ザァァァ
ZAAAA

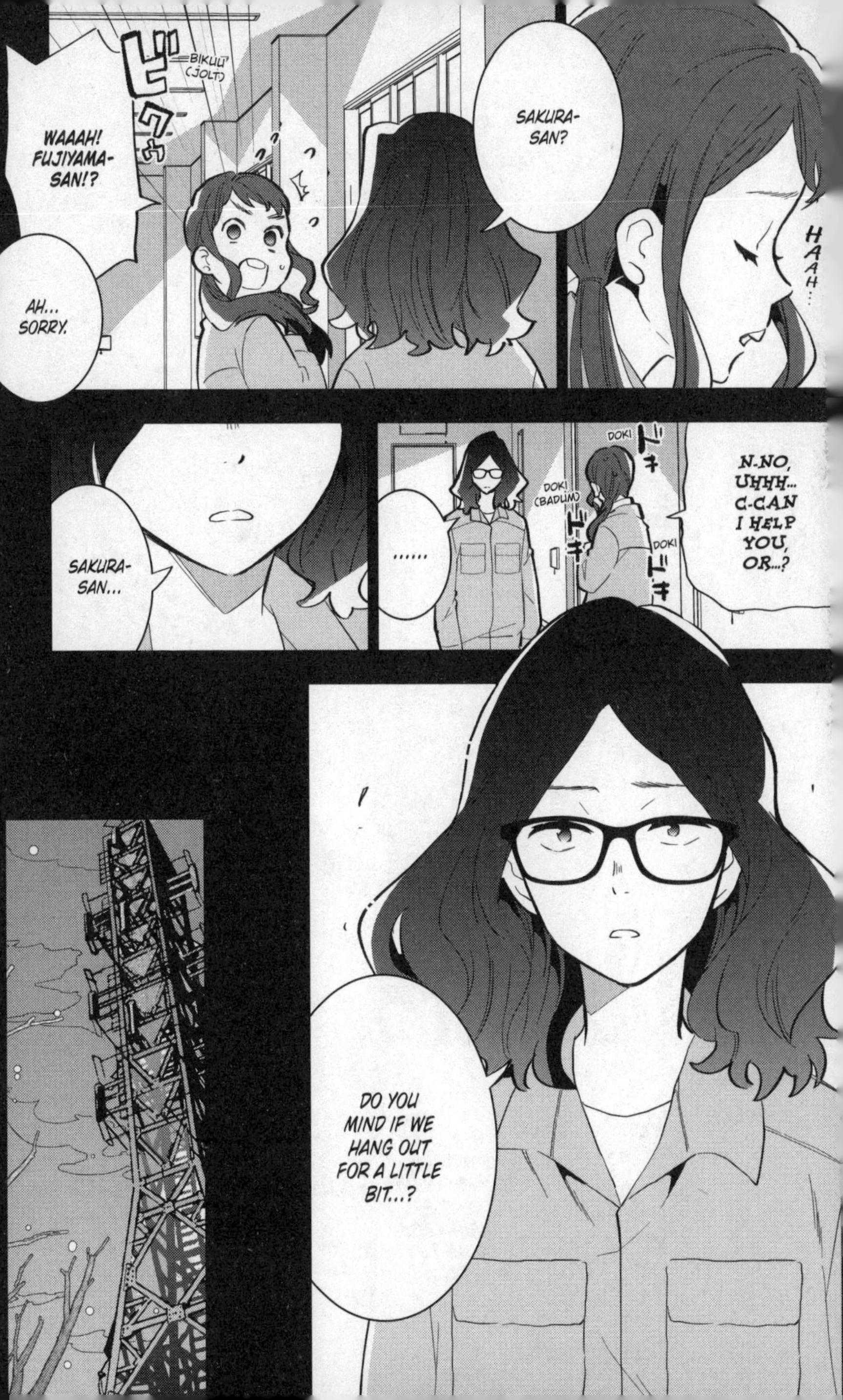
HAAAH...
SAKURA-SAN?
BIKUU' (JOLT)
WAAAH! FUJIYAMA-SAN!?
AH... SORRY.
DOKI
N-NO, UHHH... C-CAN I HELP YOU, OR...?
DOKI (BADUMP)
DOKI
......
SAKURA-SAN...
DO YOU MIND IF WE HANG OUT FOR A LITTLE BIT...?

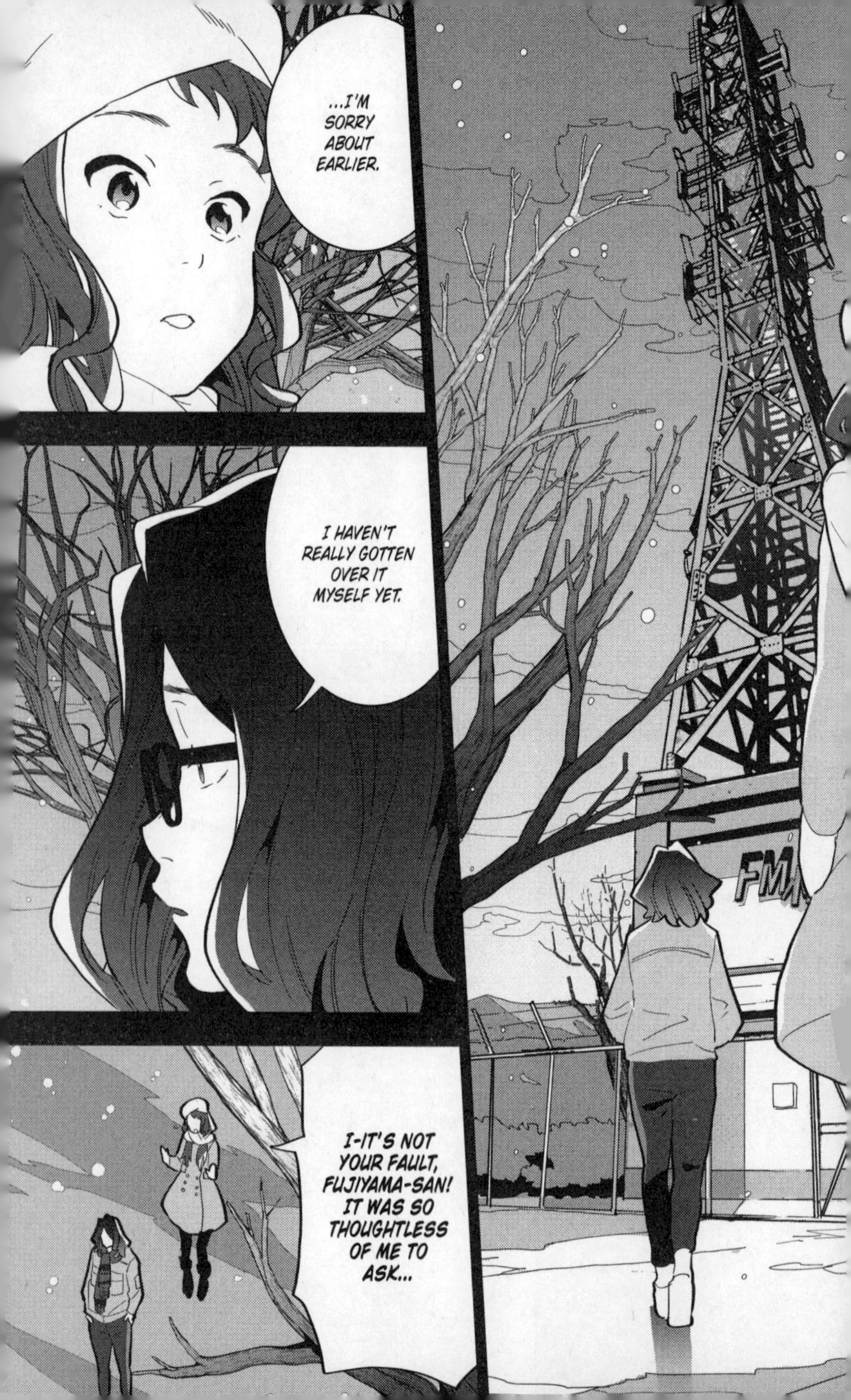
FM
...I'M SORRY ABOUT EARLIER.
I HAVEN'T REALLY GOTTEN OVER IT MYSELF YET.
I-IT'S NOT YOUR FAULT, FUJIYAMA-SAN! IT WAS SO THOUGHTLESS OF ME TO ASK...

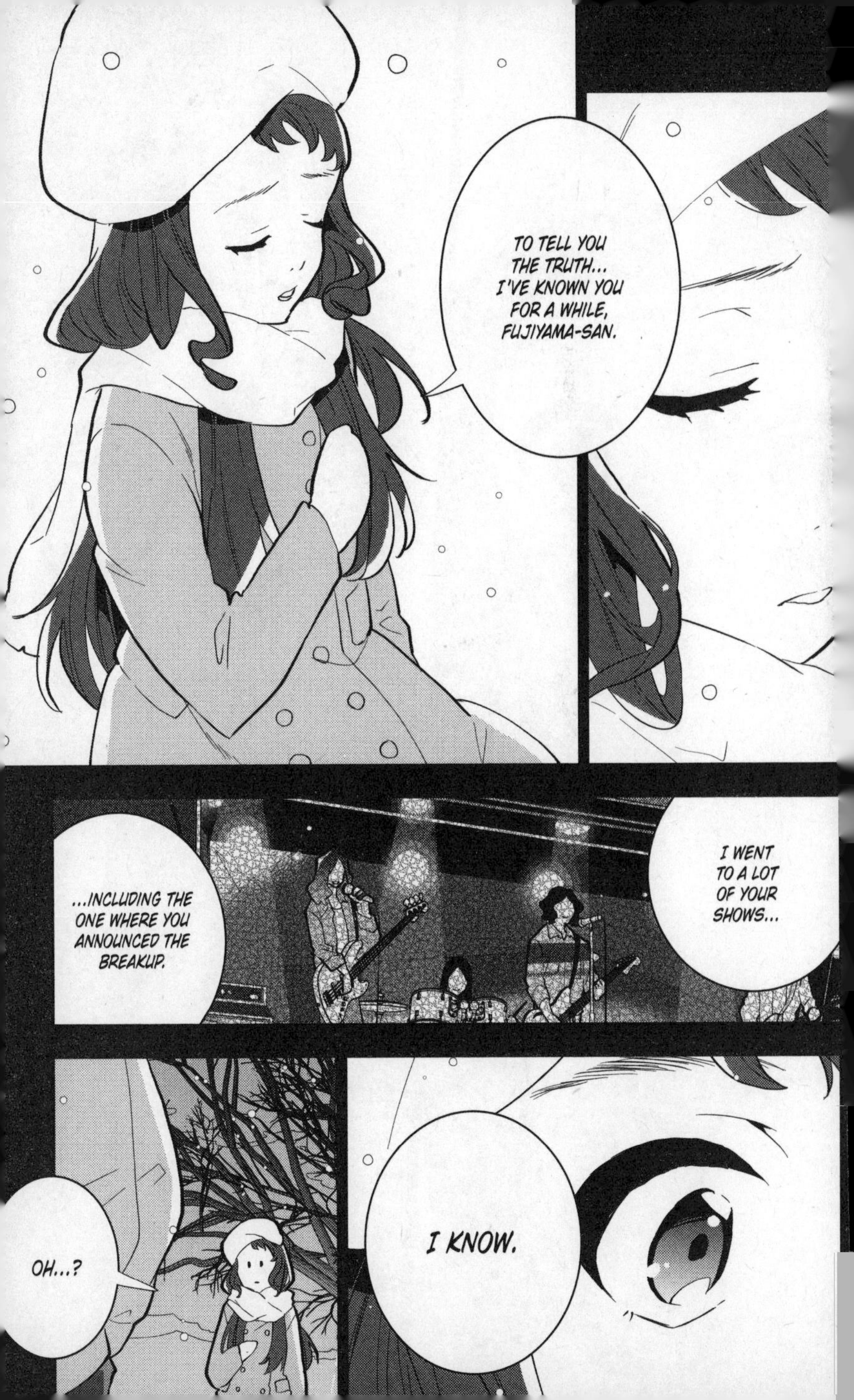
TO TELL YOU THE TRUTH... I'VE KNOWN YOU FOR A WHILE, FUJIYAMA-SAN.
I WENT TO A LOT OF YOUR SHOWS...
...INCLUDING THE ONE WHERE YOU ANNOUNCED THE BREAKUP.
I KNOW.
OH...?

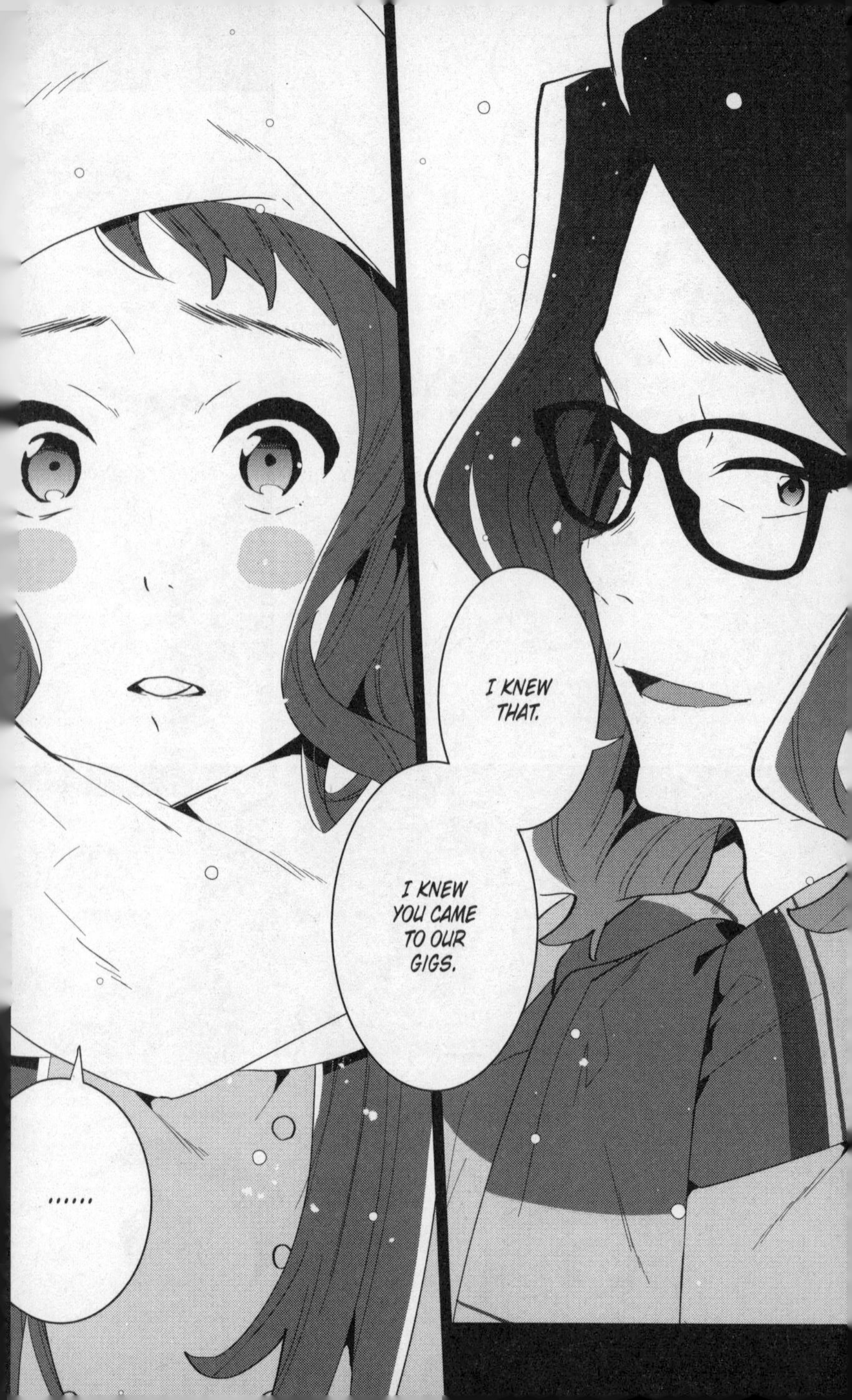
I KNEW THAT.
I KNEW YOU CAME TO OUR GIGS.
......

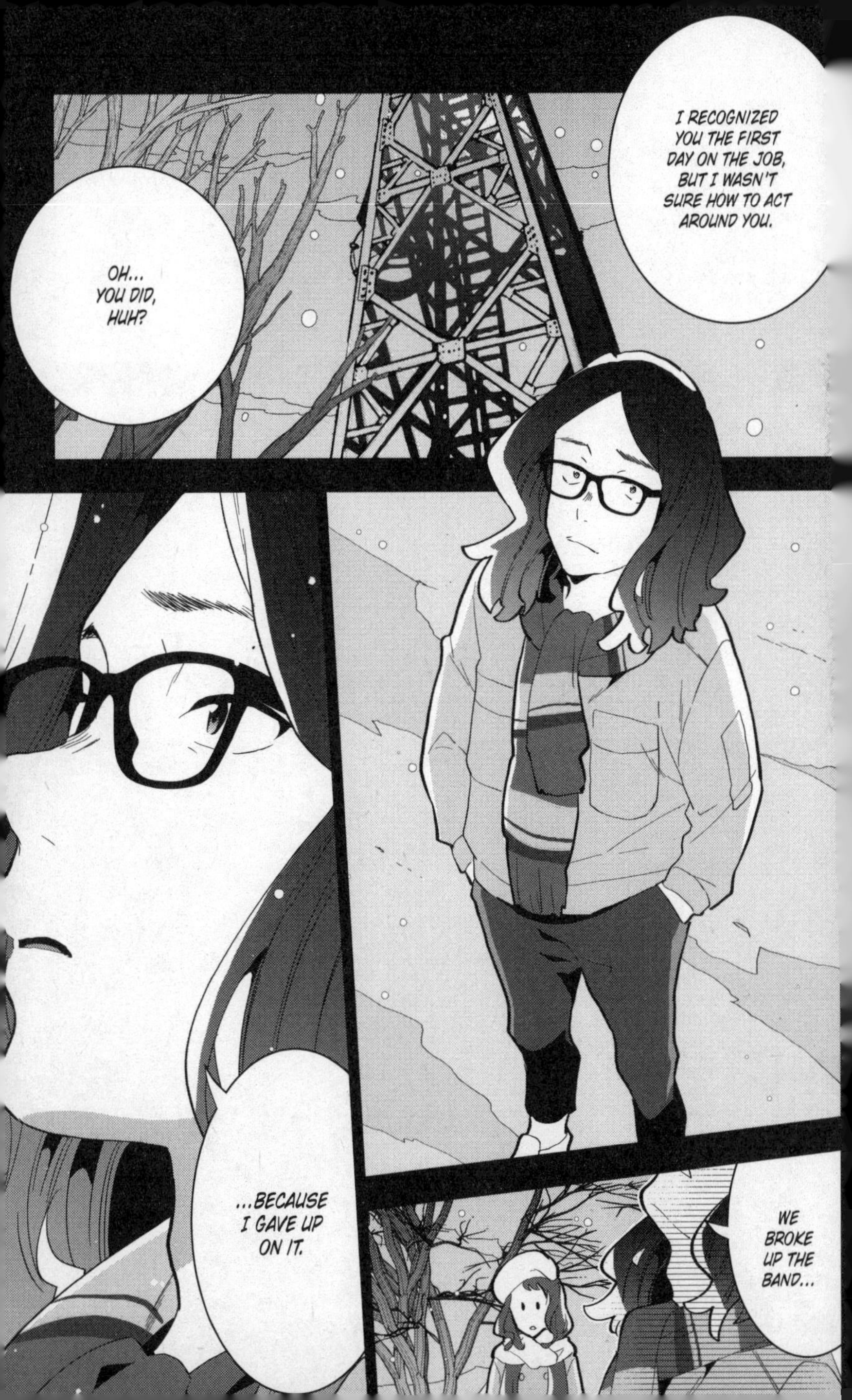
I RECOGNIZED YOU THE FIRST DAY ON THE JOB, BUT I WASN'T SURE HOW TO ACT AROUND YOU.
OH... YOU DID, HUH?
WE BROKE UP THE BAND...
...BECAUSE I GAVE UP ON IT.

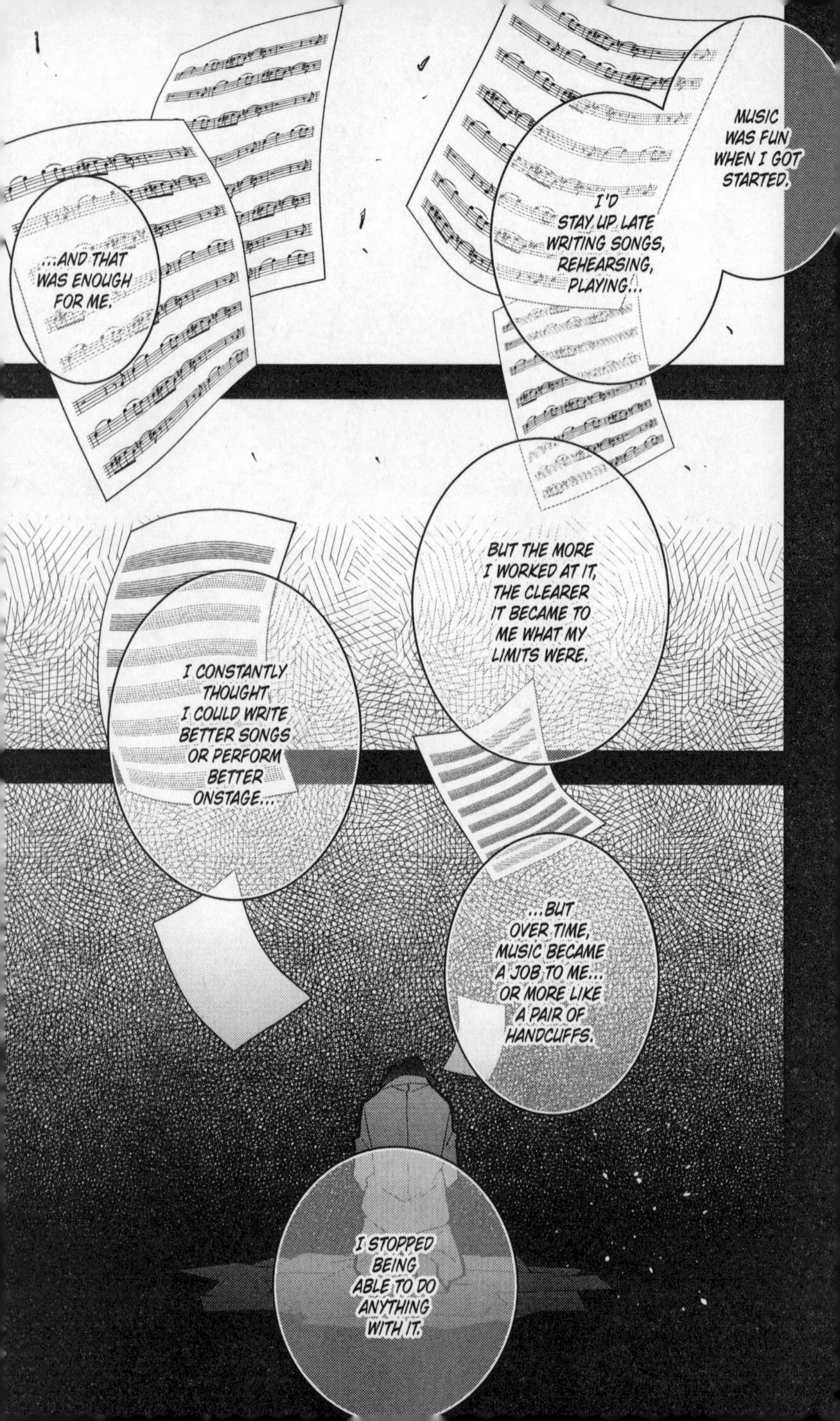
MUSIC WAS FUN WHEN I GOT STARTED.
I'D STAY UP LATE WRITING SONGS, REHEARSING, PLAYING...
...AND THAT WAS ENOUGH FOR ME.
BUT THE MORE I WORKED AT IT, THE CLEARER IT BECAME TO ME WHAT MY LIMITS WERE.
I CONSTANTLY THOUGHT I COULD WRITE BETTER SONGS OR PERFORM BETTER ONSTAGE...
...BUT OVER TIME, MUSIC BECAME A JOB TO ME... OR MORE LIKE A PAIR OF HANDCUFFS.
I STOPPED BEING ABLE TO DO ANYTHING WITH IT.

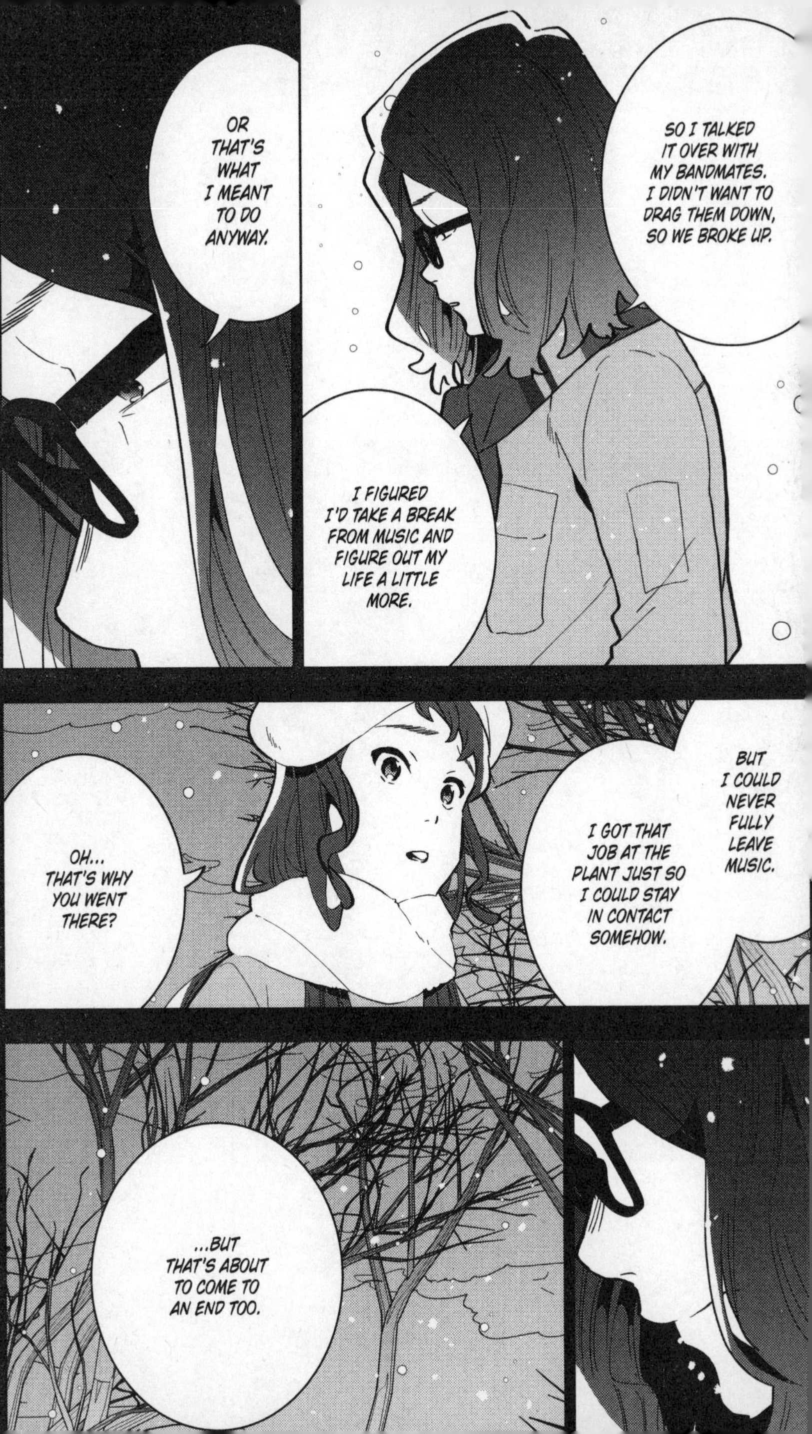
SO I TALKED IT OVER WITH MY BANDMATES. I DIDN'T WANT TO DRAG THEM DOWN, SO WE BROKE UP.
I FIGURED I'D TAKE A BREAK FROM MUSIC AND FIGURE OUT MY LIFE A LITTLE MORE.
OR THAT'S WHAT I MEANT TO DO ANYWAY.
BUT I COULD NEVER FULLY LEAVE MUSIC.
I GOT THAT JOB AT THE PLANT JUST SO I COULD STAY IN CONTACT SOMEHOW.
OH... THAT'S WHY YOU WENT THERE?
...BUT THAT'S ABOUT TO COME TO AN END TOO.

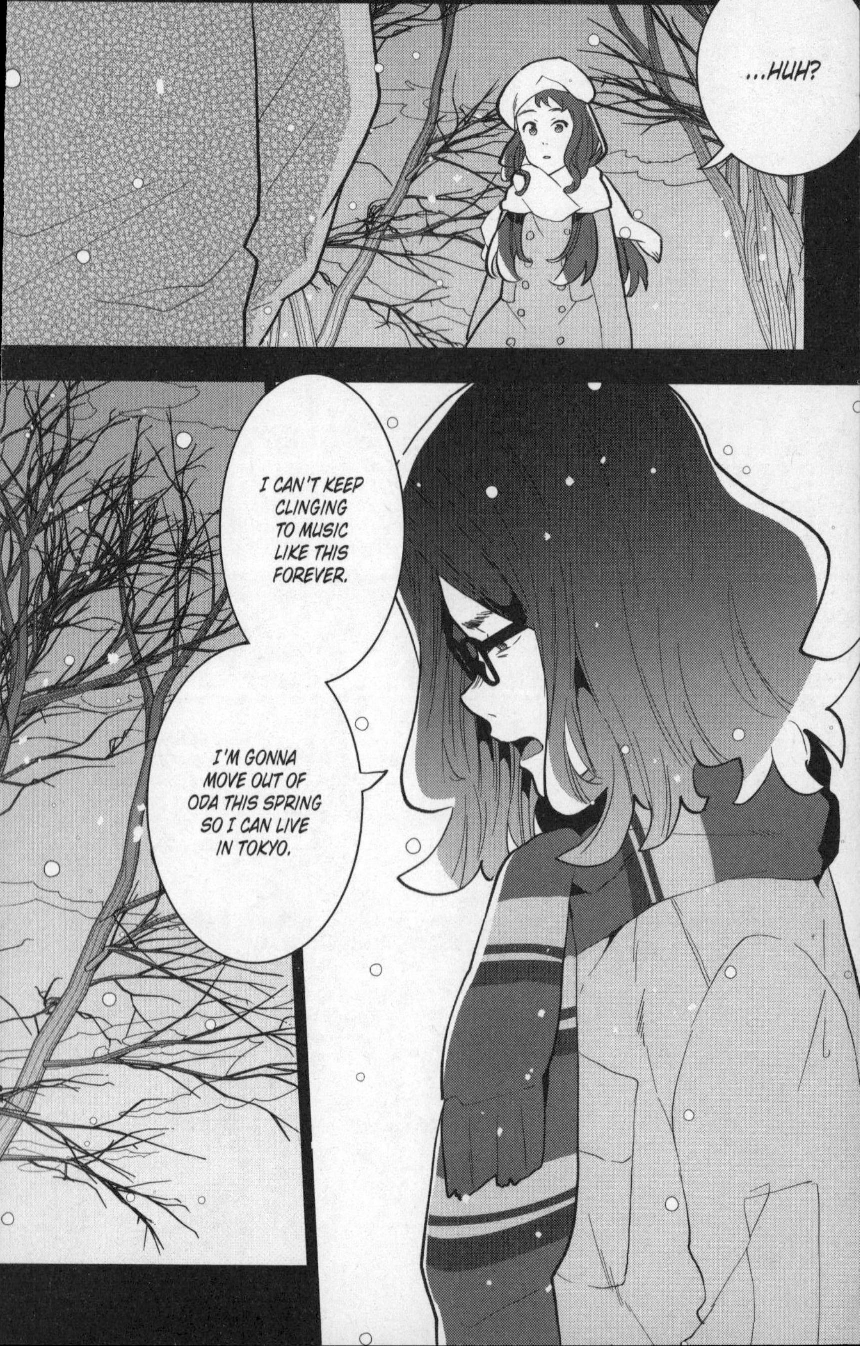
...HUH?
I CAN'T KEEP CLINGING TO MUSIC LIKE THIS FOREVER.
I'M GONNA MOVE OUT OF ODA THIS SPRING SO I CAN LIVE IN TOKYO.

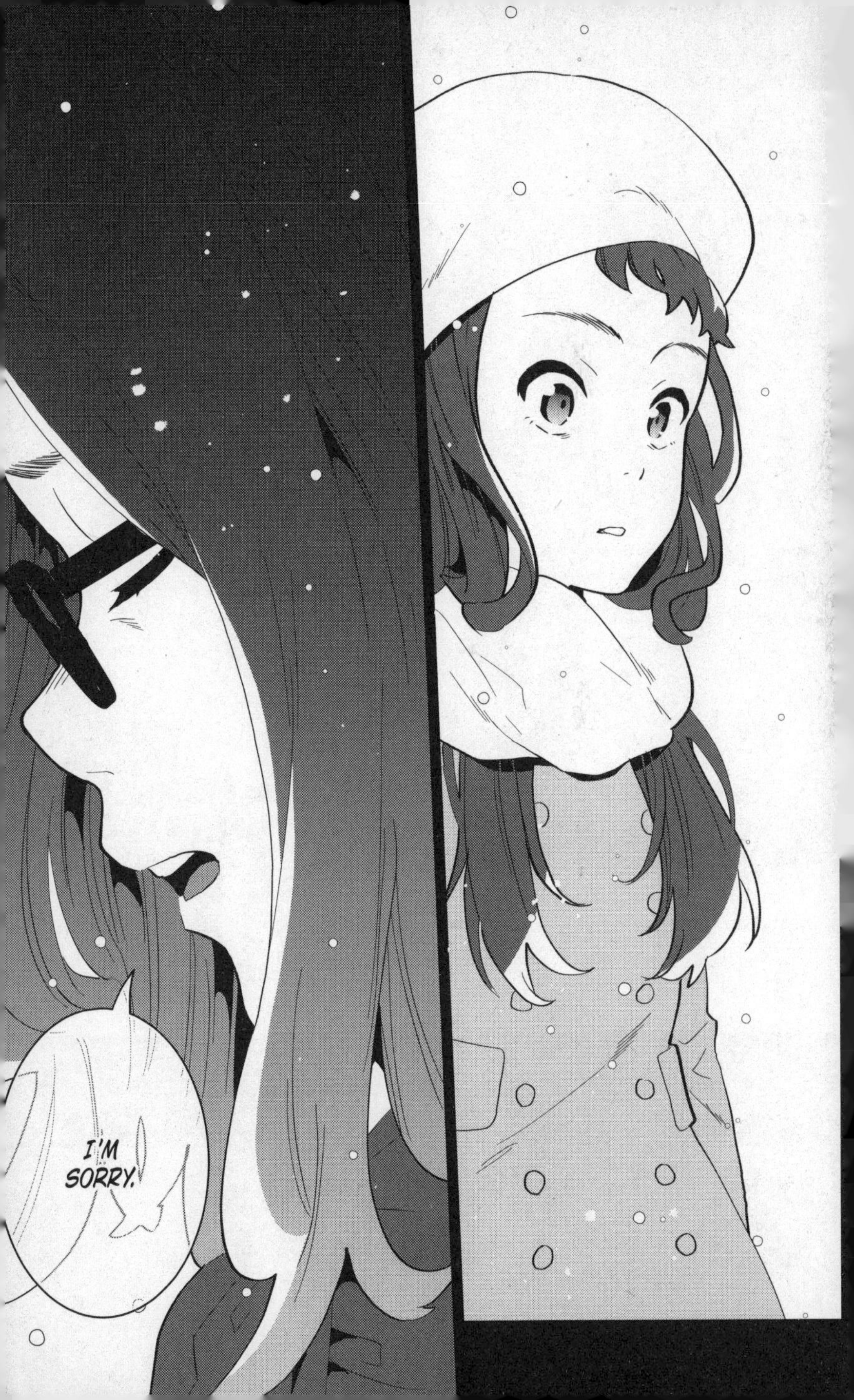
I'M SORRY.

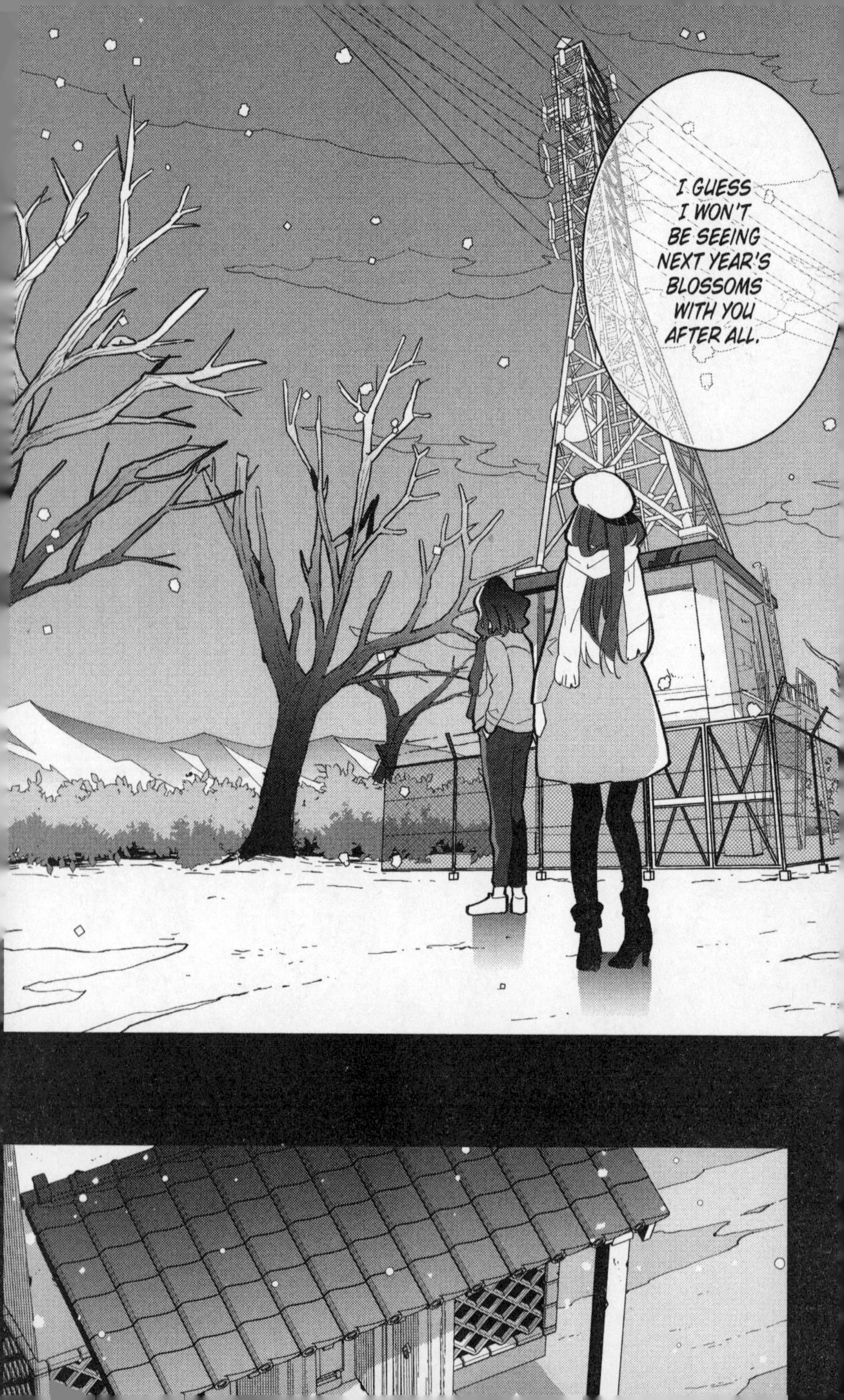
I GUESS I WON'T BE SEEING NEXT YEAR'S BLOSSOMS WITH YOU AFTER ALL.

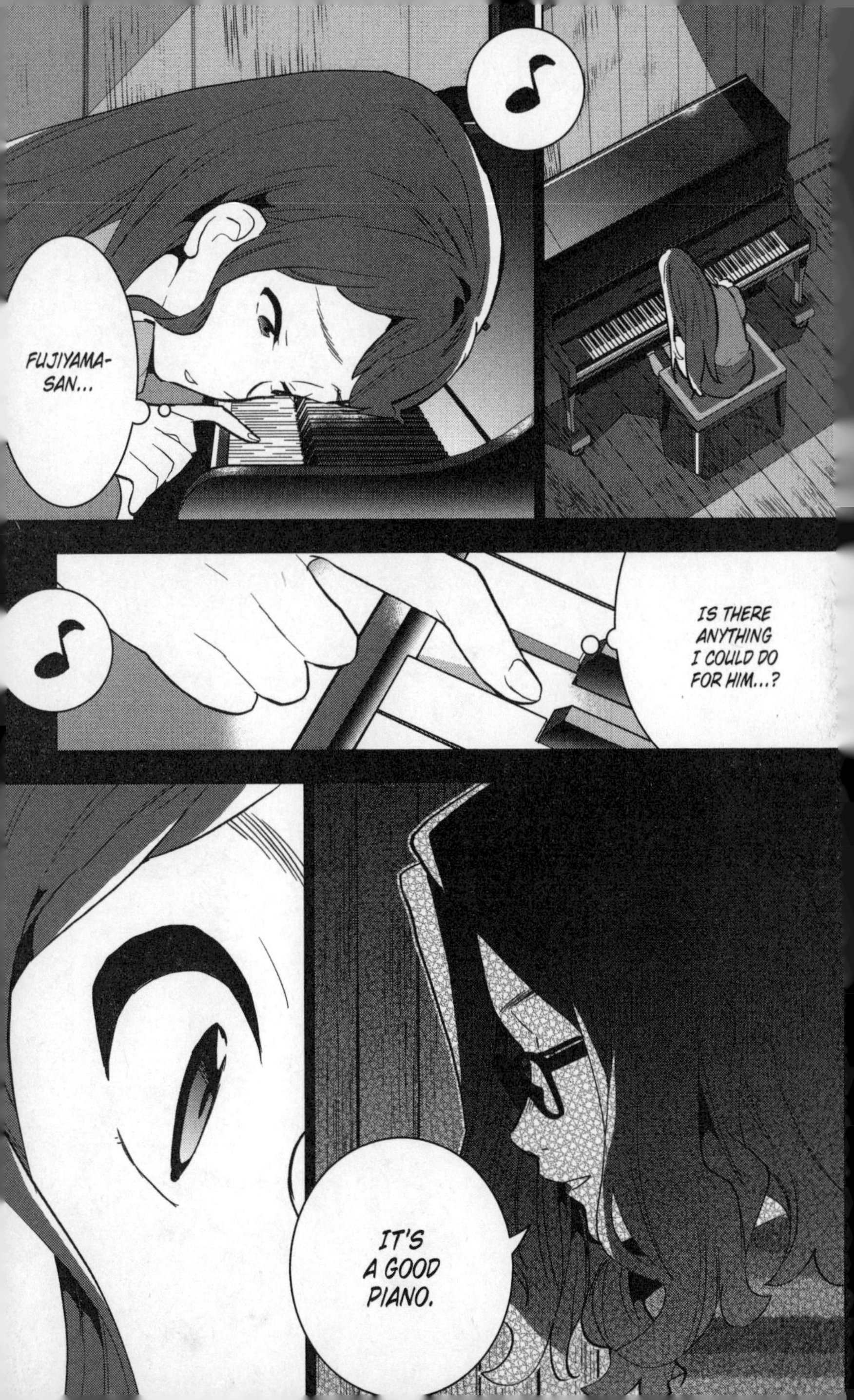
FUJIYAMA-SAN...
IS THERE ANYTHING I COULD DO FOR HIM...?
IT'S A GOOD PIANO.

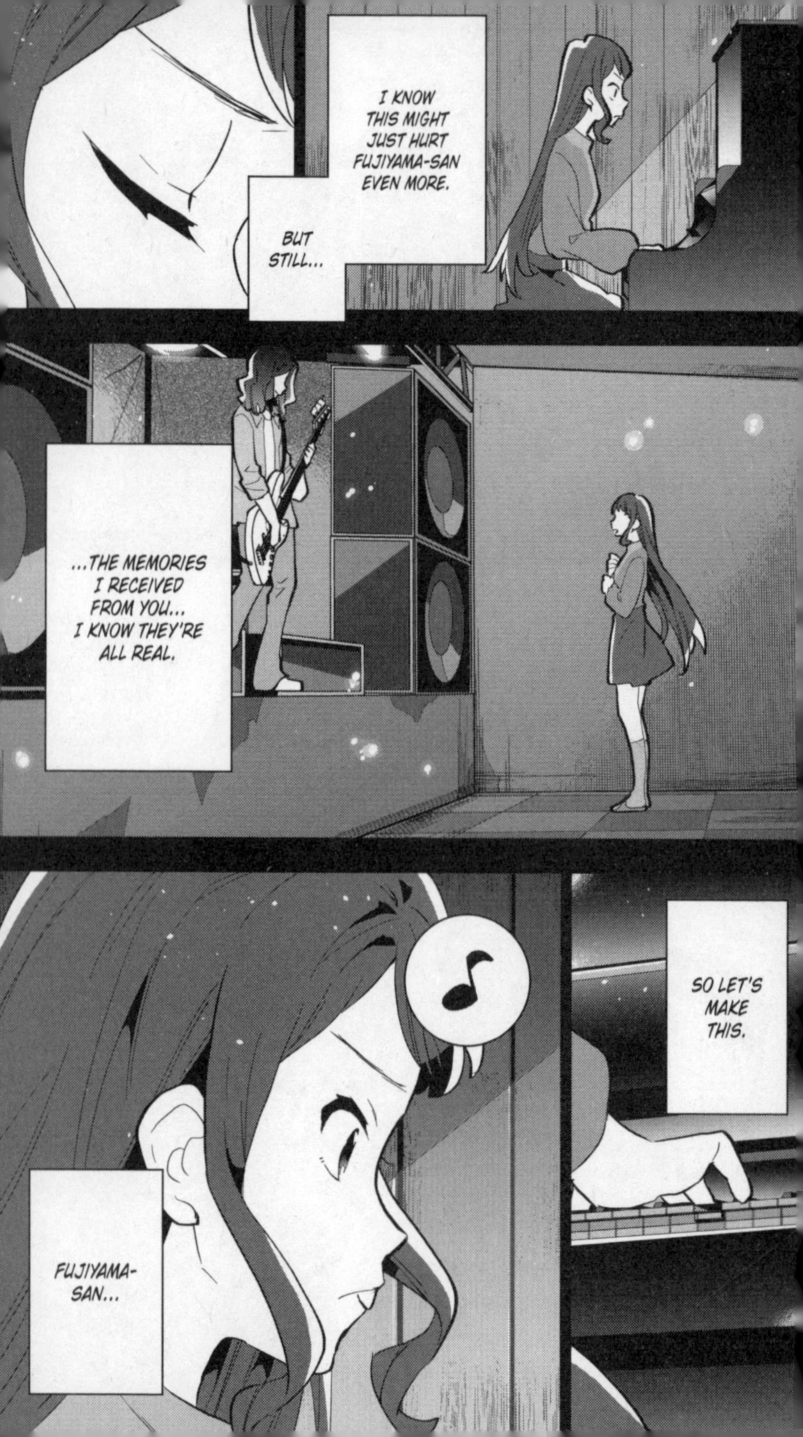
I KNOW THIS MIGHT JUST HURT FUJIYAMA-SAN EVEN MORE.
BUT STILL...
...THE MEMORIES I RECEIVED FROM YOU... I KNOW THEY'RE ALL REAL.
SO LET'S MAKE THIS.
FUJIYAMA-SAN...

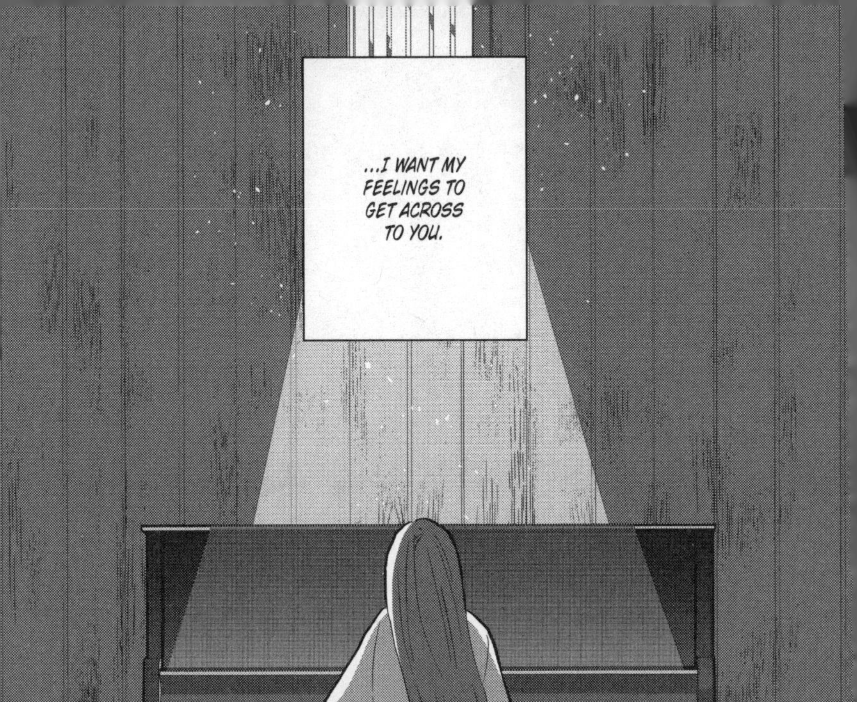
...I WANT MY FEELINGS TO GET ACROSS TO YOU.

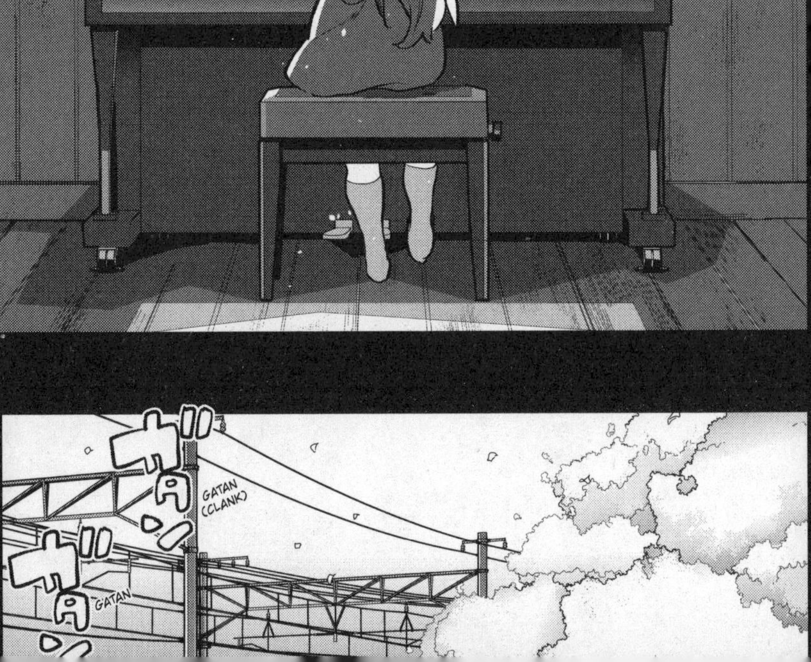
GATAN
(CLANK)
GATAN

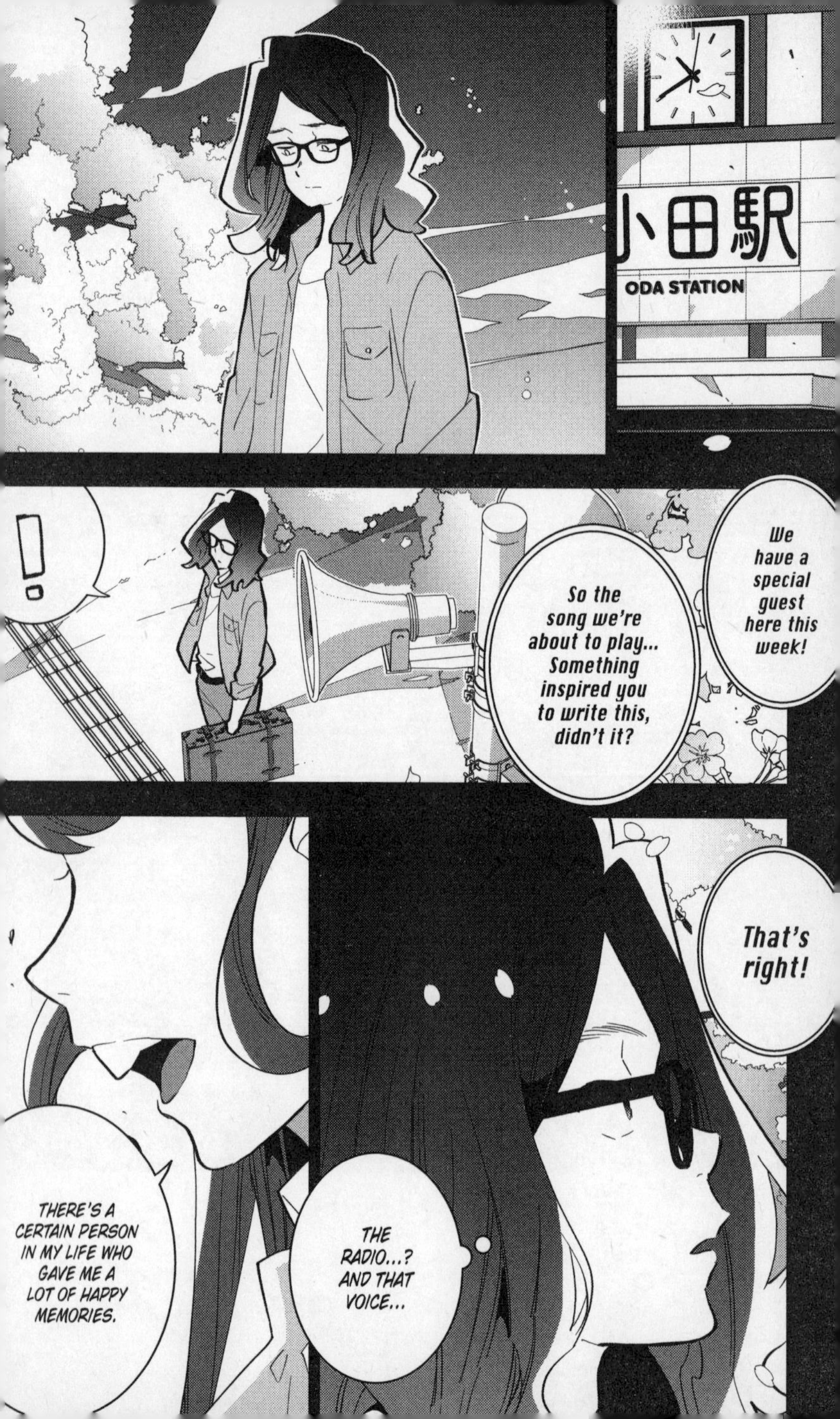

小田駅
ODA STATION
We have a special guest here this week!
So the song we're about to play... Something inspired you to write this, didn't it?
!
That's right!
THE RADIO...? AND THAT VOICE...
THERE'S A CERTAIN PERSON IN MY LIFE WHO GAVE ME A LOT OF HAPPY MEMORIES.

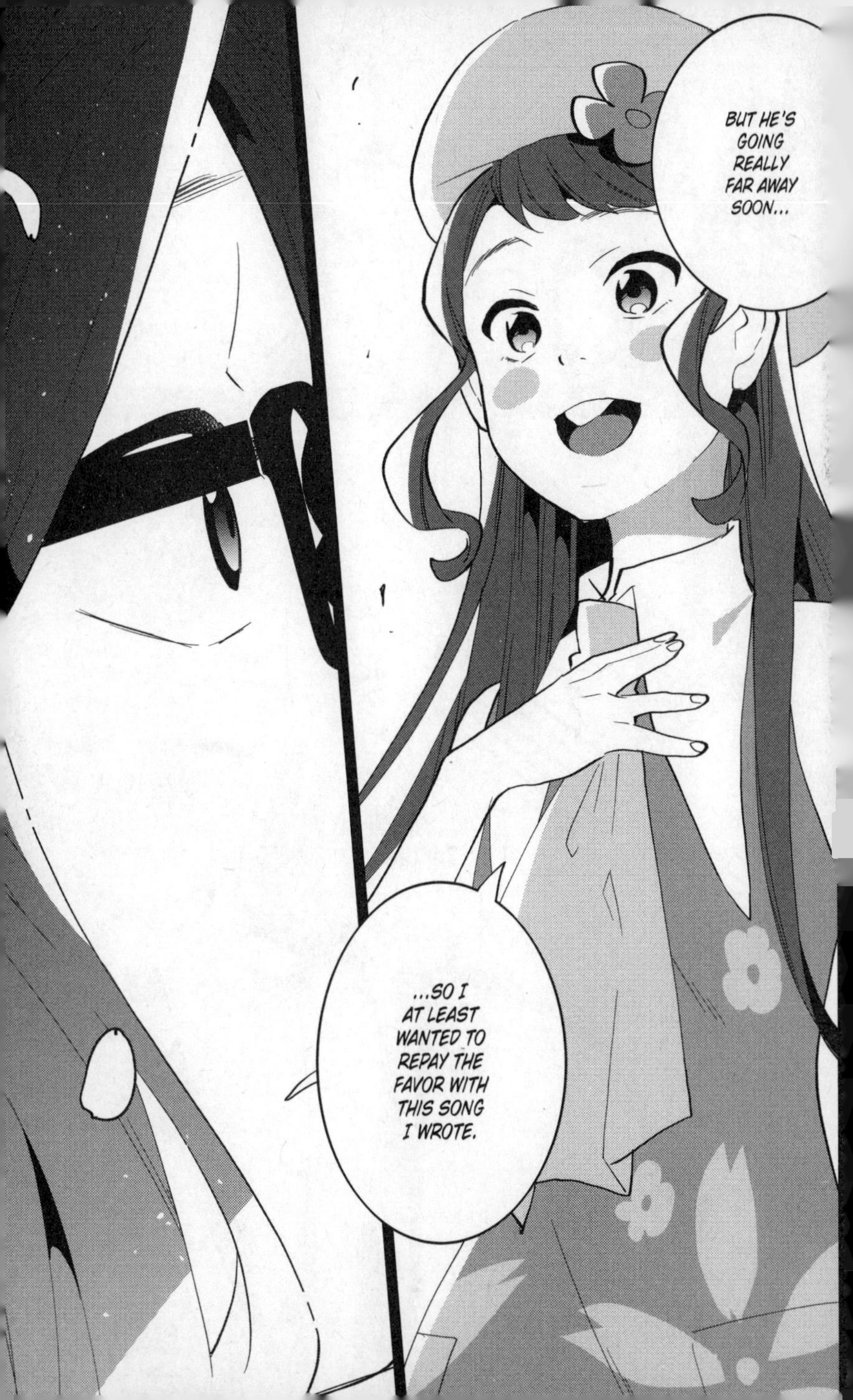
BUT HE'S GOING REALLY FAR AWAY SOON...
...SO I AT LEAST WANTED TO REPAY THE FAVOR WITH THIS SONG I WROTE.

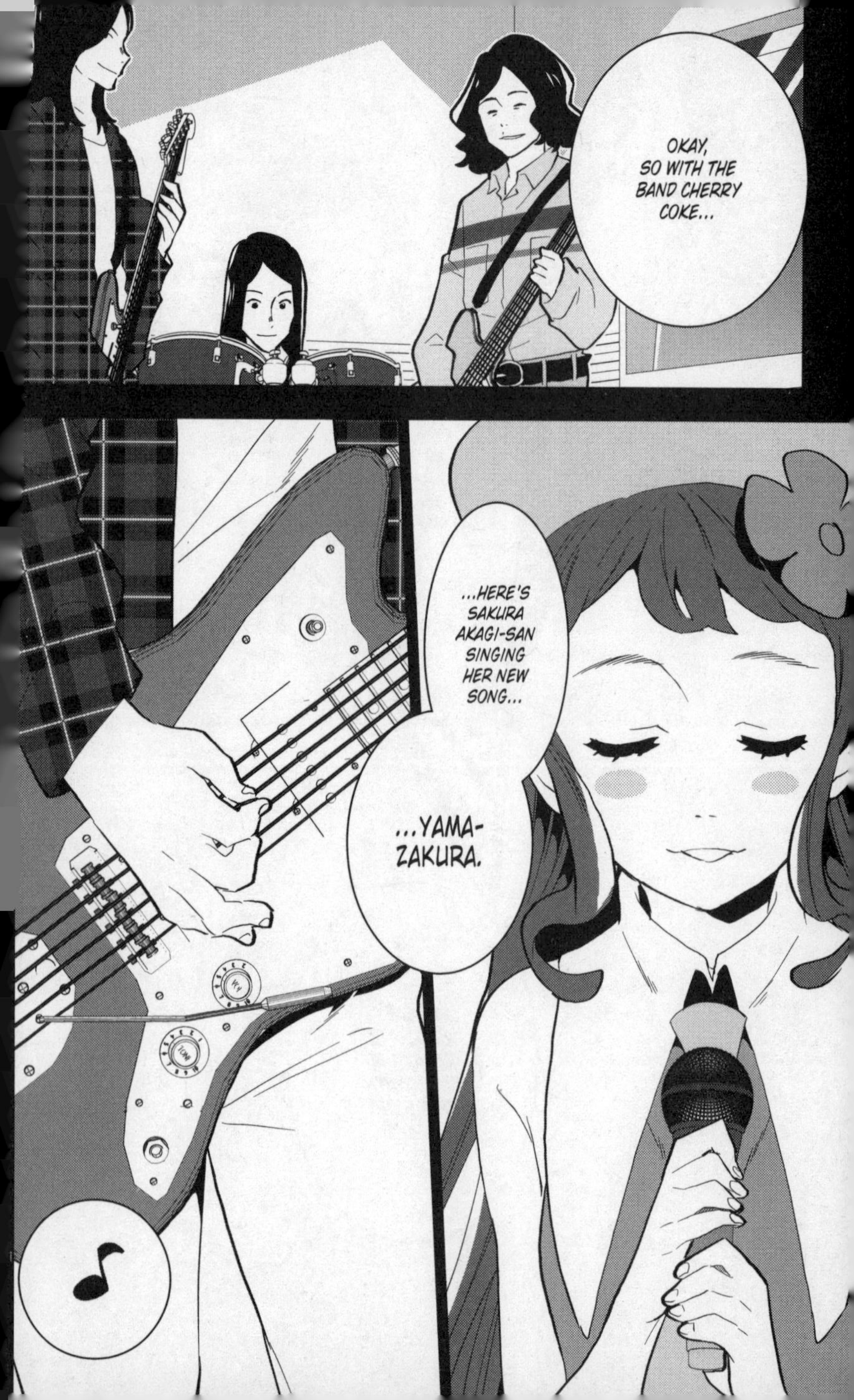
OKAY, SO WITH THE BAND CHERRY COKE...
...HERE'S SAKURA AKAGI-SAN SINGING HER NEW SONG...
...YAMA-ZAKURA.

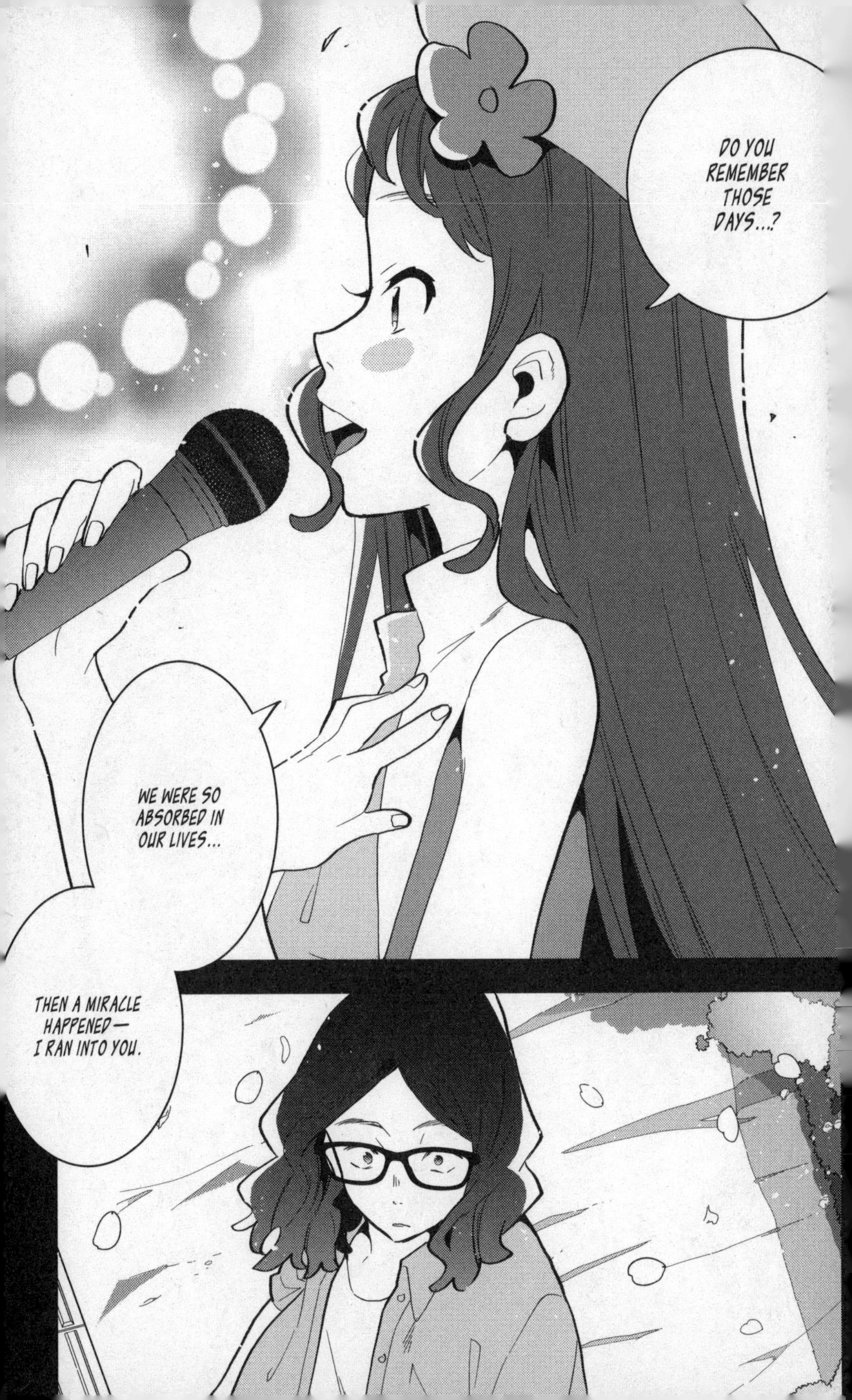
DO YOU REMEMBER THOSE DAYS...?
WE WERE SO ABSORBED IN OUR LIVES...
THEN A MIRACLE HAPPENED— I RAN INTO YOU.

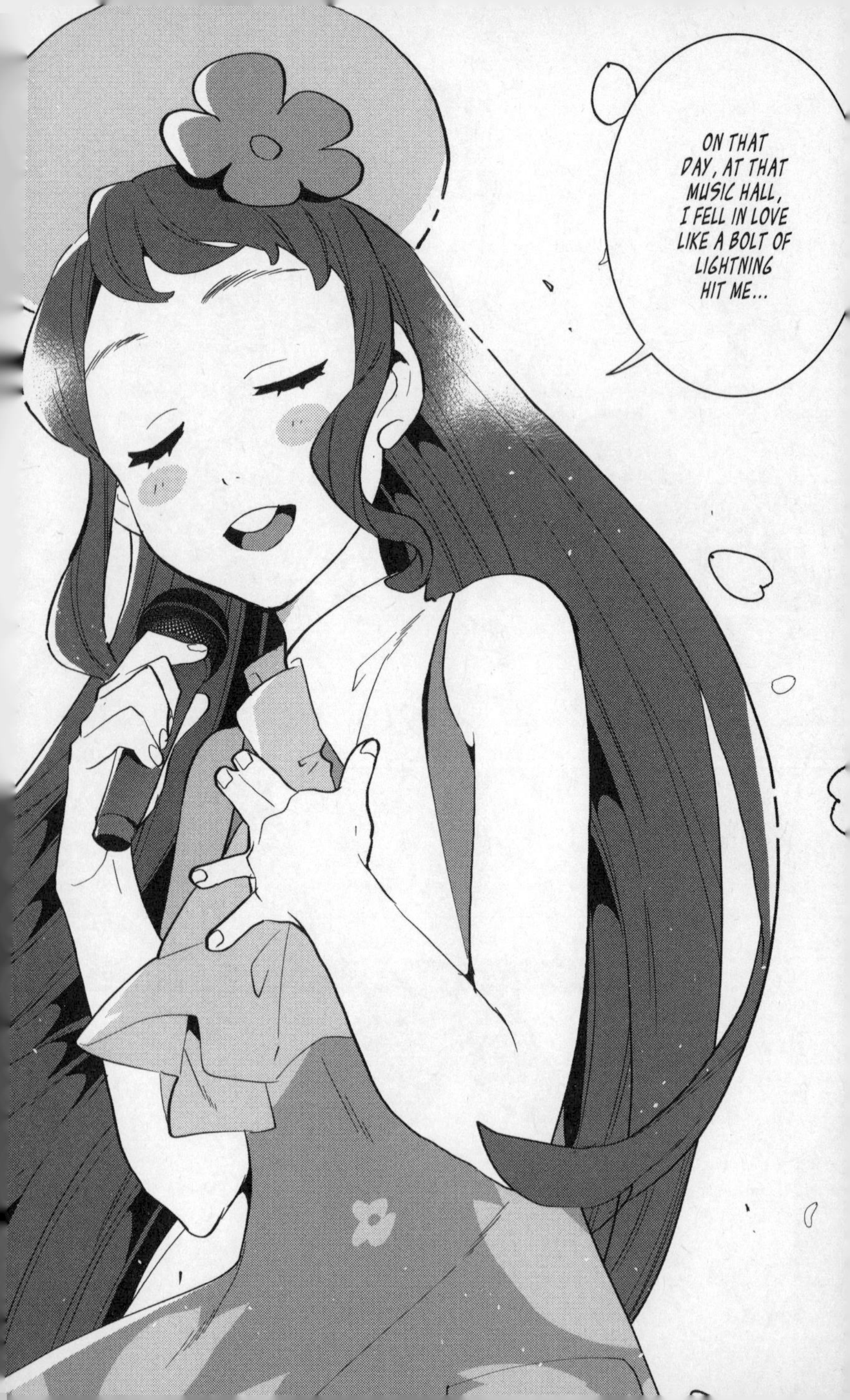
ON THAT DAY, AT THAT MUSIC HALL, I FELL IN LOVE LIKE A BOLT OF LIGHTNING HIT ME...

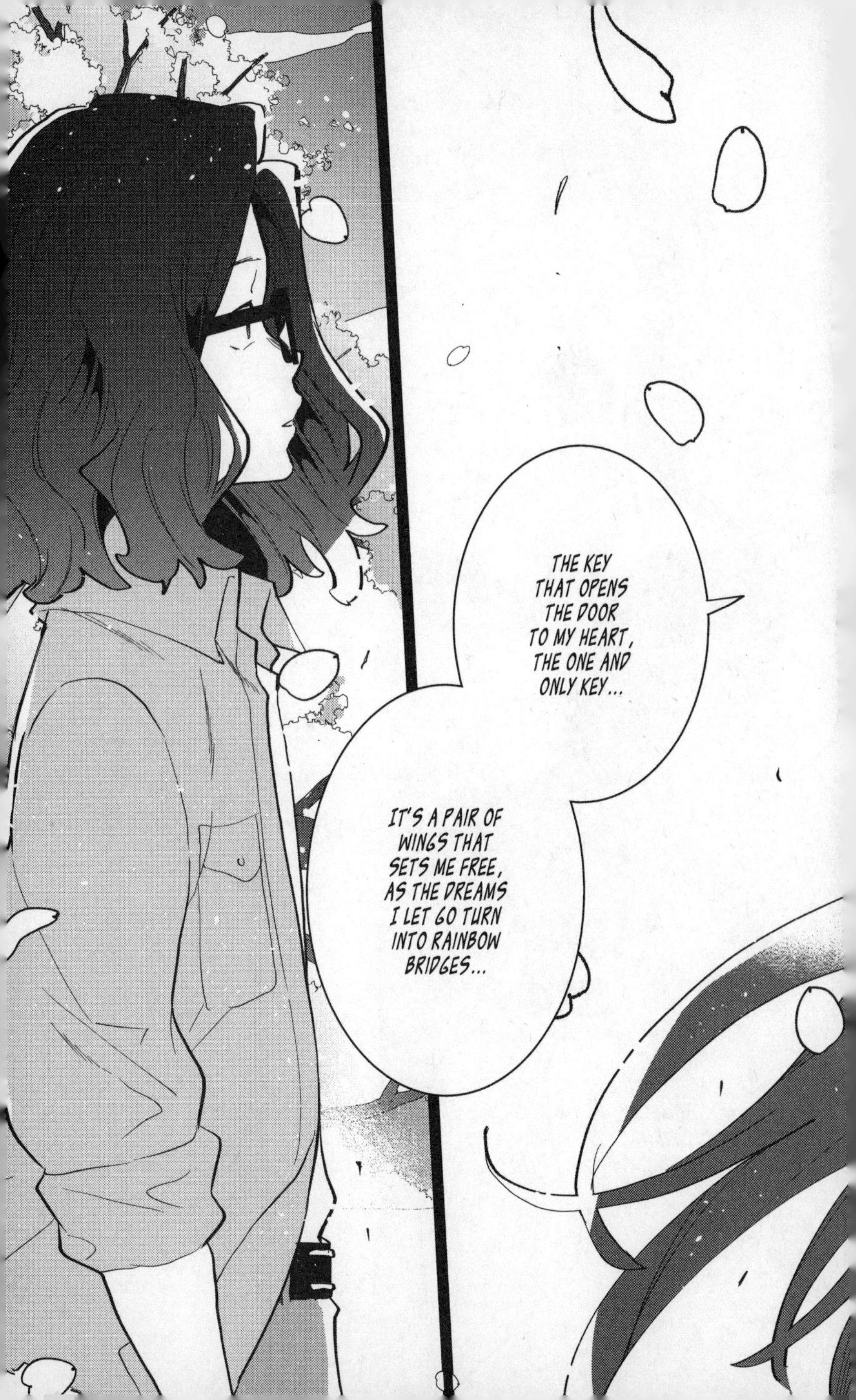
THE KEY THAT OPENS THE DOOR TO MY HEART, THE ONE AND ONLY KEY...
IT'S A PAIR OF WINGS THAT SETS ME FREE, AS THE DREAMS I LET GO TURN INTO RAINBOW BRIDGES...

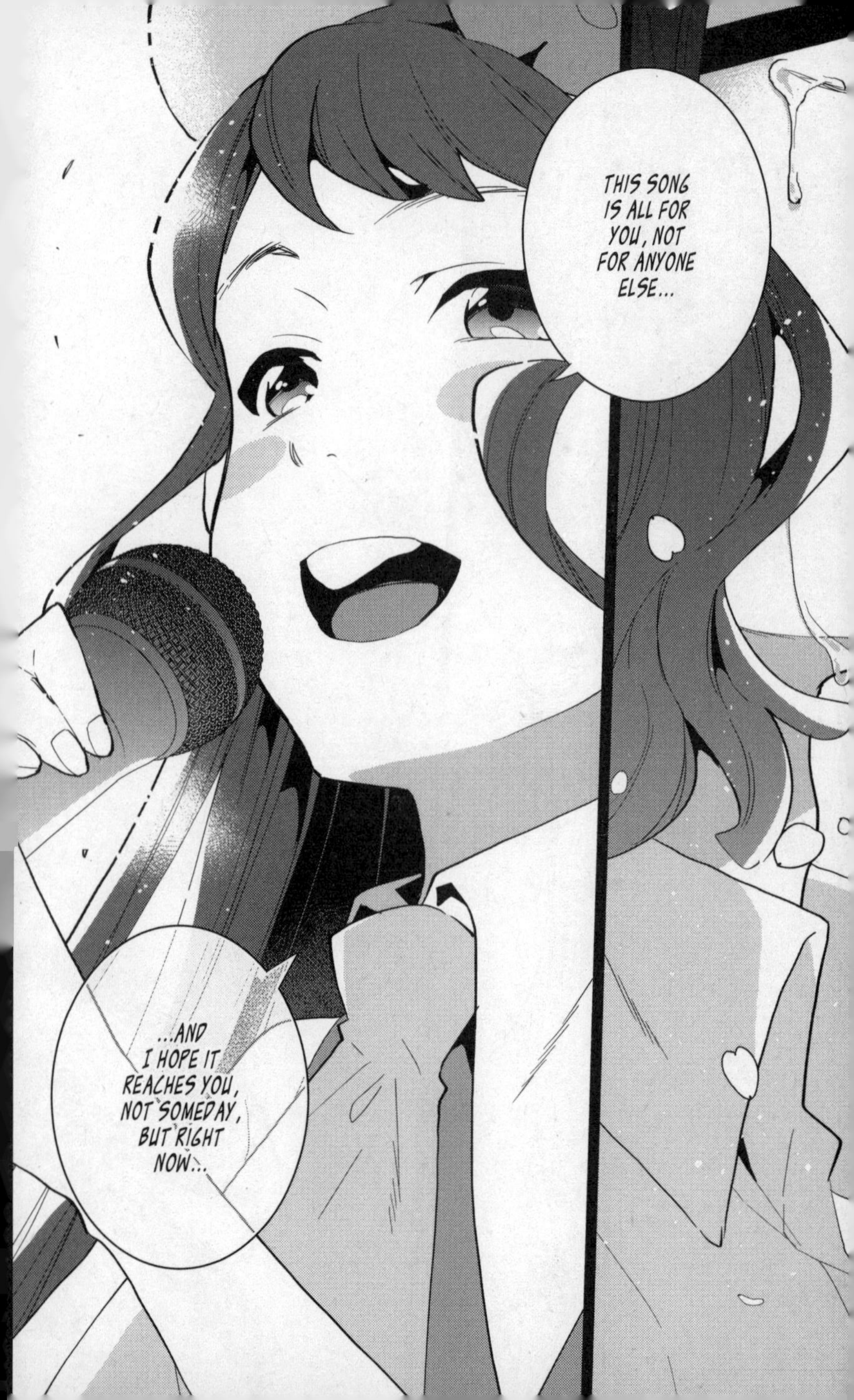
THIS SONG IS ALL FOR YOU, NOT FOR ANYONE ELSE...
...AND I HOPE IT REACHES YOU, NOT SOMEDAY, BUT RIGHT NOW...

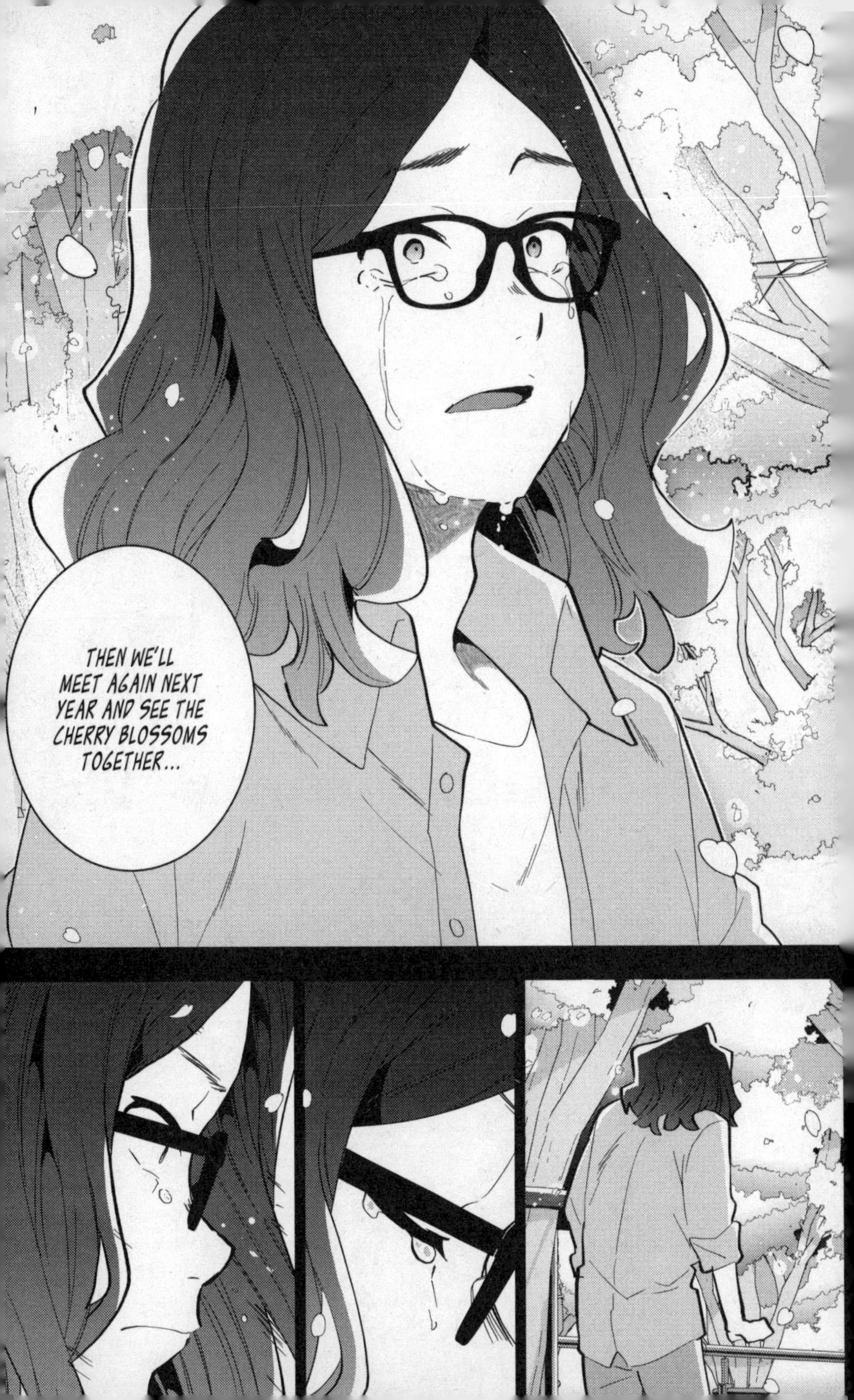
THEN WE'LL MEET AGAIN NEXT YEAR AND SEE THE CHERRY BLOSSOMS TOGETHER...

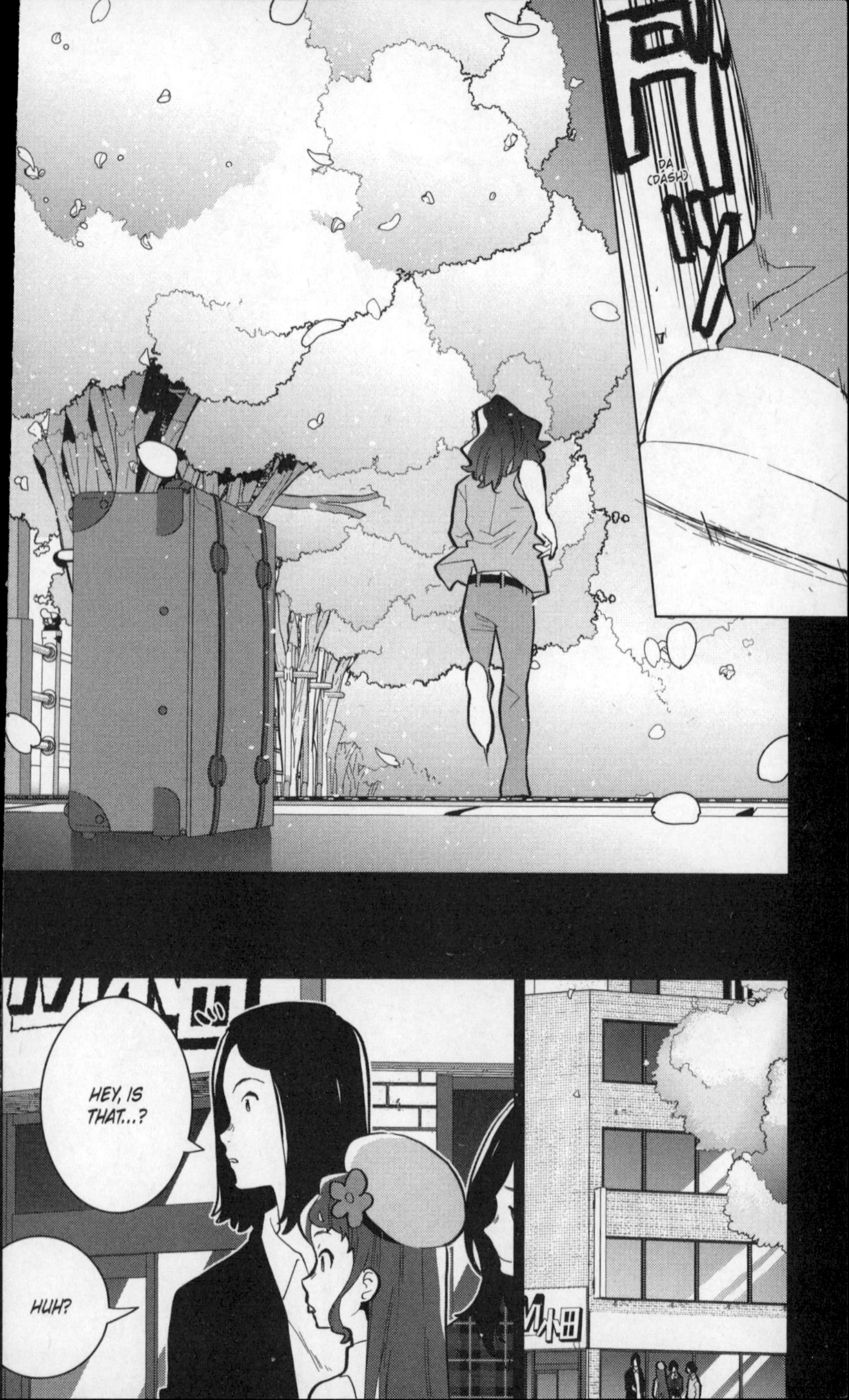
DA (DASH)
HEY, IS THAT...?
HUH?

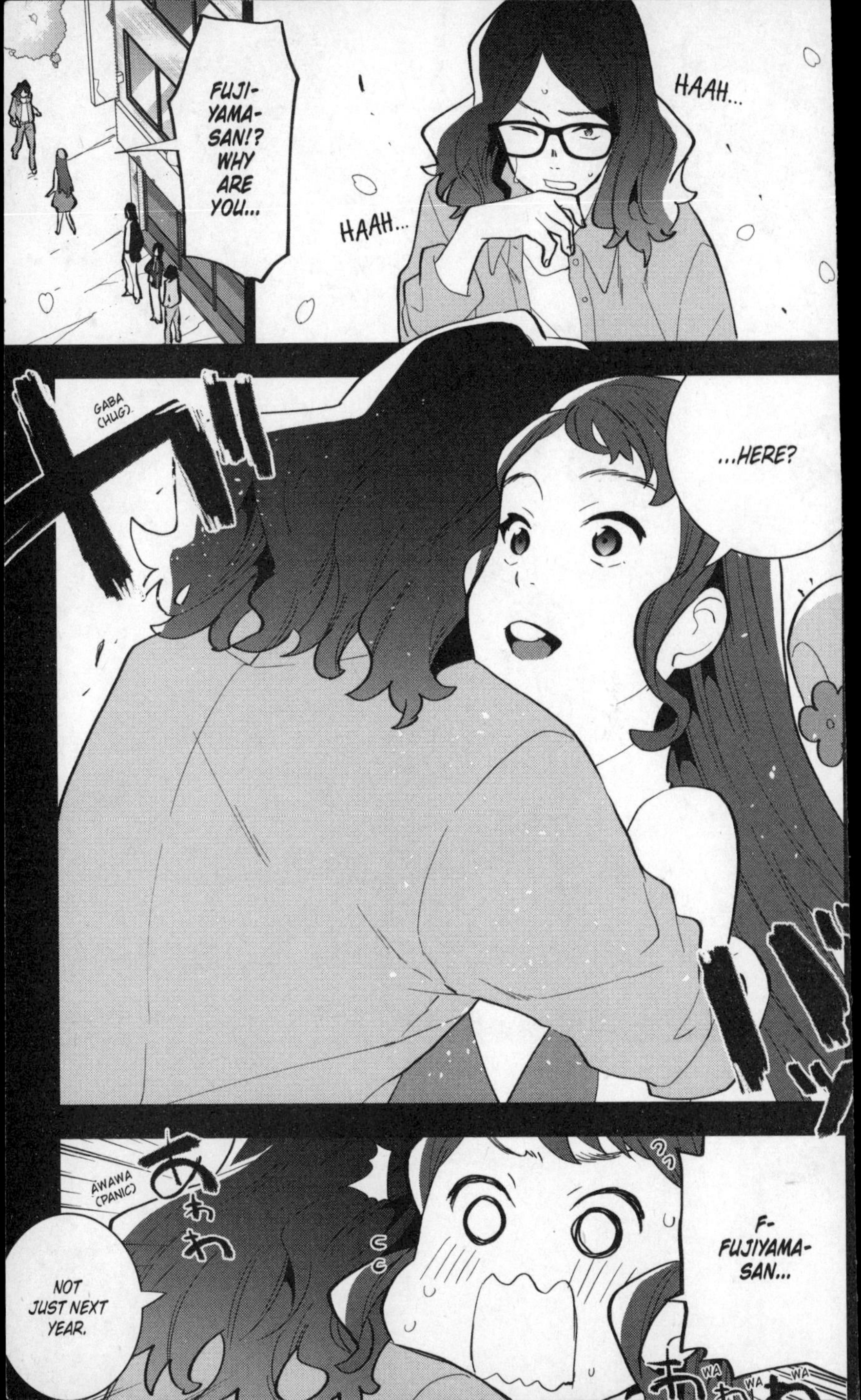
HAAH...
HAAH...
FUJI-YAMA-SAN!? WHY ARE YOU...
...HERE?
GABA (HUG)
F-FUJIYAMA-SAN...
AWAWA (PANIC)
NOT JUST NEXT YEAR.
WA WA WA

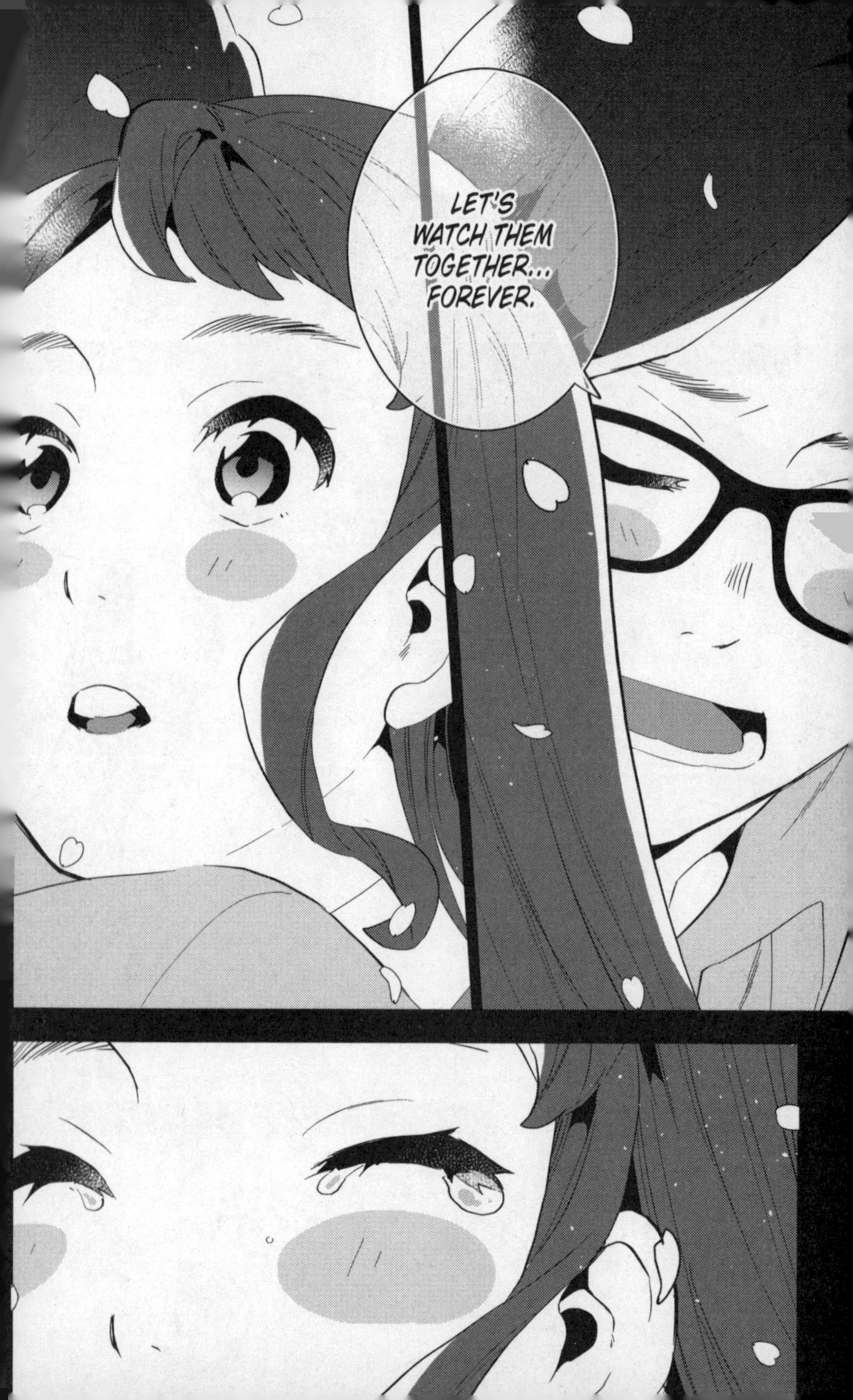
LET'S WATCH THEM TOGETHER... FOREVER.

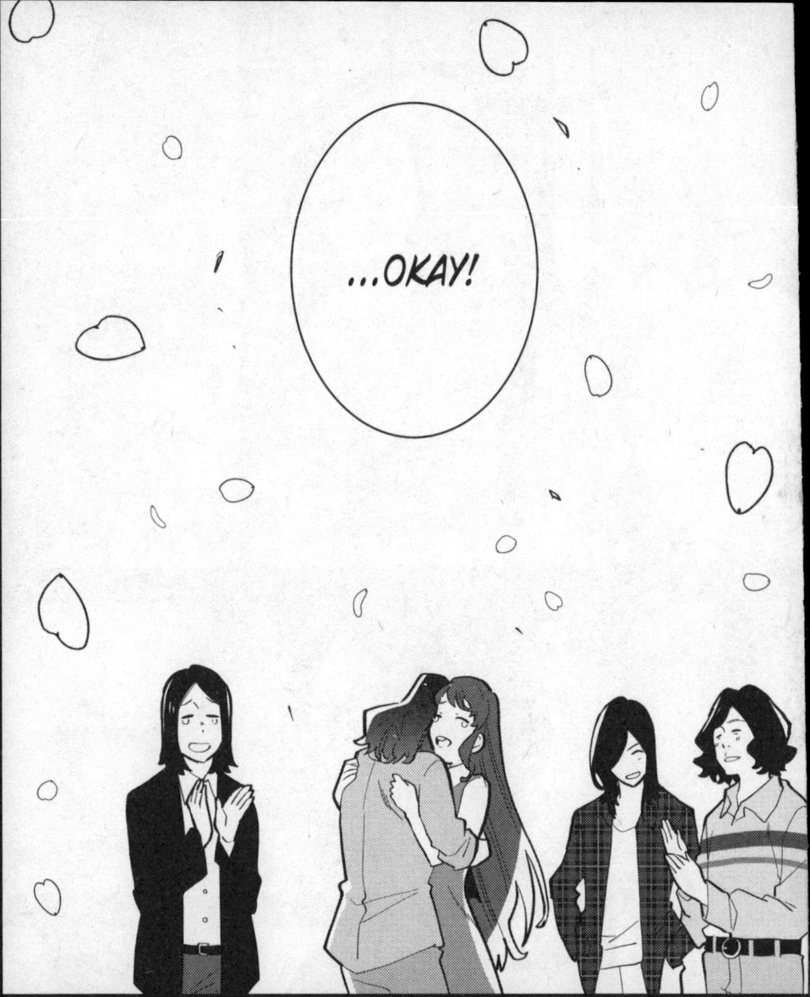
...OKAY!

SIGN: 3RD ANNUAL MT. ODA DARUMA FESTIVAL

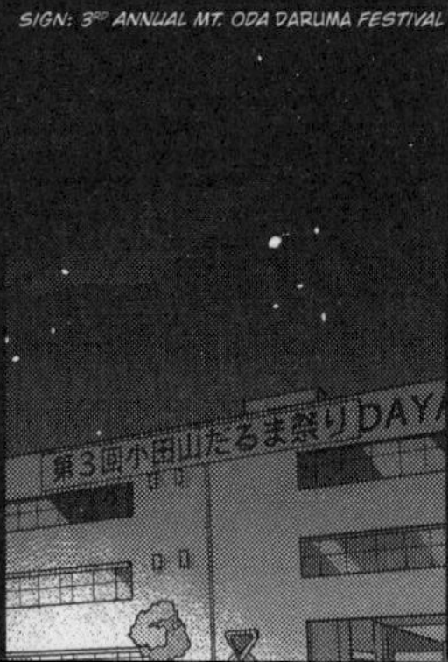
第3回小田山だるま祭りDAY

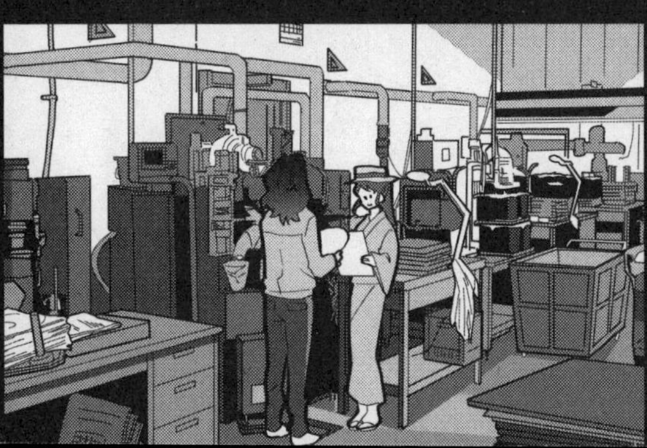

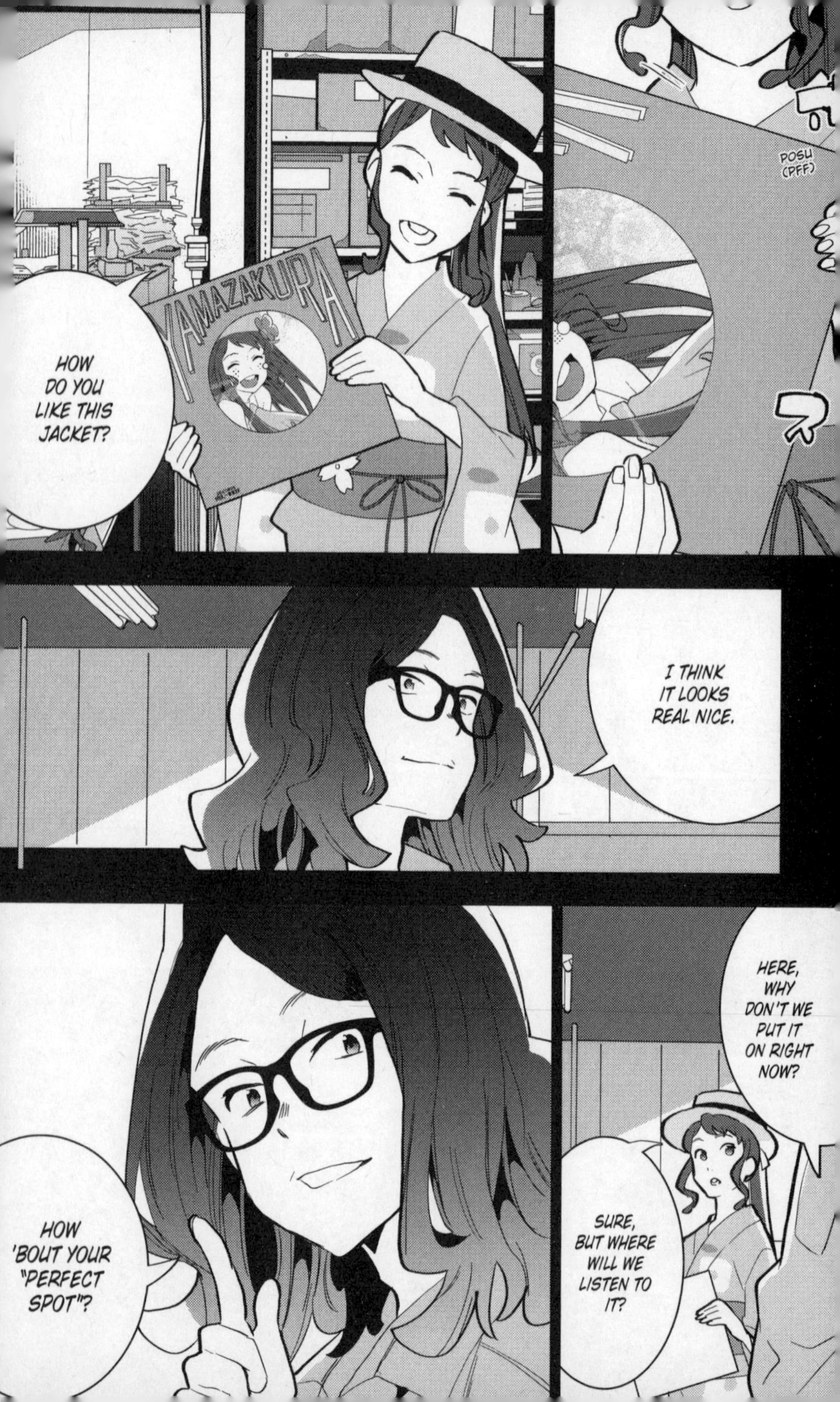
POSU (PFF)
YAMAZAKURA
HOW DO YOU LIKE THIS JACKET?
I THINK IT LOOKS REAL NICE.
HERE, WHY DON'T WE PUT IT ON RIGHT NOW?
SURE, BUT WHERE WILL WE LISTEN TO IT?
HOW 'BOUT YOUR "PERFECT SPOT"?

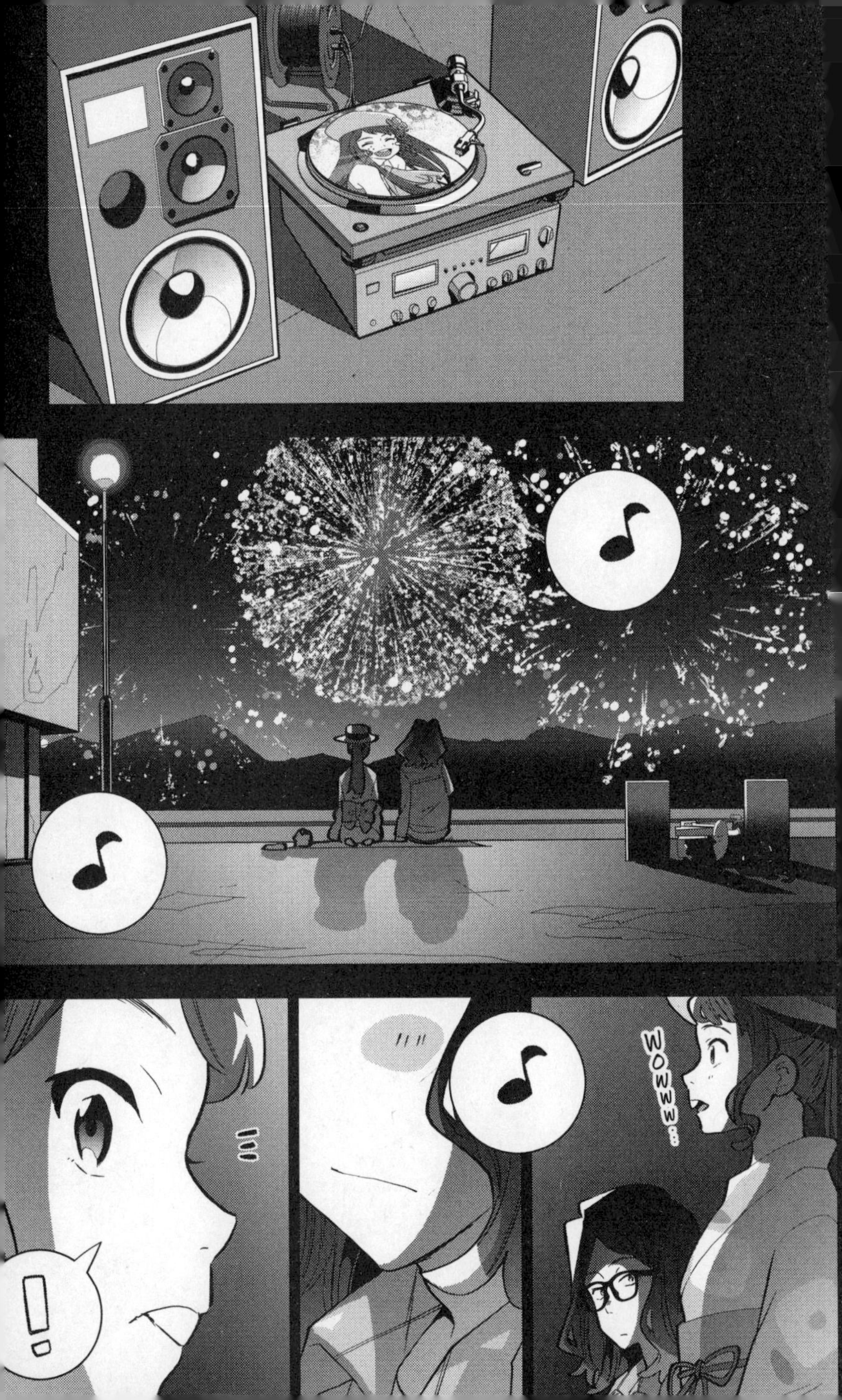
WOWWW...
!

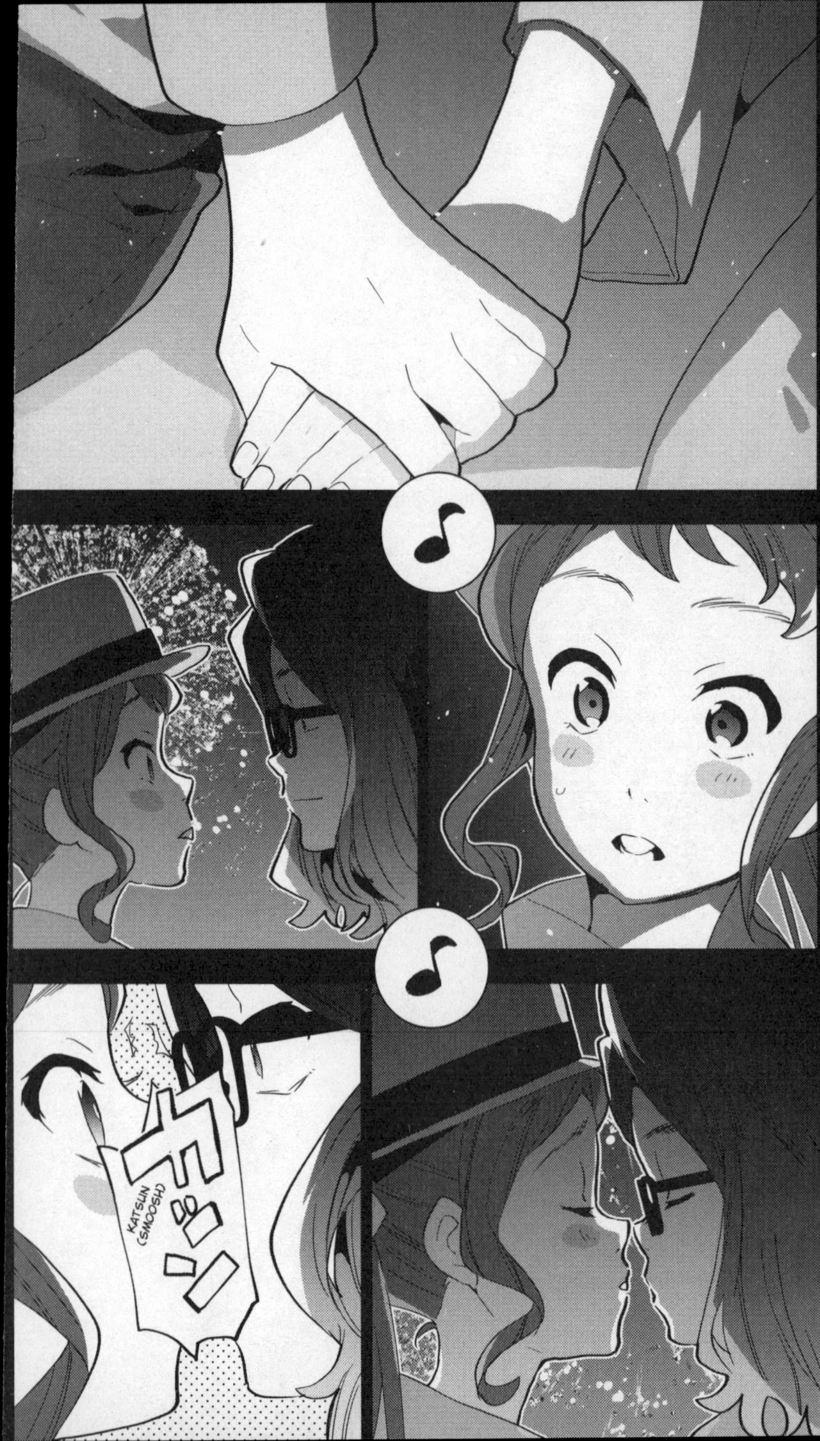
KATSUN (SMOOSH)

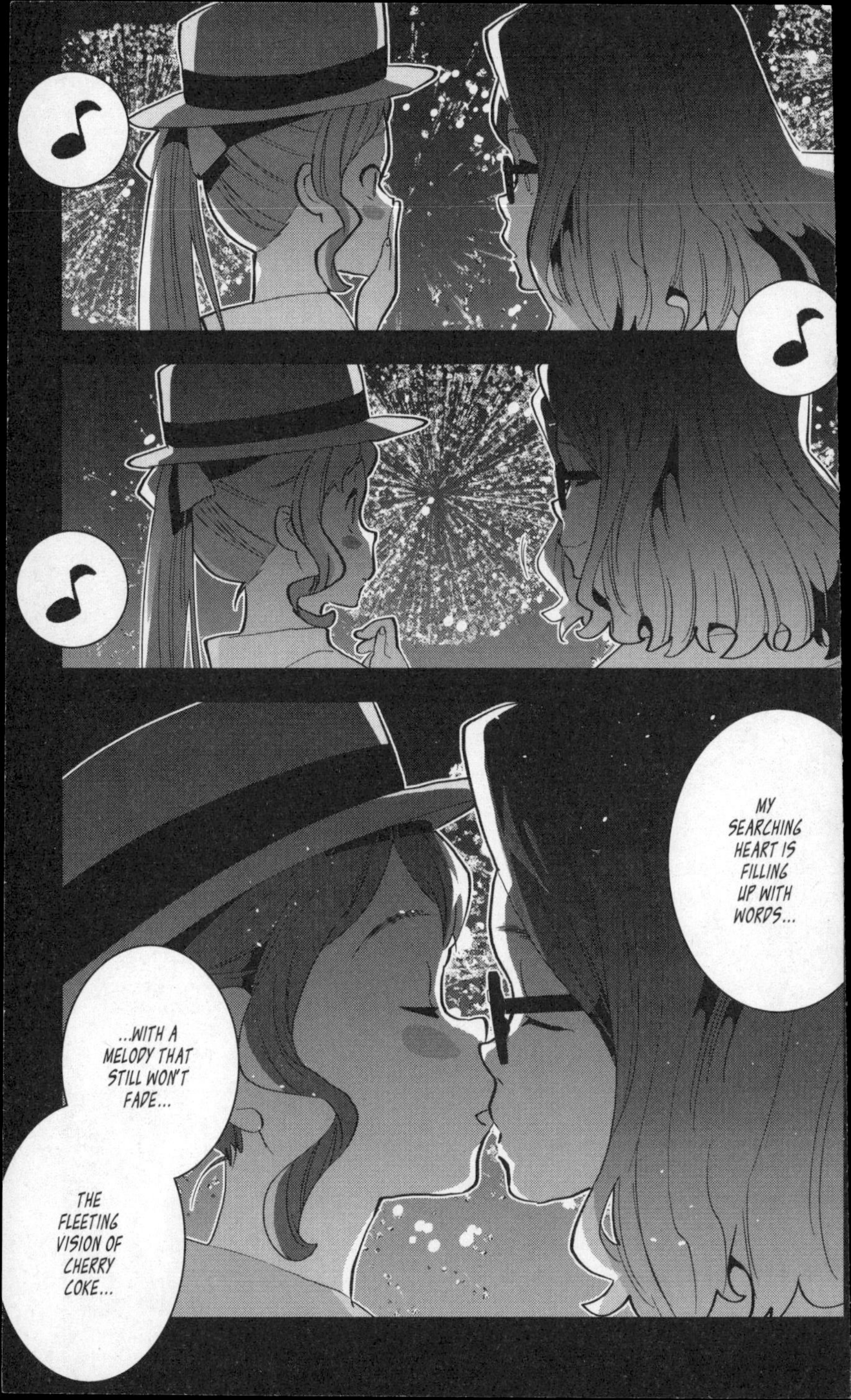
MY SEARCHING HEART IS FILLING UP WITH WORDS...
...WITH A MELODY THAT STILL WON'T FADE...
THE FLEETING VISION OF CHERRY COKE...

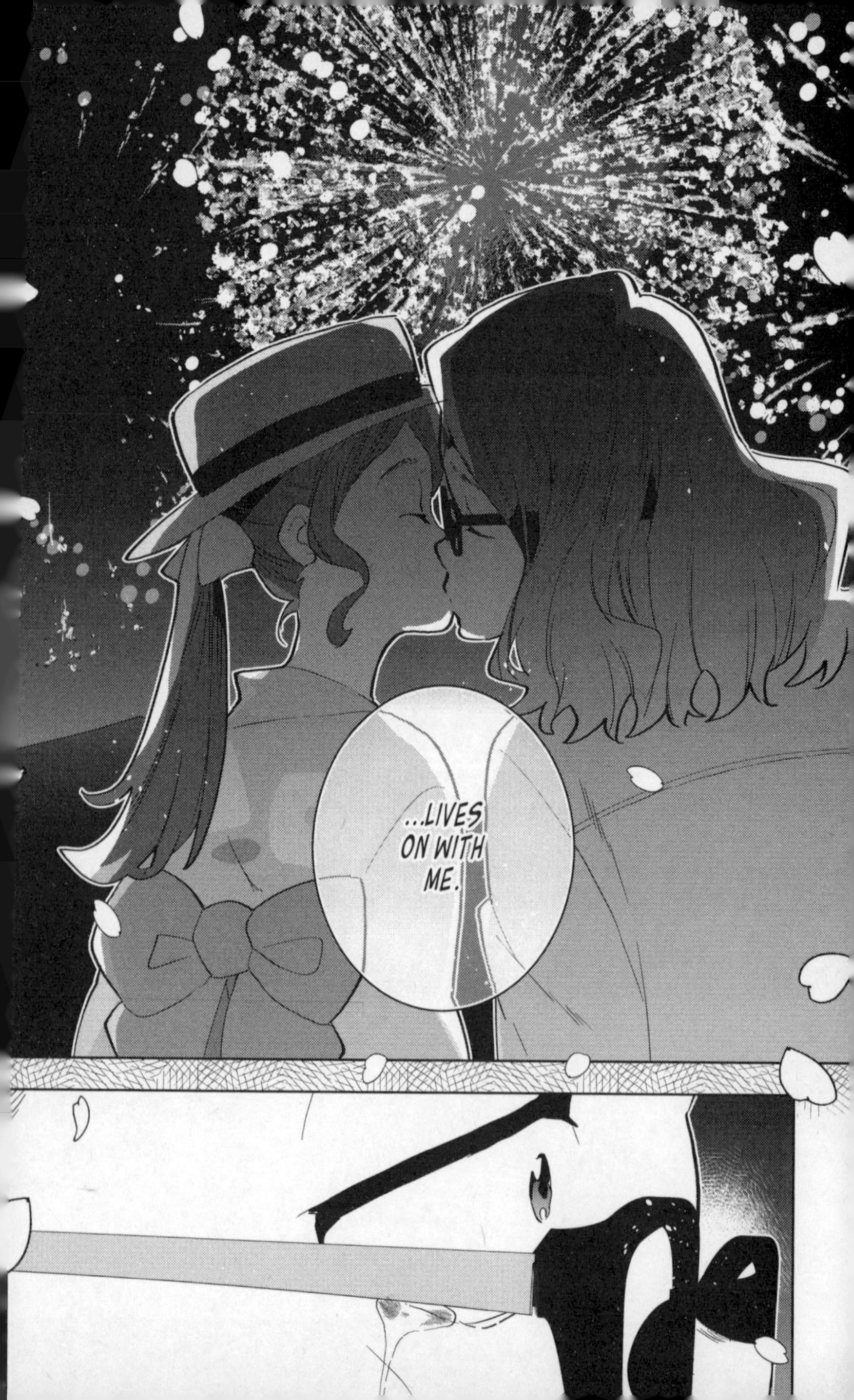
...LIVES ON WITH ME.

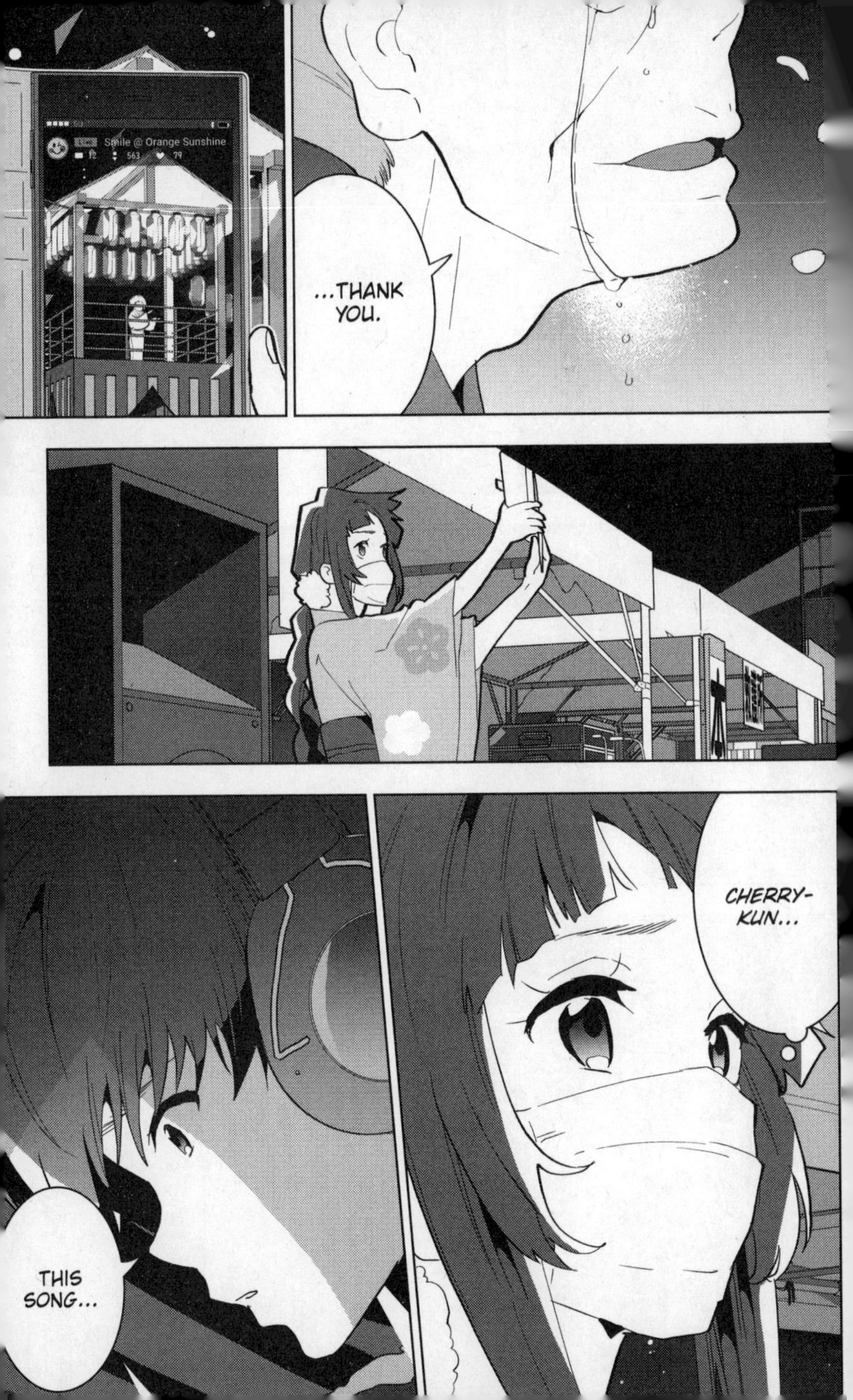
...THANK YOU.
Smile @ Orange Sunshine
12
563
79
CHERRY-KUN...
THIS SONG...

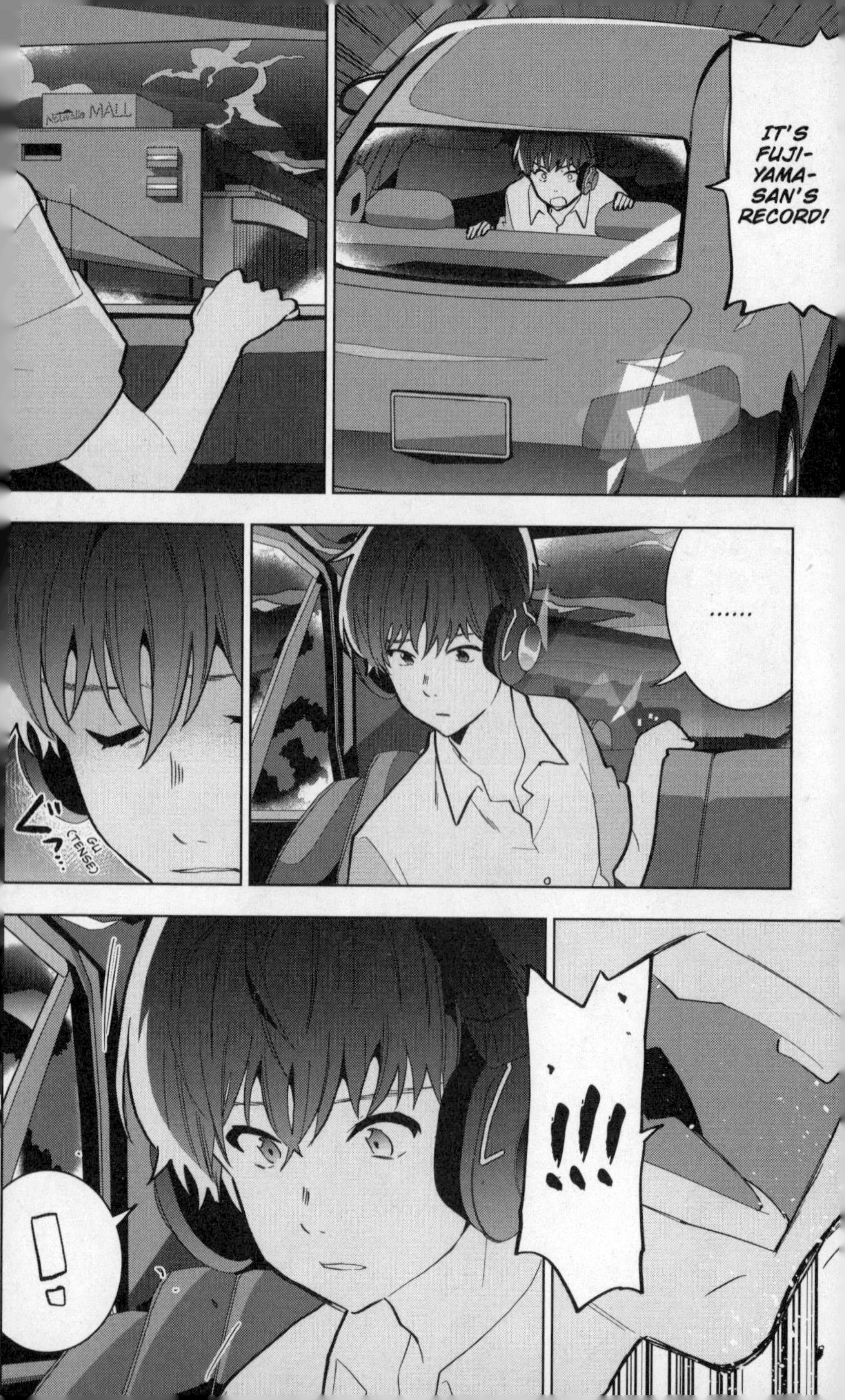
IT'S FUJI-YAMA-SAN'S RECORD!
MALL
......
ぐっ...
GU (TENSE)
!!!
!

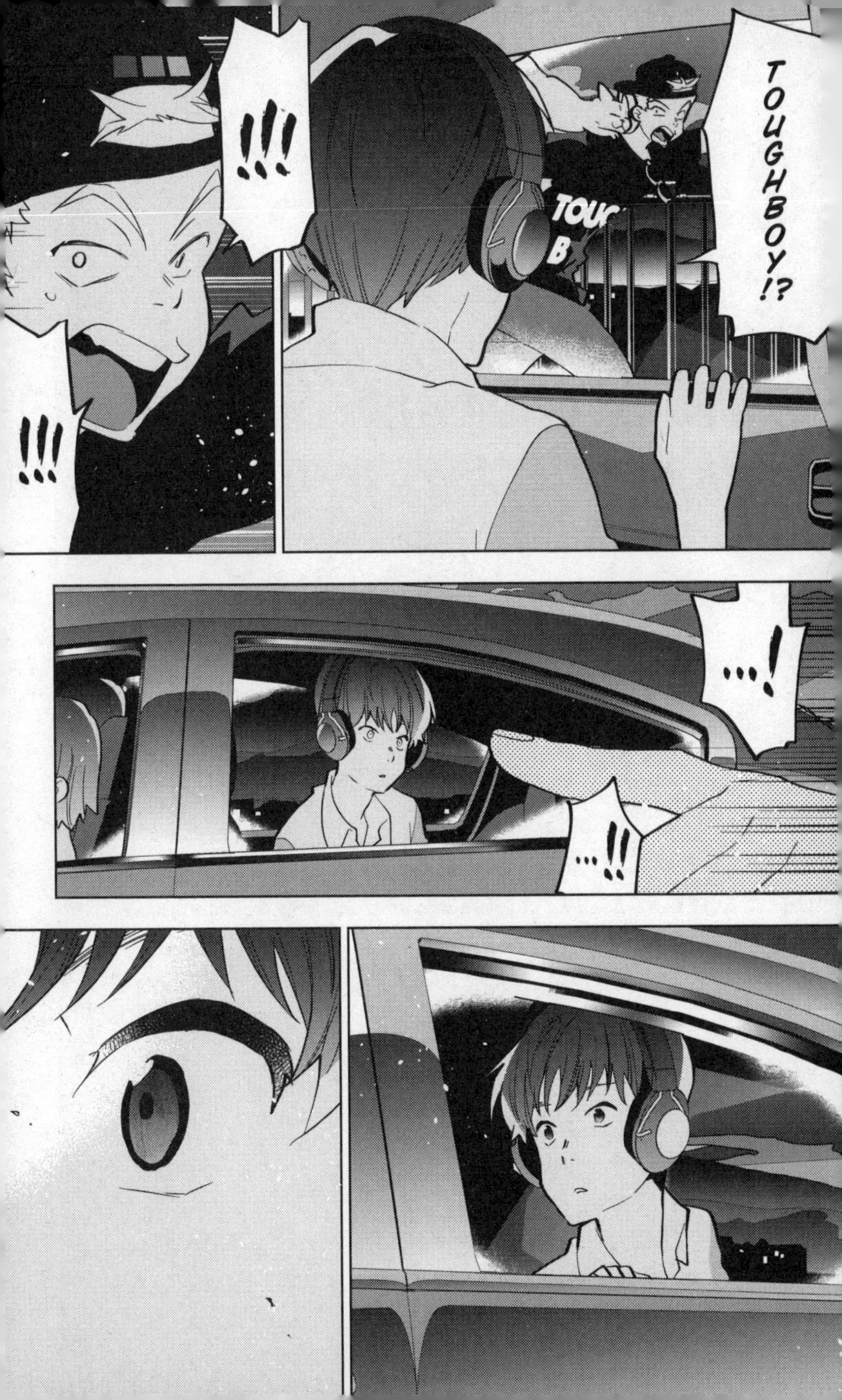
TOUGHBOY!?
!!!
!!!
...!
...!!

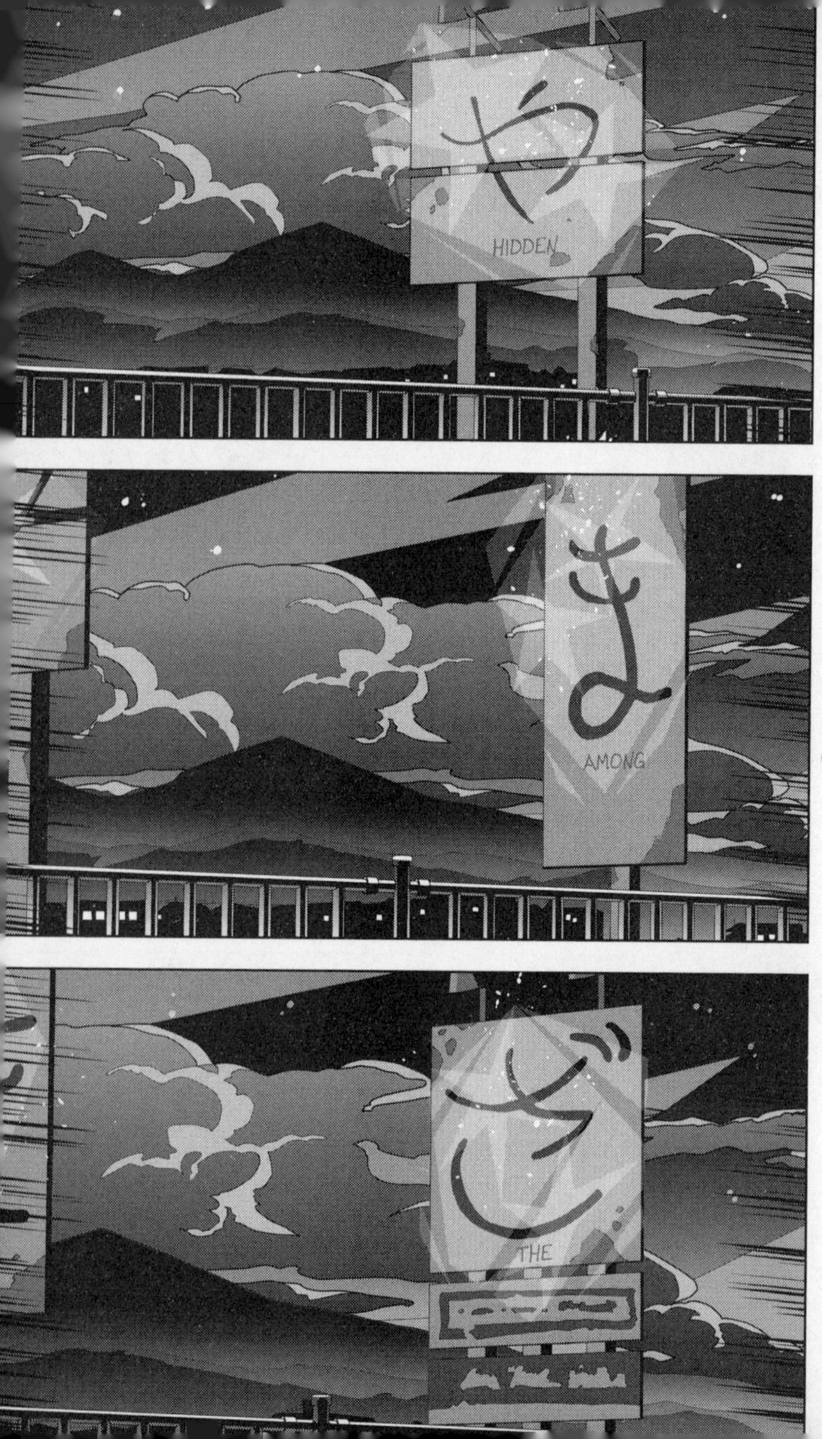
や
HIDDEN
ま
AMONG
ご
THE

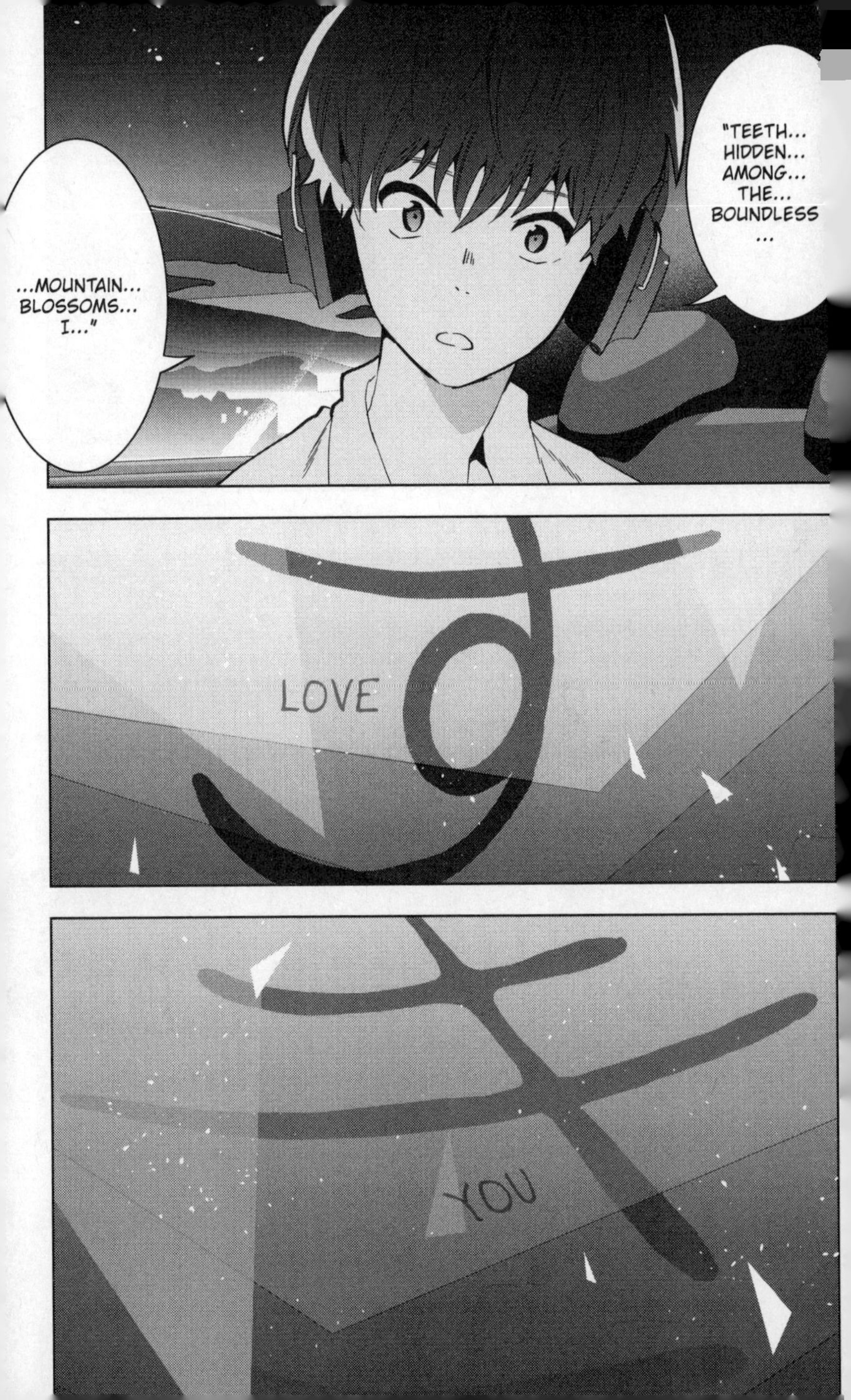
"TEETH... HIDDEN... AMONG... THE... BOUNDLESS ...
...MOUNTAIN... BLOSSOMS... I..."
LOVE
YOU

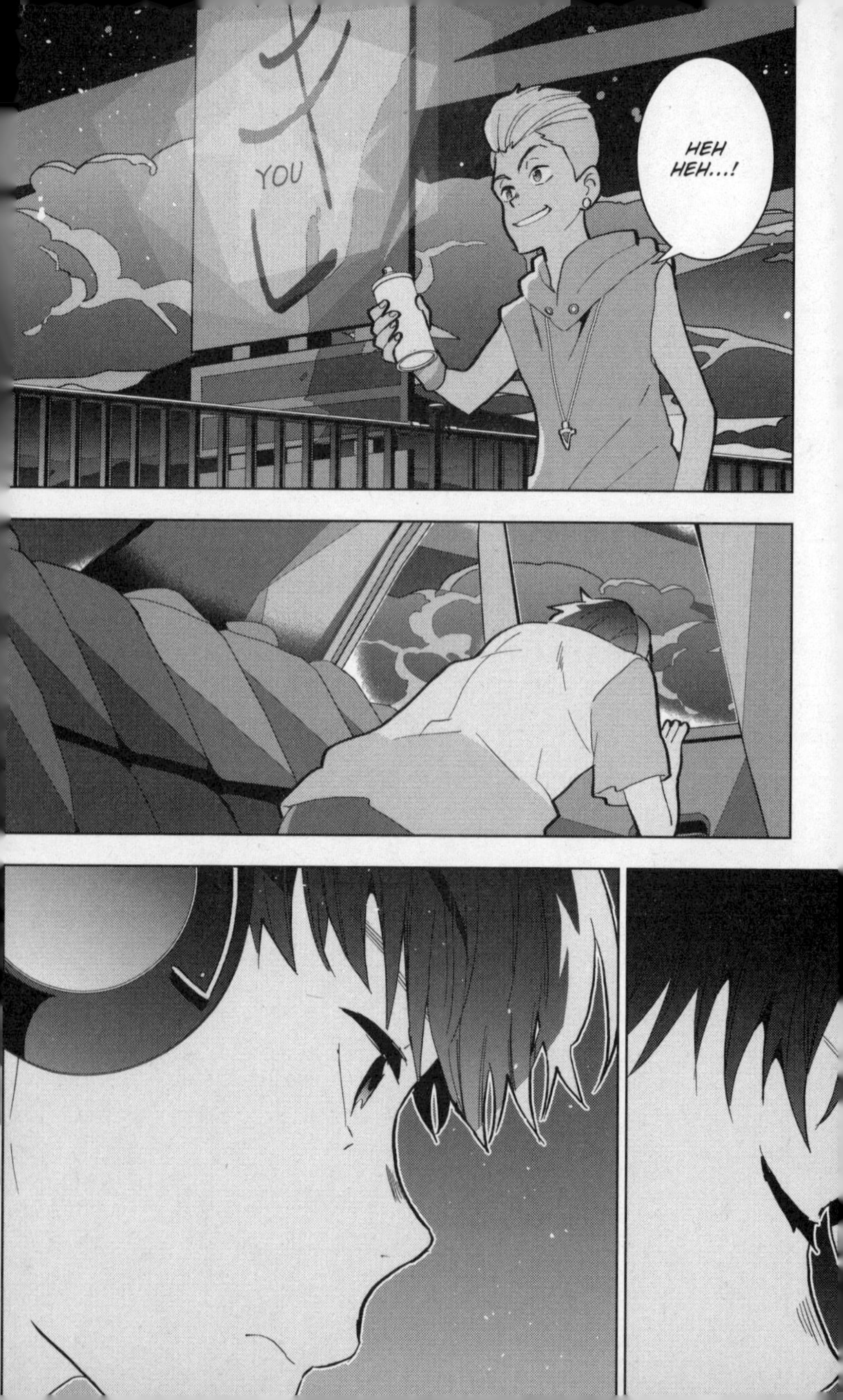
HEH HEH...!
YOU

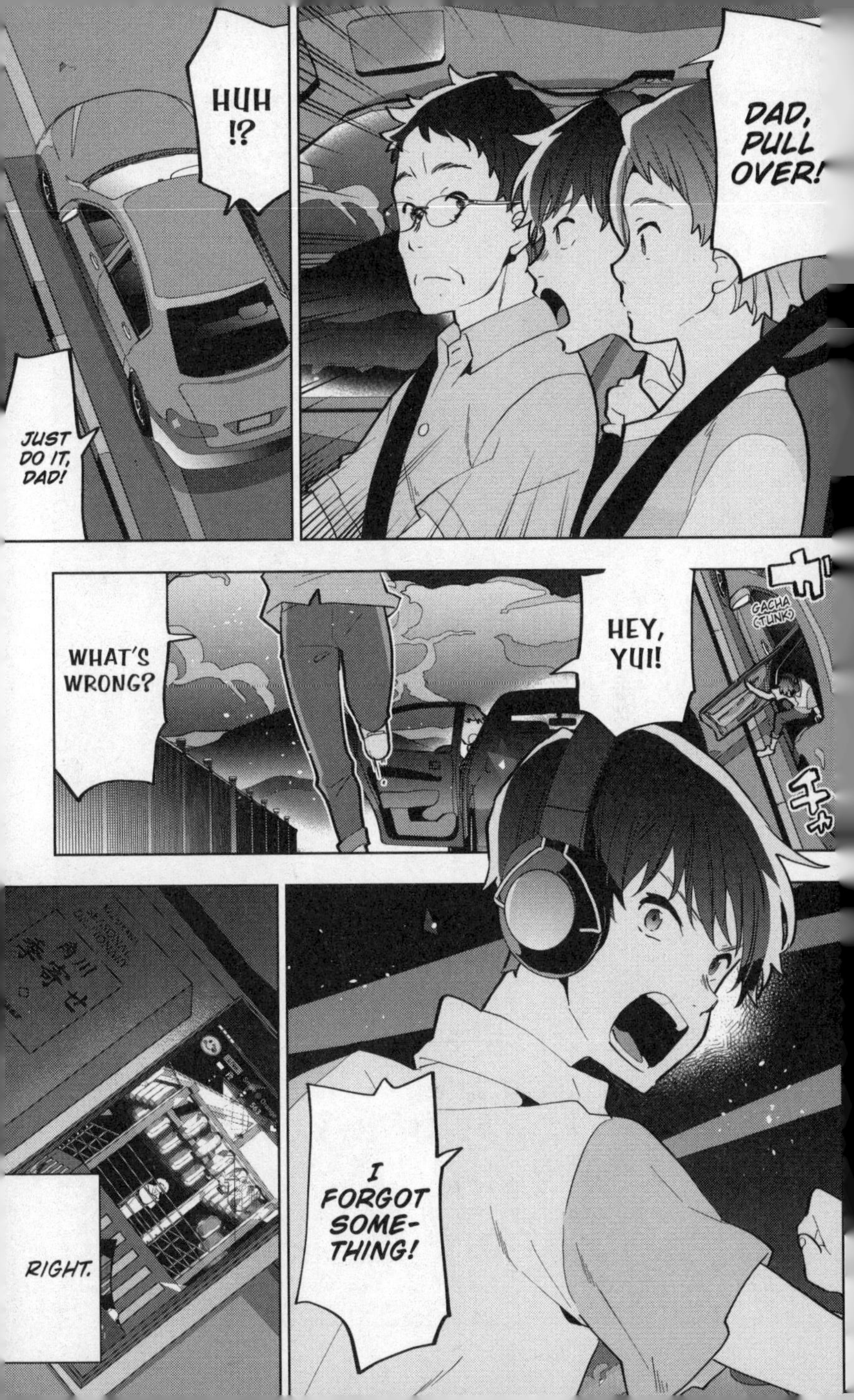
DAD, PULL OVER!
HUH !?
JUST DO IT, DAD!
GACHA (TUNK)
HEY, YUI!
WHAT'S WRONG?
I FORGOT SOME-THING!
RIGHT.

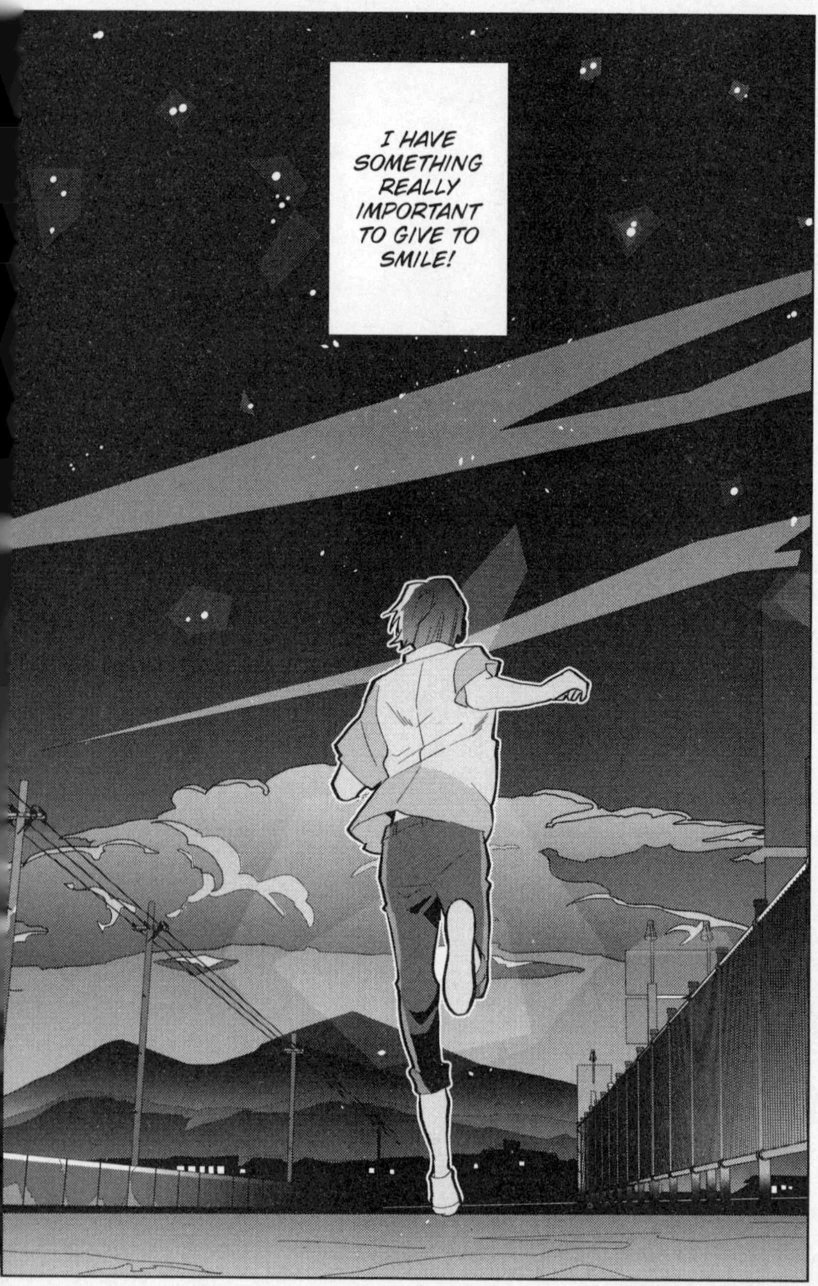
I HAVE SOMETHING REALLY IMPORTANT TO GIVE TO SMILE!

Words Bubble Up
Like Soda Pop

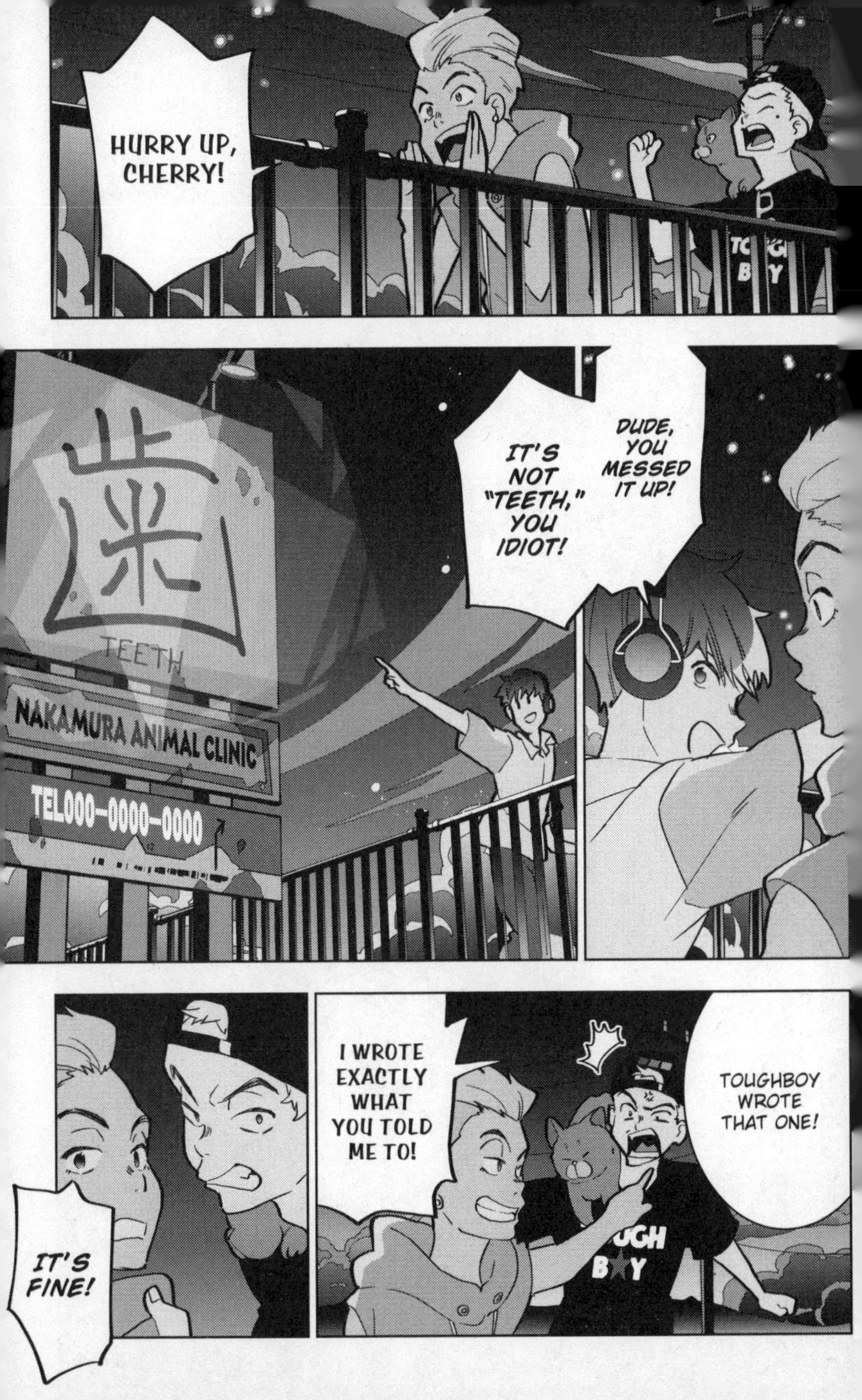
HURRY UP, CHERRY!
DUDE, YOU MESSED IT UP!
IT'S NOT "TEETH," YOU IDIOT!
TEETH
NAKAMURA ANIMAL CLINIC
TEL000-0000-0000
TOUGHBOY WROTE THAT ONE!
I WROTE EXACTLY WHAT YOU TOLD ME TO!
IT'S FINE!

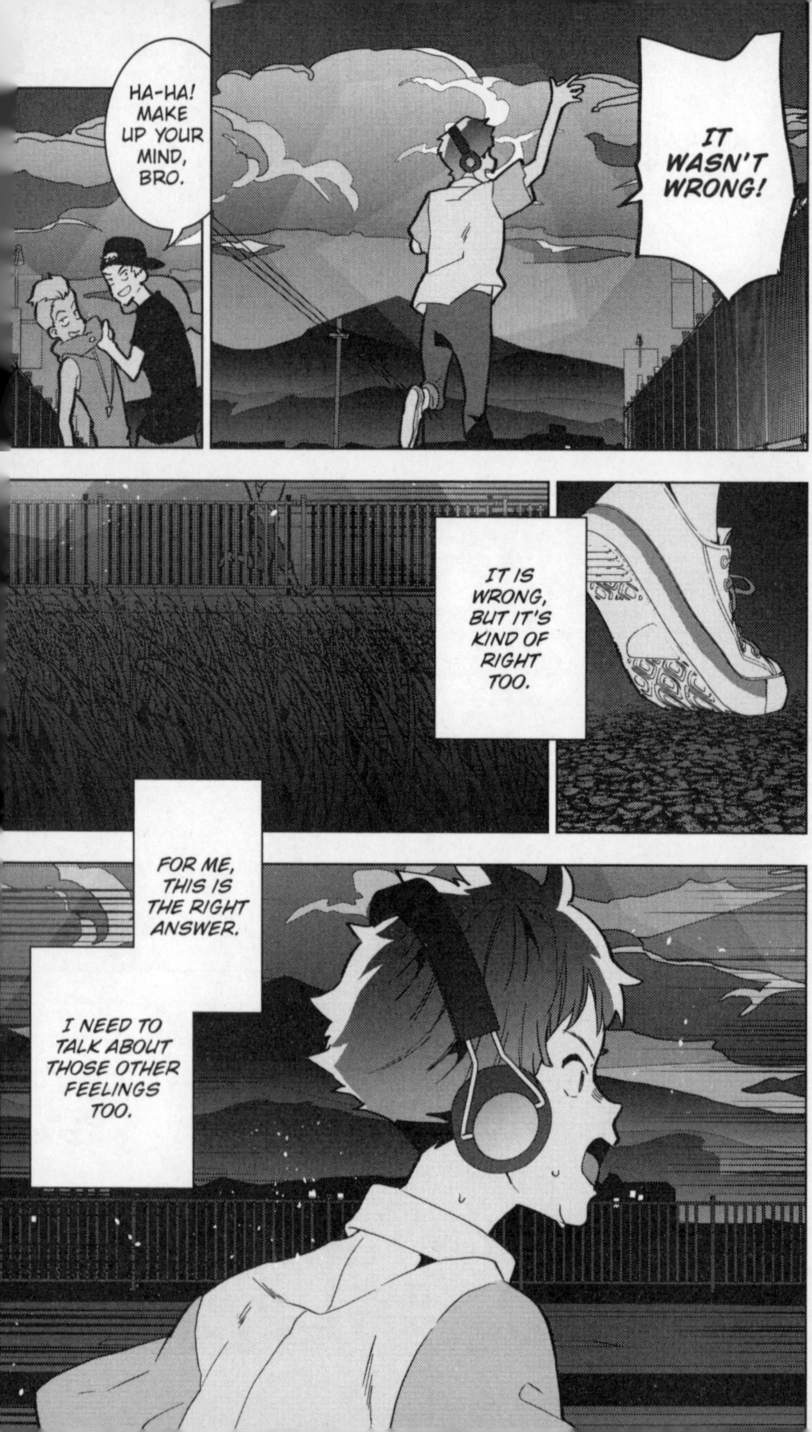
IT WASN'T WRONG!
HA-HA! MAKE UP YOUR MIND, BRO.
IT IS WRONG, BUT IT'S KIND OF RIGHT TOO.
FOR ME, THIS IS THE RIGHT ANSWER.
I NEED TO TALK ABOUT THOSE OTHER FEELINGS TOO.

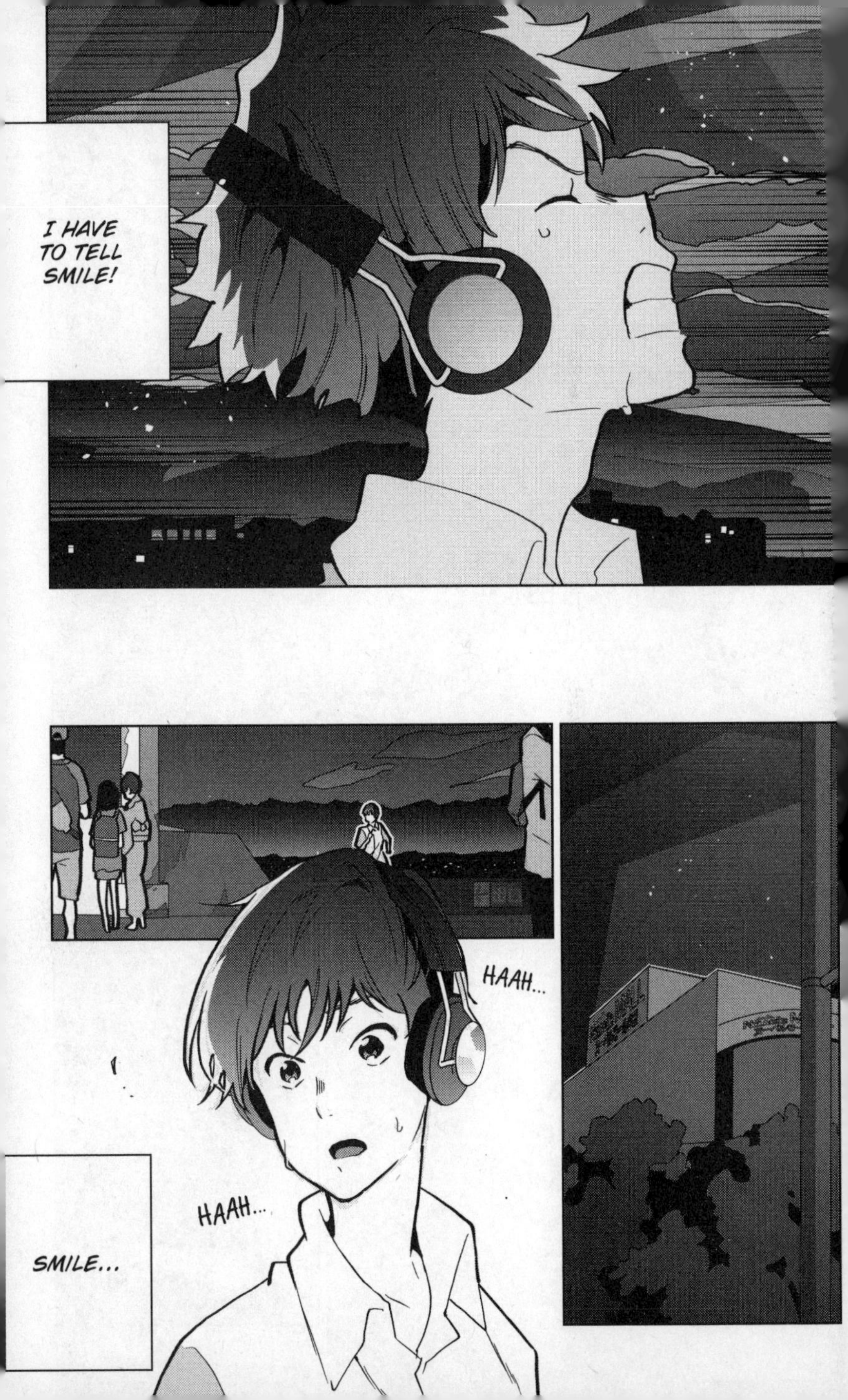
I HAVE TO TELL SMILE!
HAAH...
HAAH...
SMILE...

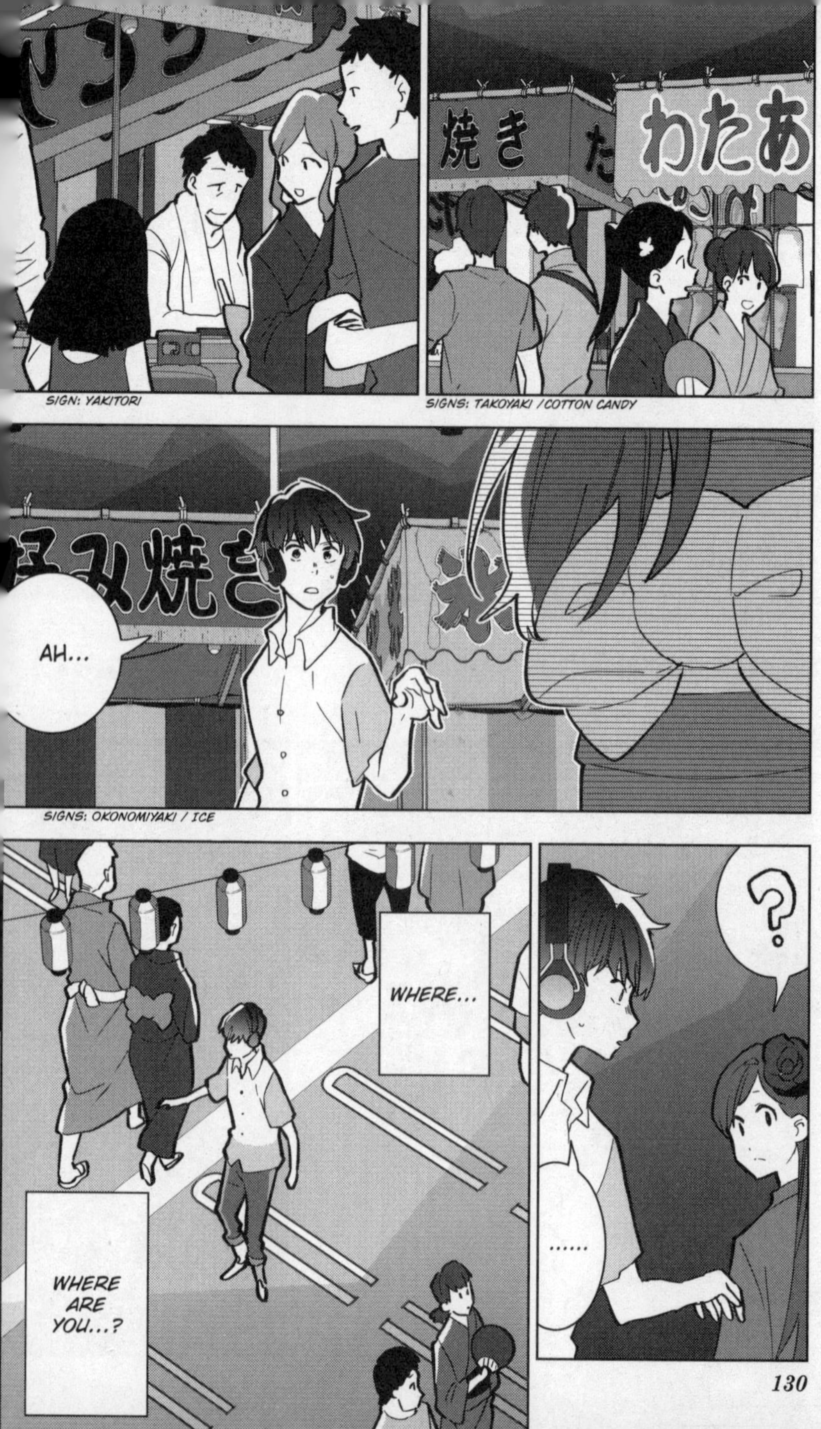
焼き
た
わたあ
SIGNS: TAKOYAKI / COTTON CANDY
SIGN: YAKITORI
み焼き
AH...
SIGNS: OKONOMIYAKI / ICE
?
......
WHERE...
WHERE ARE YOU...?

I CAME ALL THIS WAY...

...AND I'M STILL NOT GONNA GET TO SEE YOU...?

DON'T GIVE UP.

NO.

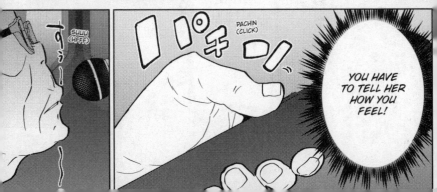

SUUU
(HFFF)

PACHIN
(CLICK)

YOU HAVE TO TELL HER HOW YOU FEEL!

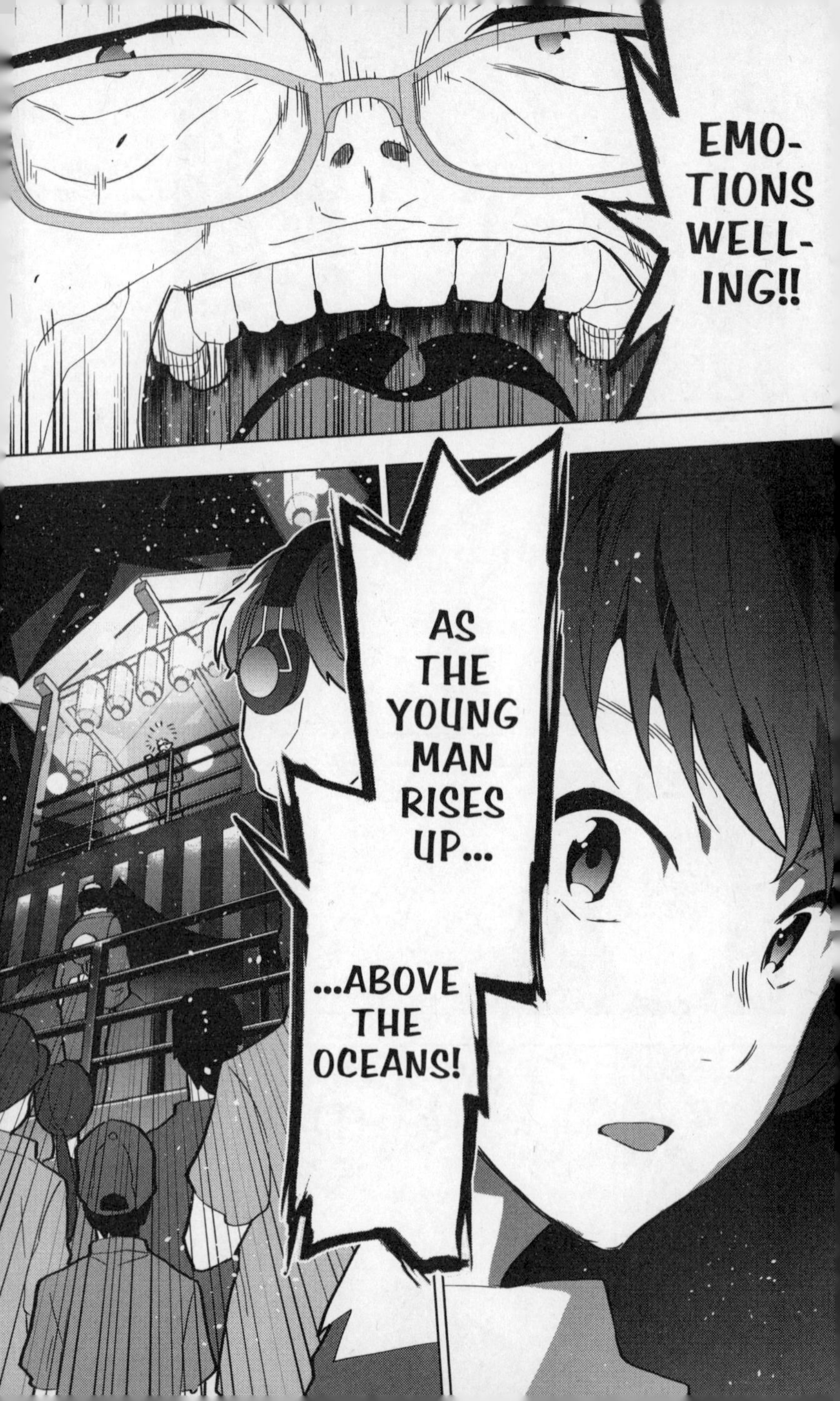
EMO-
TIONS
WELL-
ING!!
AS
THE
YOUNG
MAN
RISES
UP...
...ABOVE
THE
OCEANS!

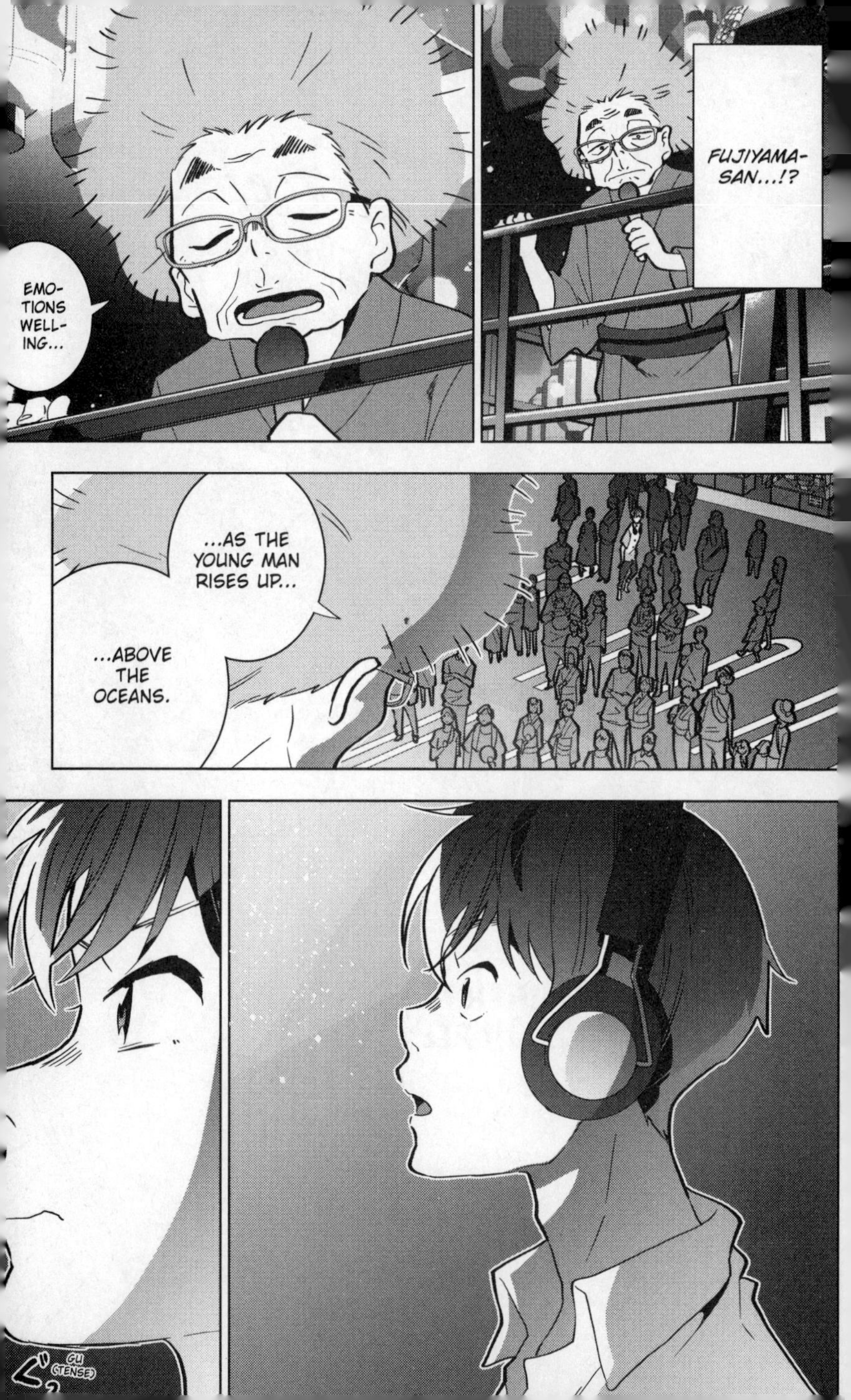
FUJIYAMA-SAN...!?
EMOTIONS WELLING...
...AS THE YOUNG MAN RISES UP...
...ABOVE THE OCEANS.
GU (TENSE)

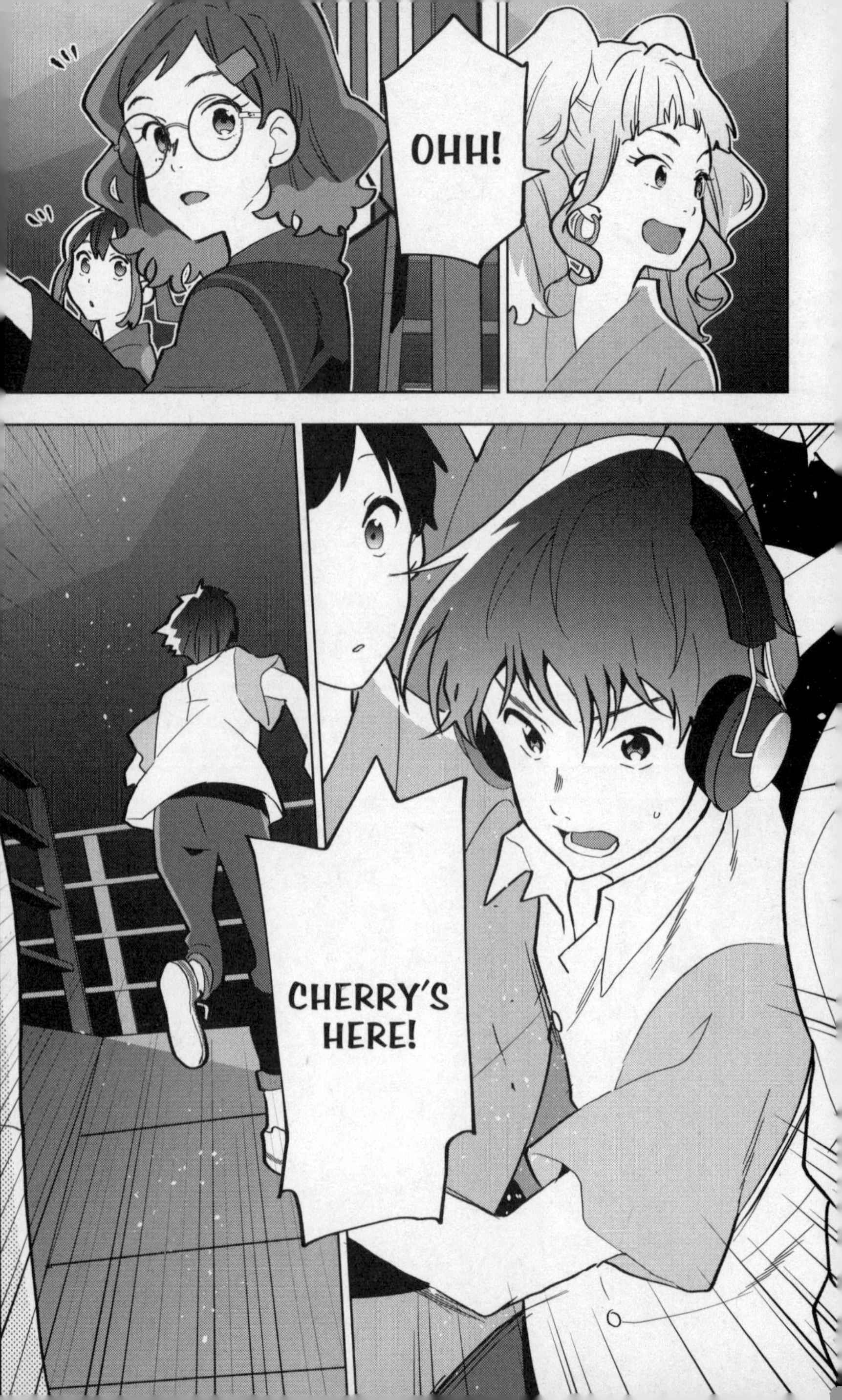
OHH!
CHERRY'S
HERE!

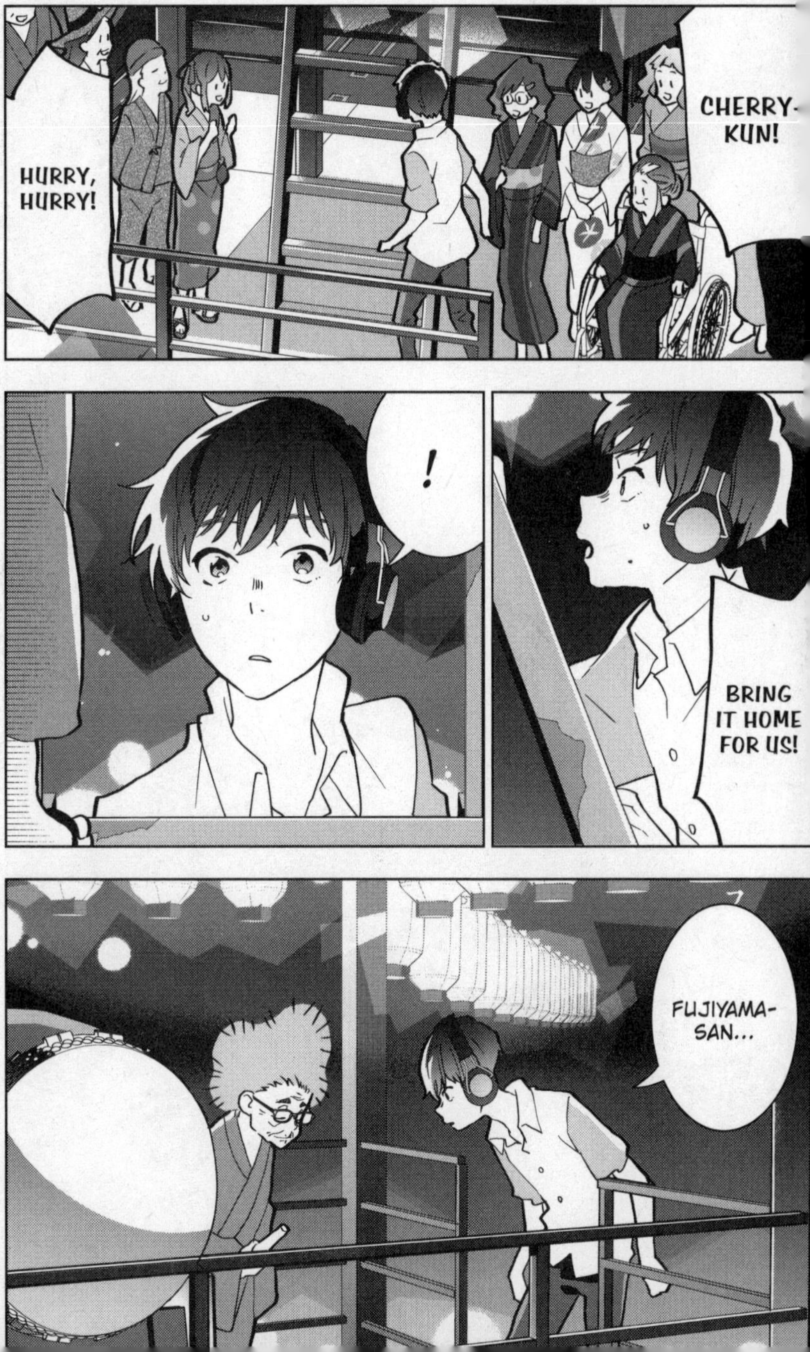
CHERRY-KUN!
HURRY, HURRY!
BRING IT HOME FOR US!
!
FUJIYAMA-SAN...

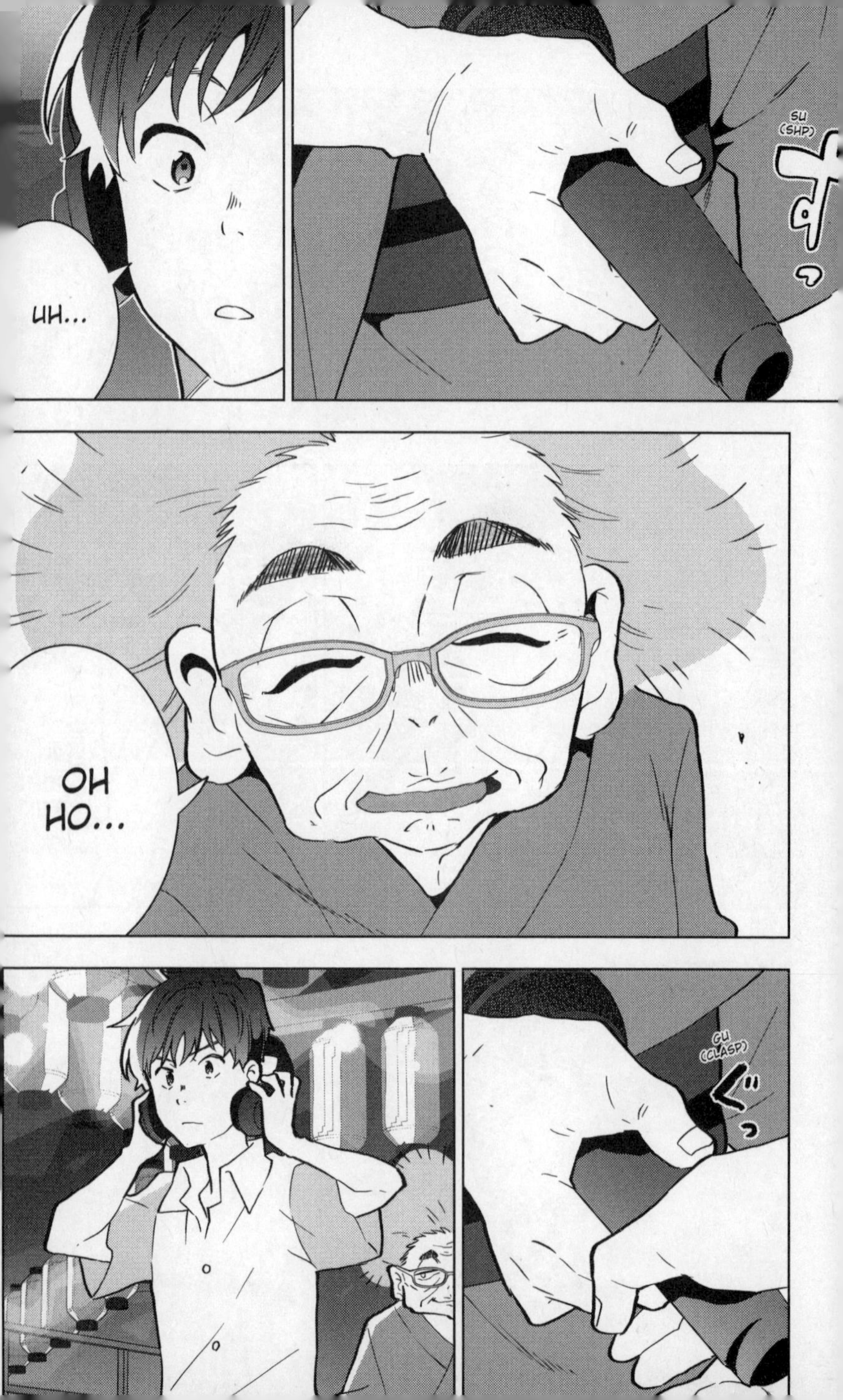
SU (SHP)
すっ
UH...
OH HO...
GU (CLASP)
ぐっ

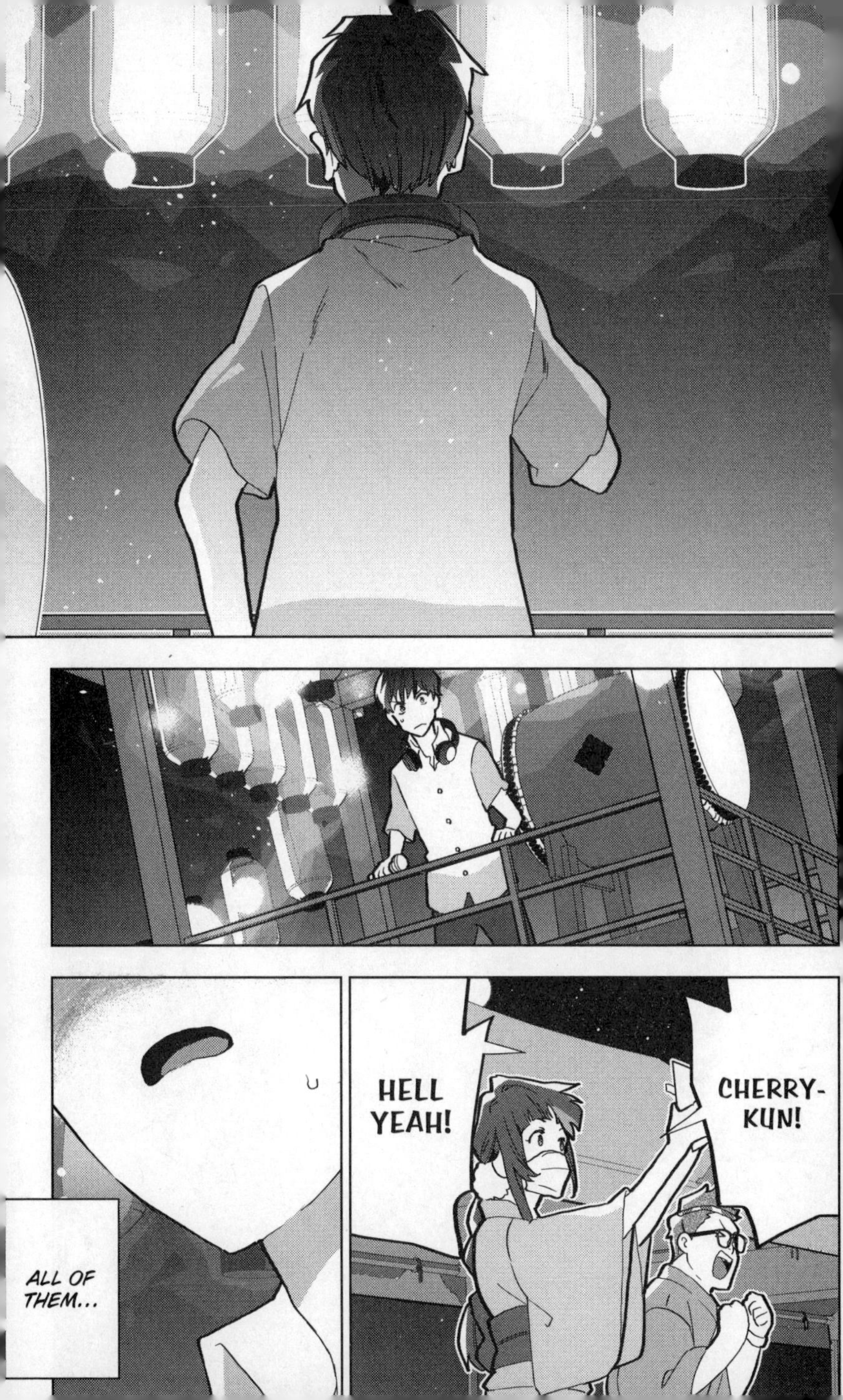
CHERRY-KUN!
HELL YEAH!
ALL OF THEM...

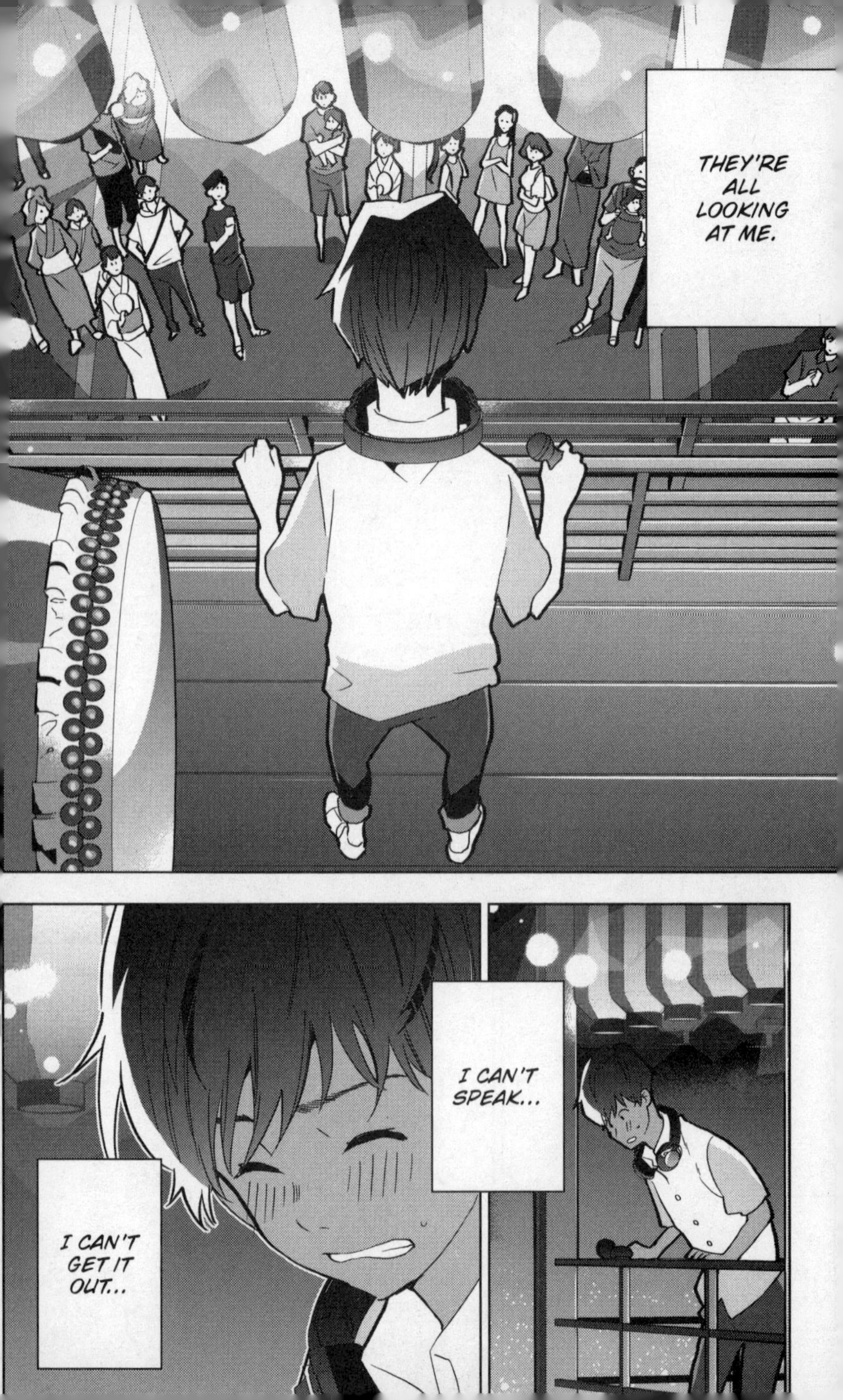
THEY'RE ALL LOOKING AT ME.
I CAN'T SPEAK...
I CAN'T GET IT OUT...

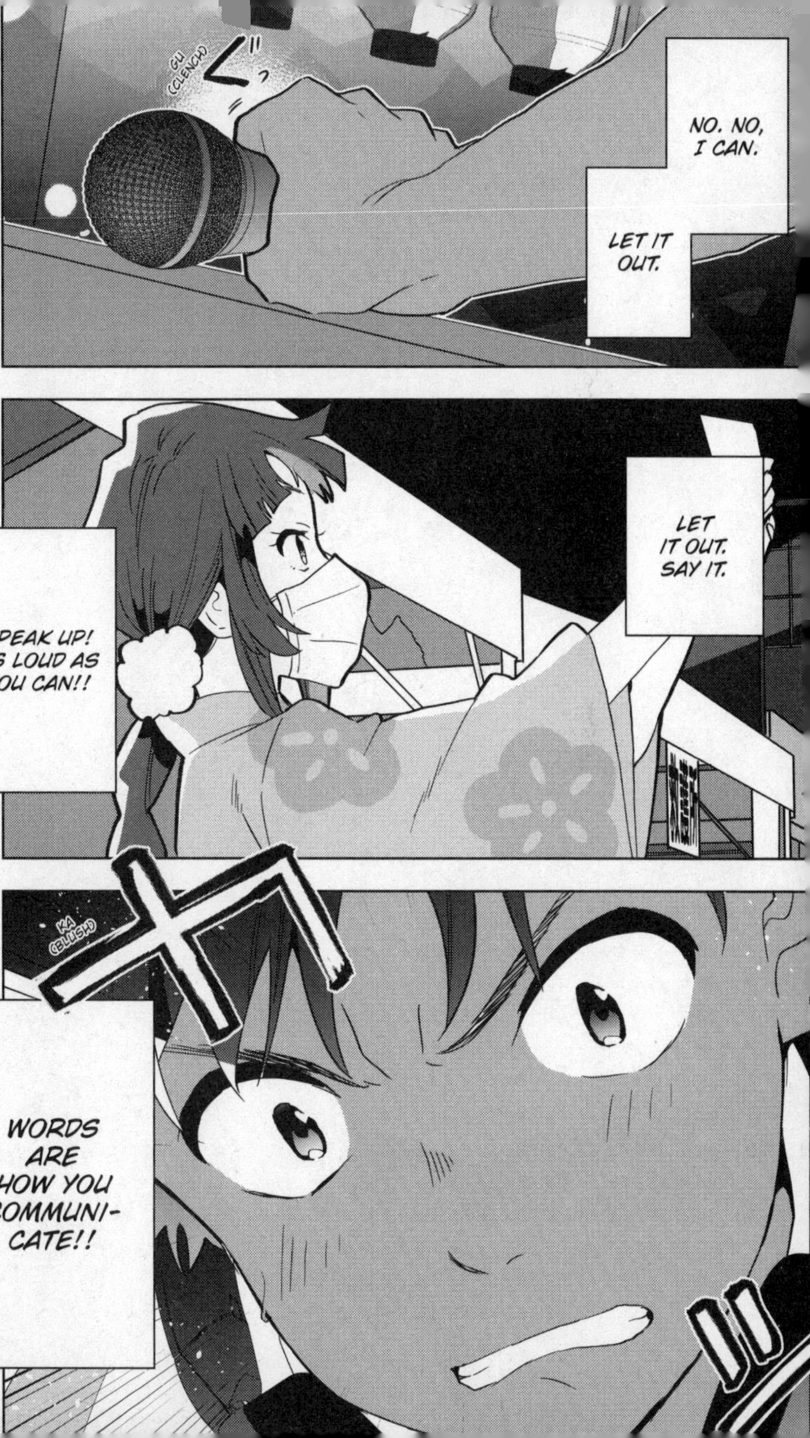
NO. NO, I CAN.
LET IT OUT.
GU (CLENCH)
LET IT OUT. SAY IT.
SPEAK UP! AS LOUD AS YOU CAN!!
KA (BLUSH)
WORDS ARE HOW YOU COMMUNI-CATE!!

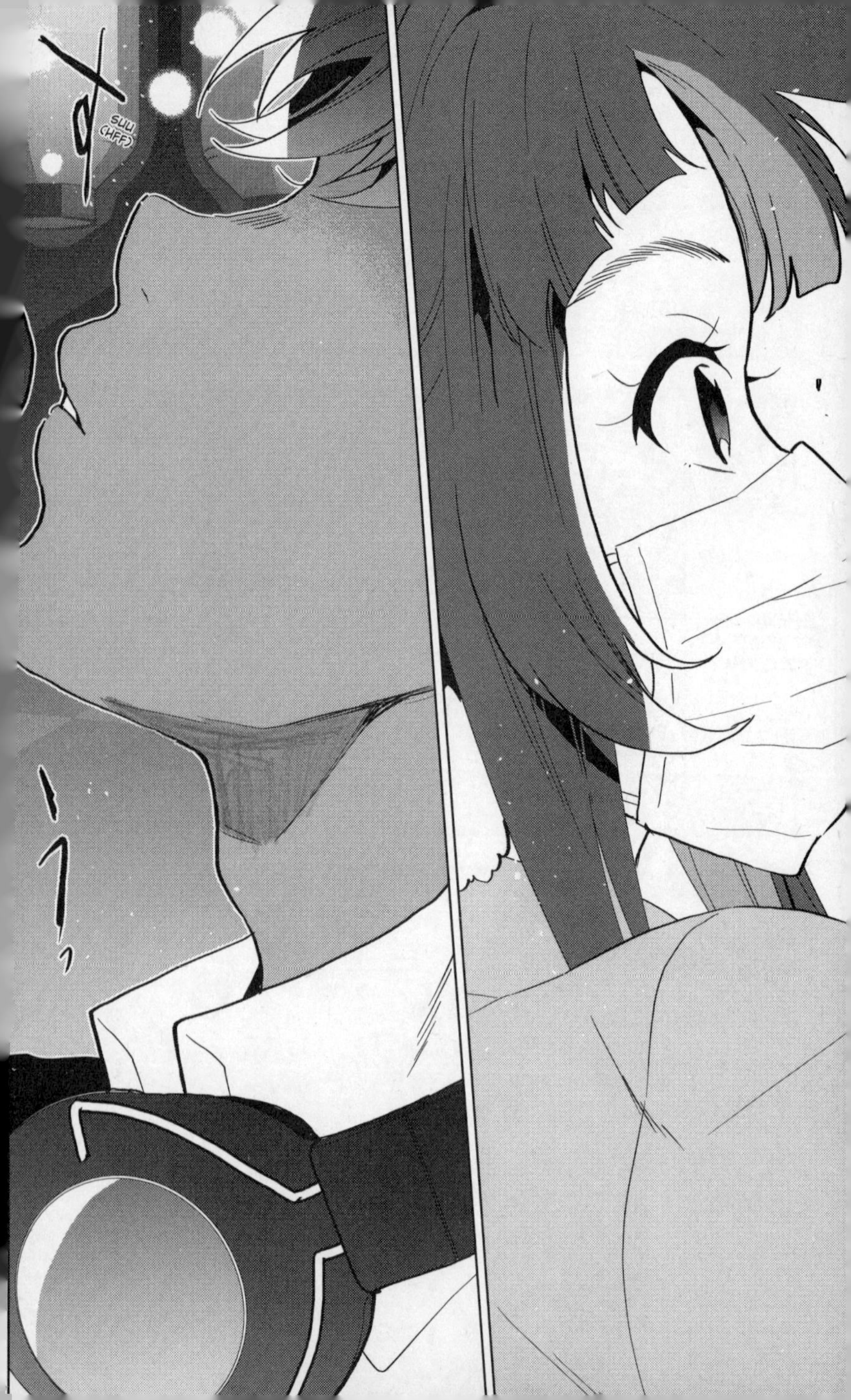
SUU
(HFF)

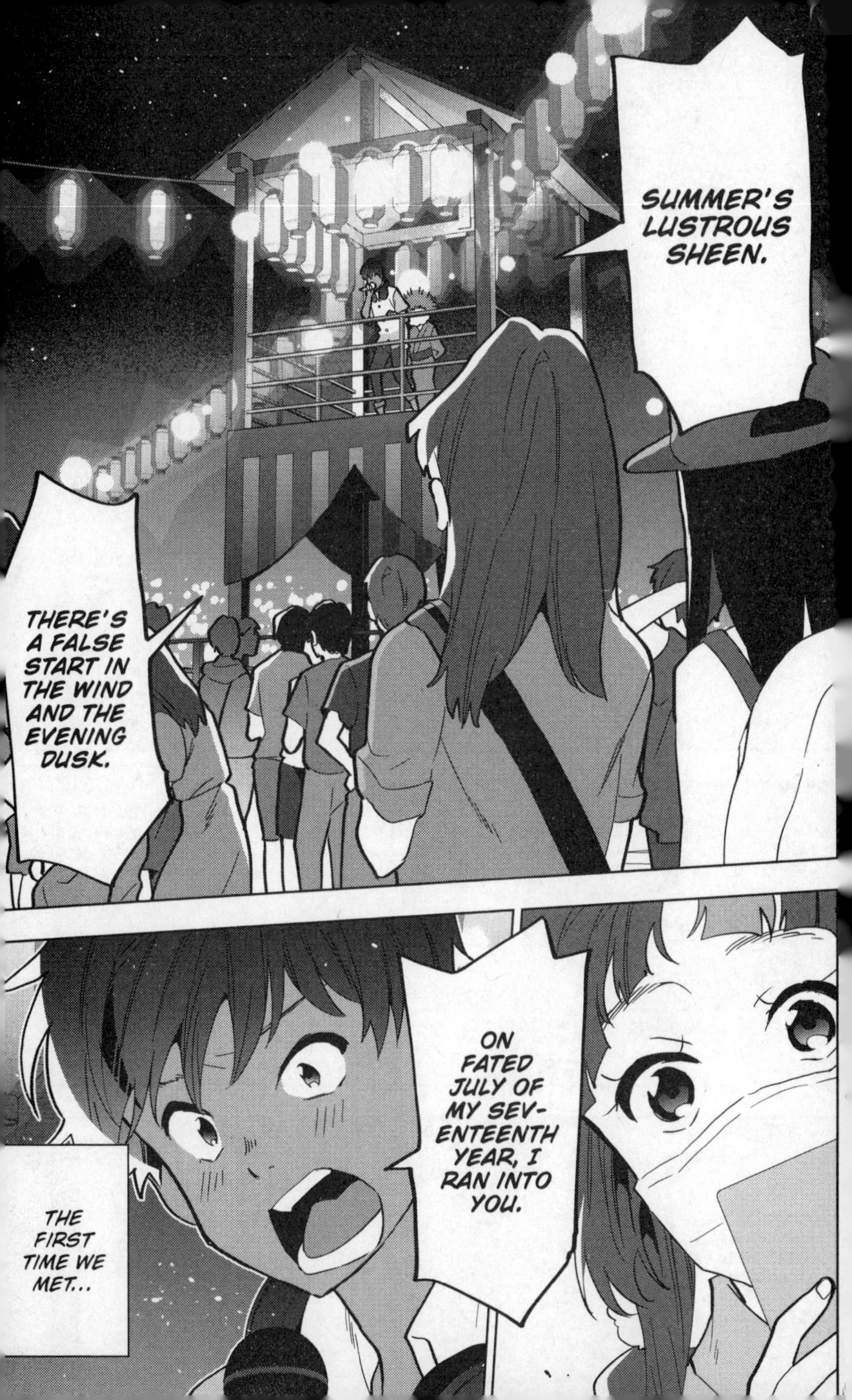
SUMMER'S LUSTROUS SHEEN.
THERE'S A FALSE START IN THE WIND AND THE EVENING DUSK.
ON FATED JULY OF MY SEV-ENTEENTH YEAR, I RAN INTO YOU.
THE FIRST TIME WE MET...

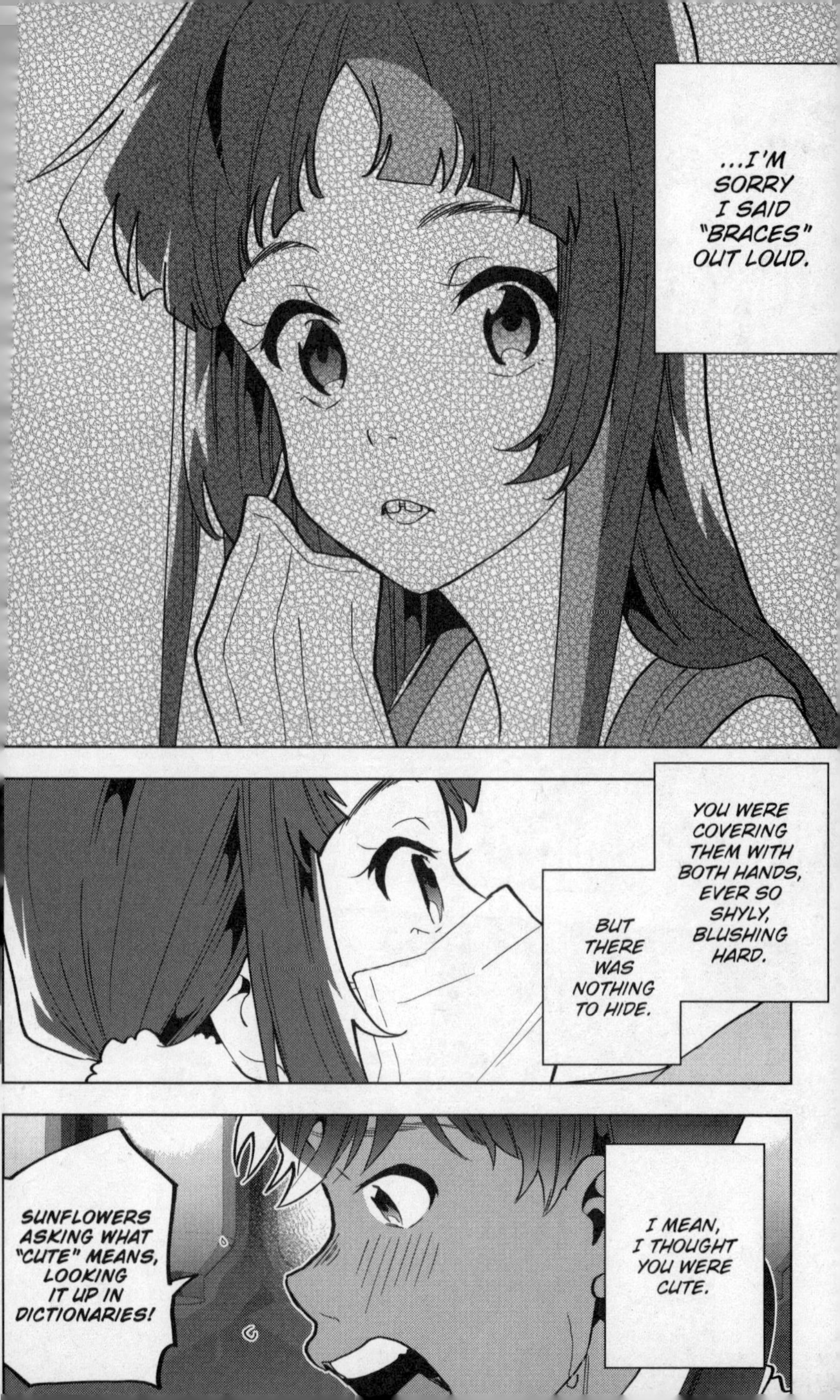
...I'M SORRY I SAID "BRACES" OUT LOUD.
YOU WERE COVERING THEM WITH BOTH HANDS, EVER SO SHYLY, BLUSHING HARD.
BUT THERE WAS NOTHING TO HIDE.
I MEAN, I THOUGHT YOU WERE CUTE.
SUNFLOWERS ASKING WHAT "CUTE" MEANS, LOOKING IT UP IN DICTIONARIES!

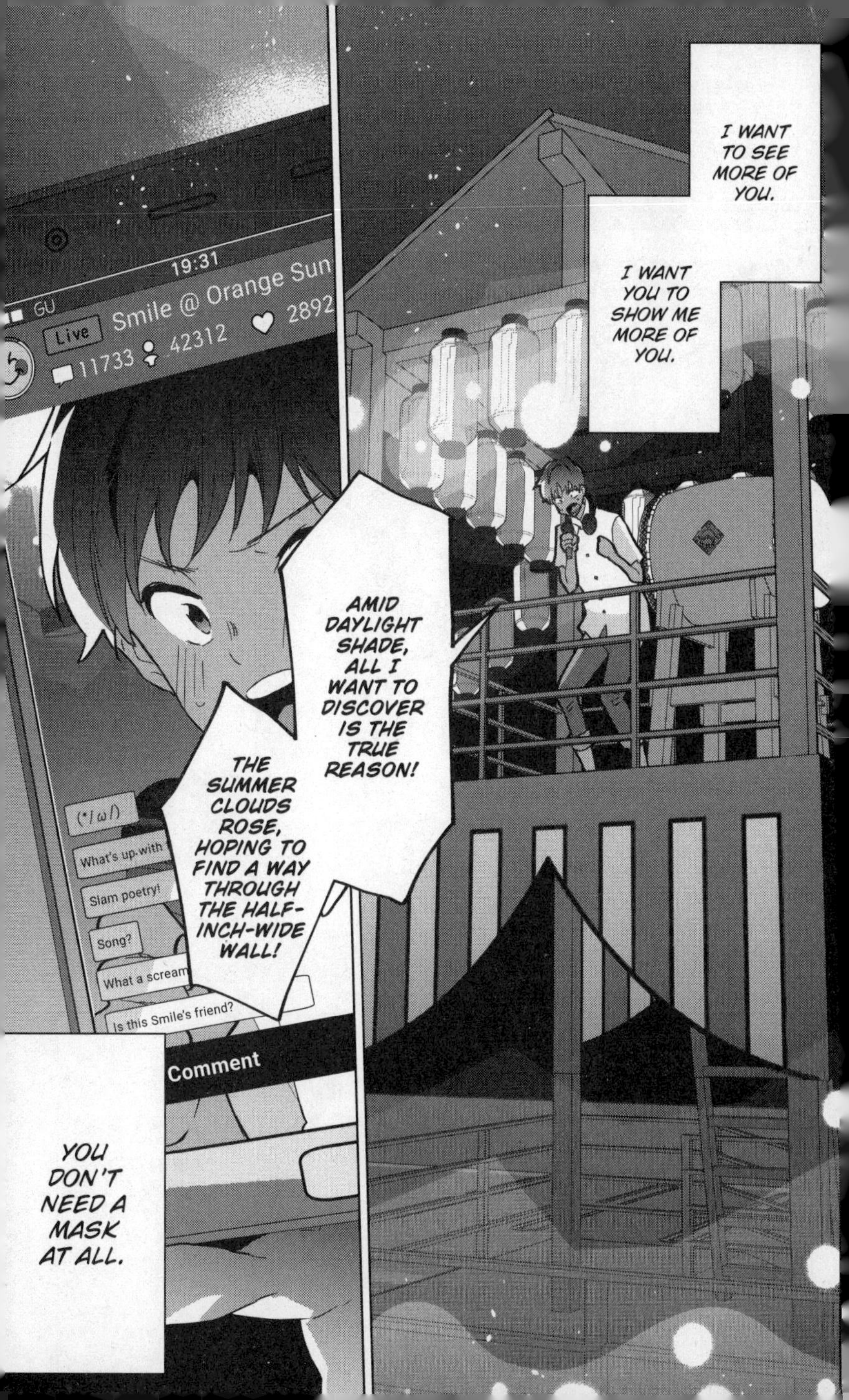
I WANT TO SEE MORE OF YOU.
I WANT YOU TO SHOW ME MORE OF YOU.
AMID DAYLIGHT SHADE, ALL I WANT TO DISCOVER IS THE TRUE REASON!
THE SUMMER CLOUDS ROSE, HOPING TO FIND A WAY THROUGH THE HALF-INCH-WIDE WALL!
19:31
GU
Smile @ Orange Sun
Live
2892
11733
42312
(*/ω/)
What's up with
Slam poetry!
Song?
What a scream
Is this Smile's friend?
Comment
YOU DON'T NEED A MASK AT ALL.

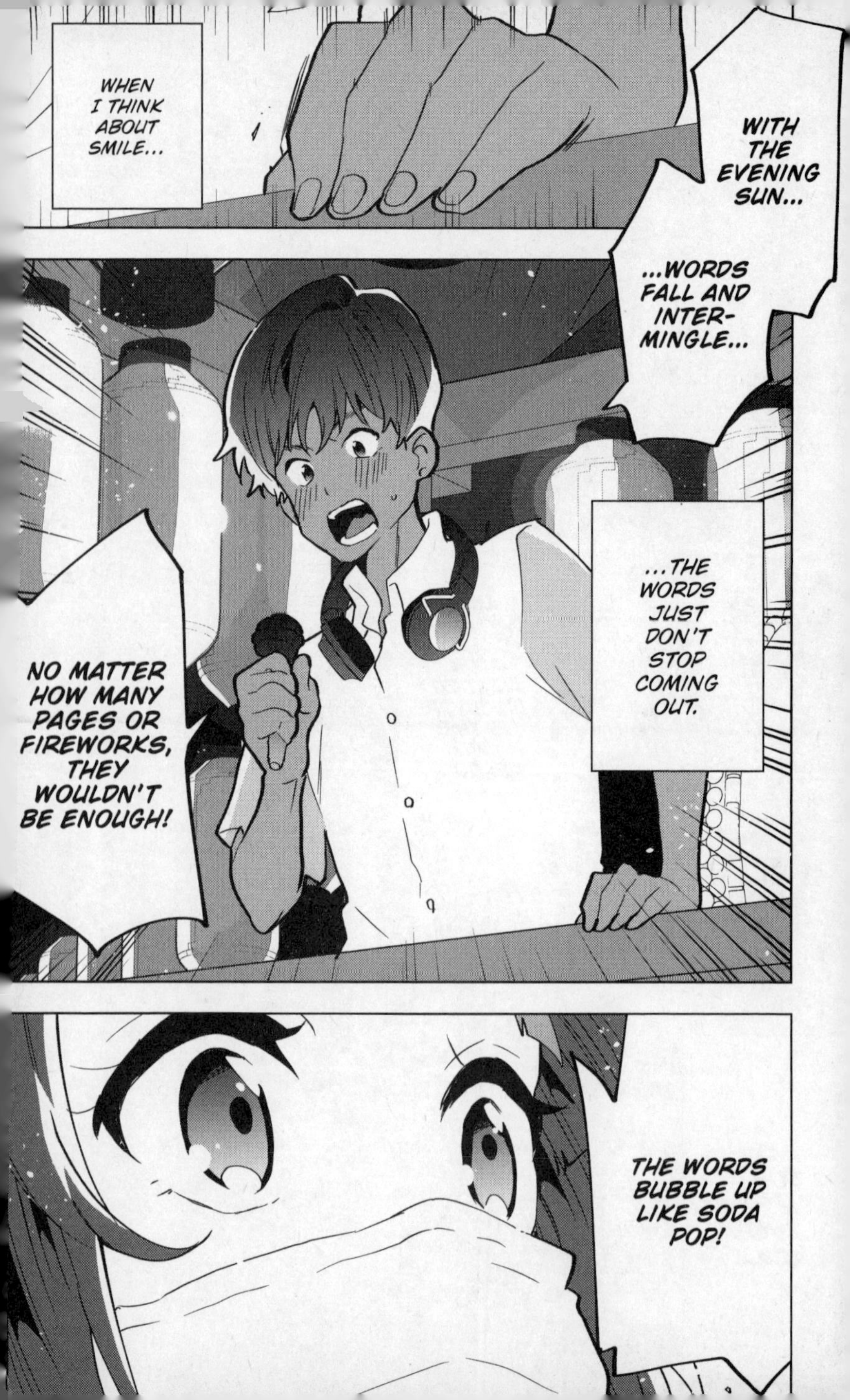

WITH THE EVENING SUN...
...WORDS FALL AND INTER-MINGLE...
WHEN I THINK ABOUT SMILE...
...THE WORDS JUST DON'T STOP COMING OUT.
NO MATTER HOW MANY PAGES OR FIREWORKS, THEY WOULDN'T BE ENOUGH!
THE WORDS BUBBLE UP LIKE SODA POP!

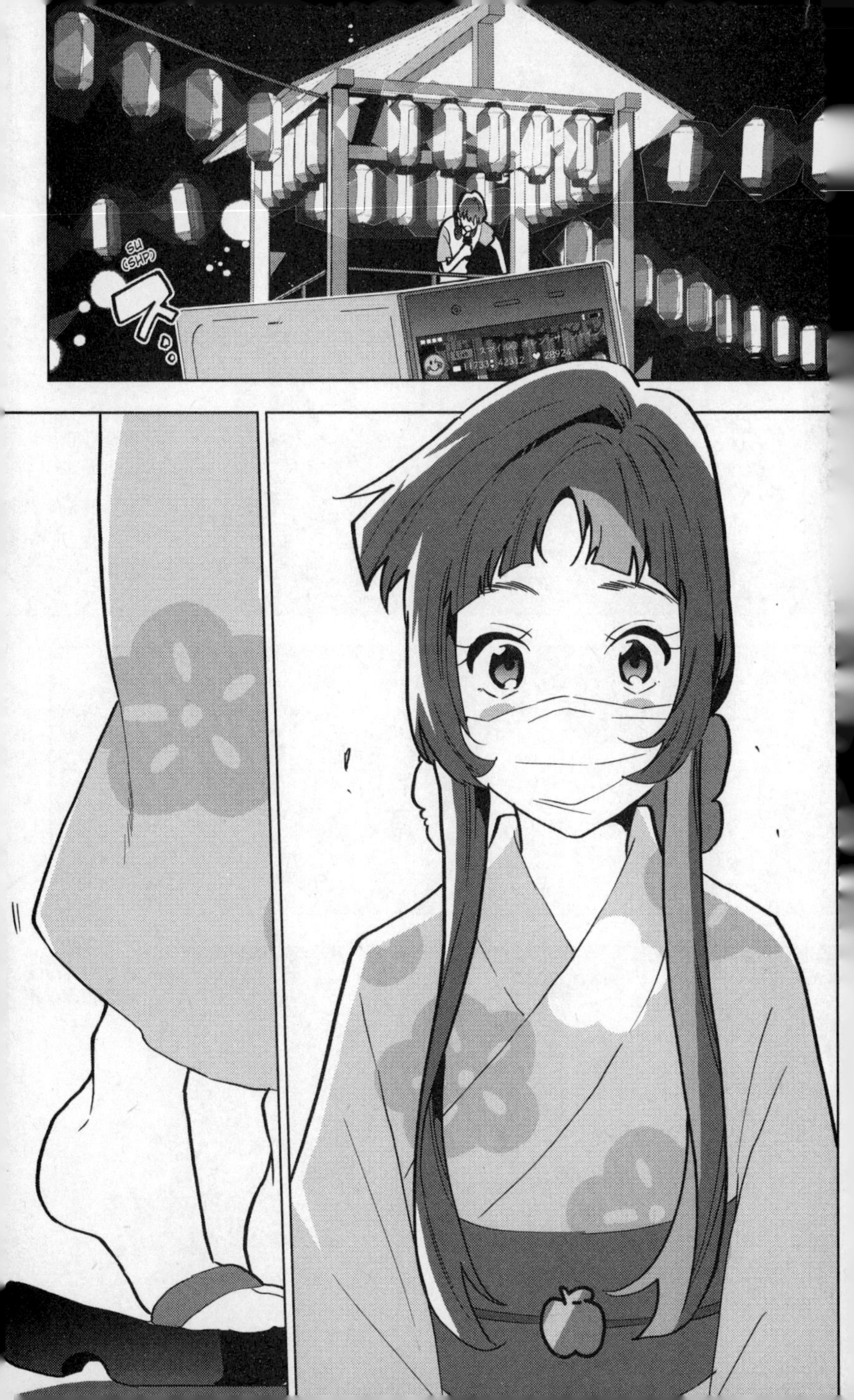
スッ
SU (SHP)

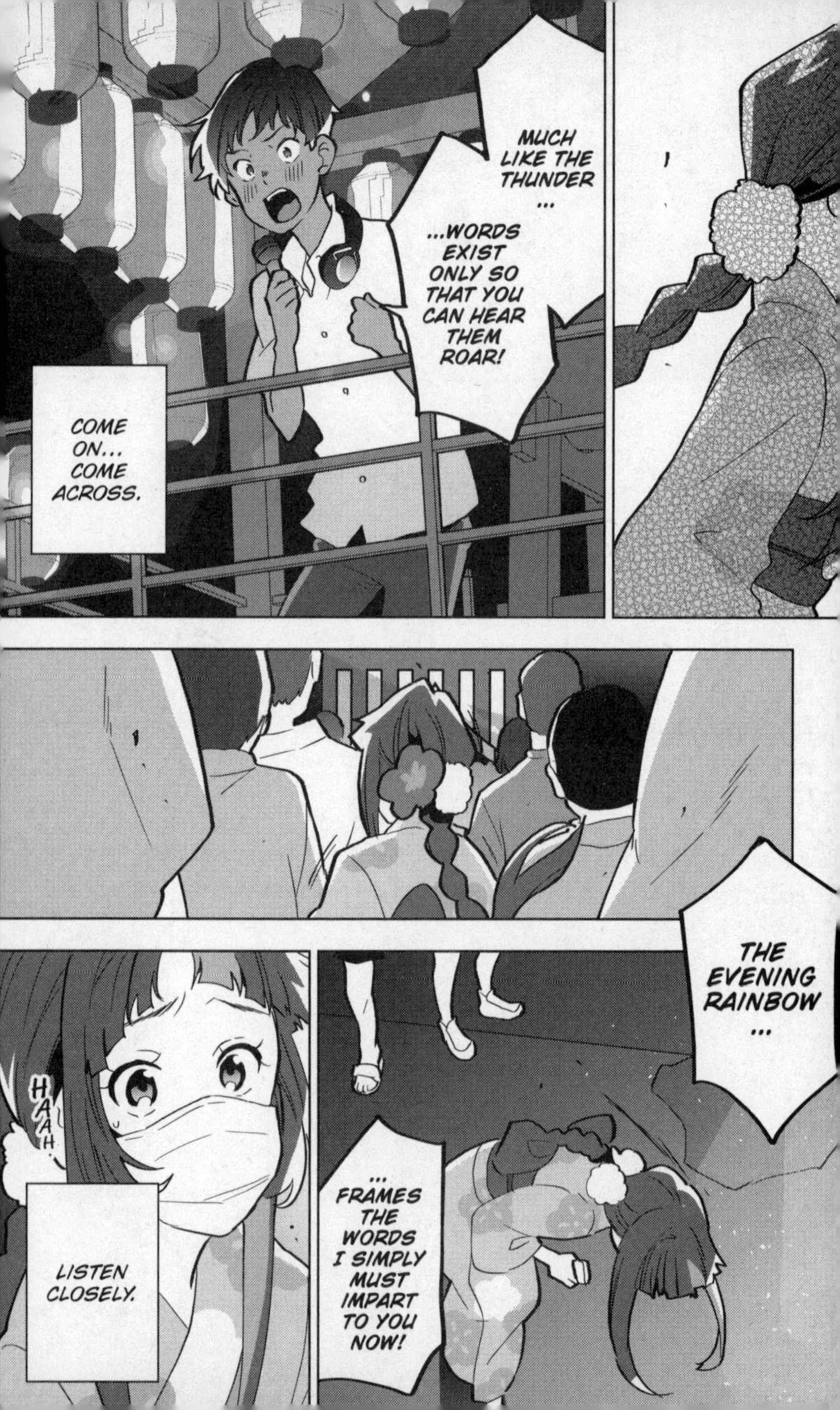
MUCH LIKE THE THUNDER...
...WORDS EXIST ONLY SO THAT YOU CAN HEAR THEM ROAR!
COME ON... COME ACROSS.
THE EVENING RAINBOW...
...FRAMES THE WORDS I SIMPLY MUST IMPART TO YOU NOW!
HAAAH
LISTEN CLOSELY.

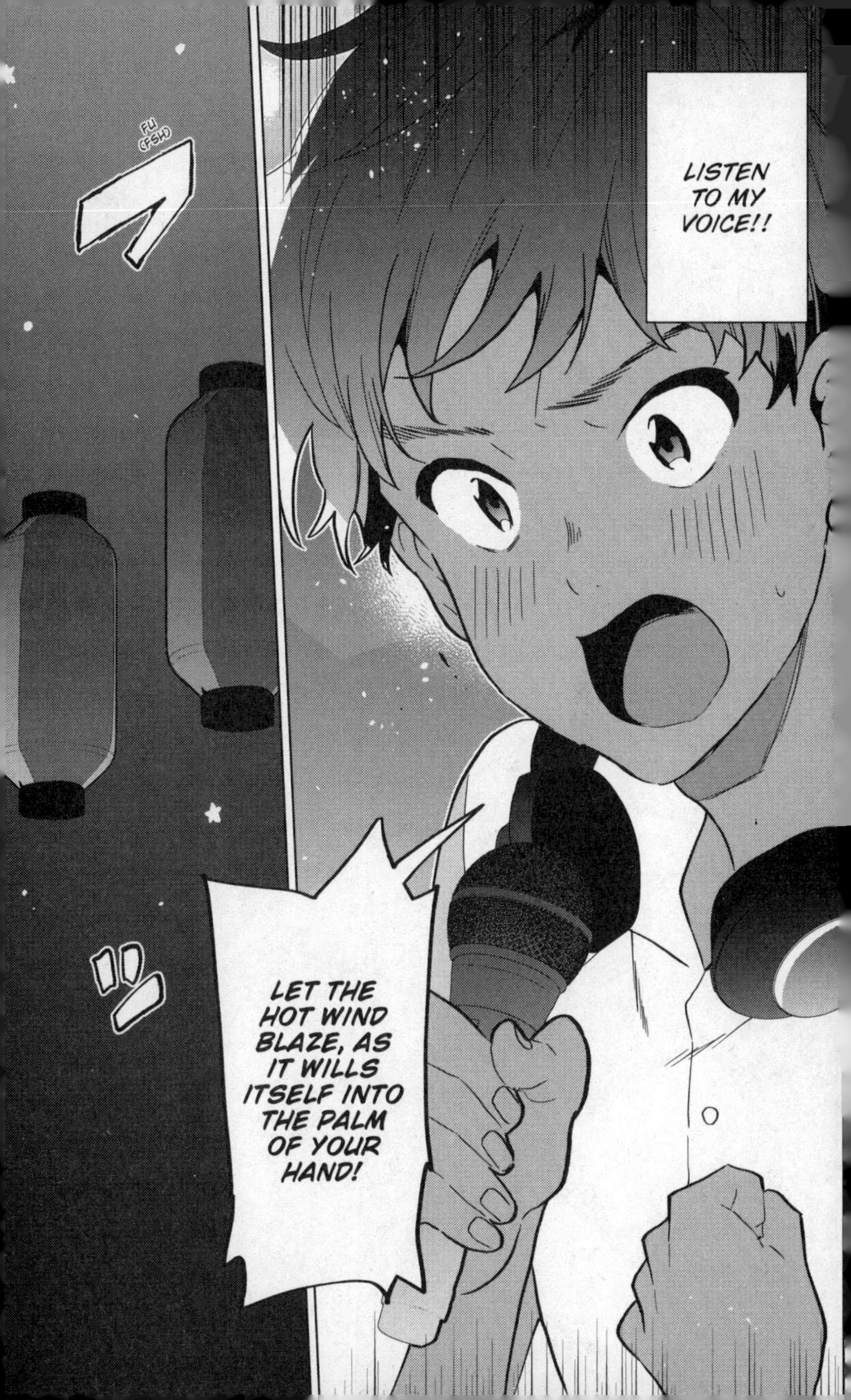
LISTEN TO MY VOICE!!
LET THE HOT WIND BLAZE, AS IT WILLS ITSELF INTO THE PALM OF YOUR HAND!
FU (FSH)

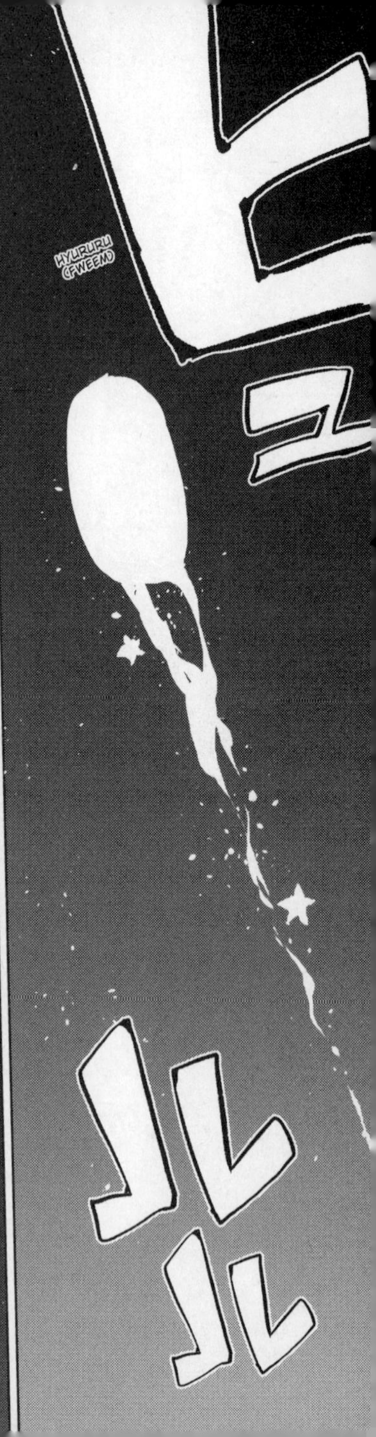
HYURURU
(FWEEM)
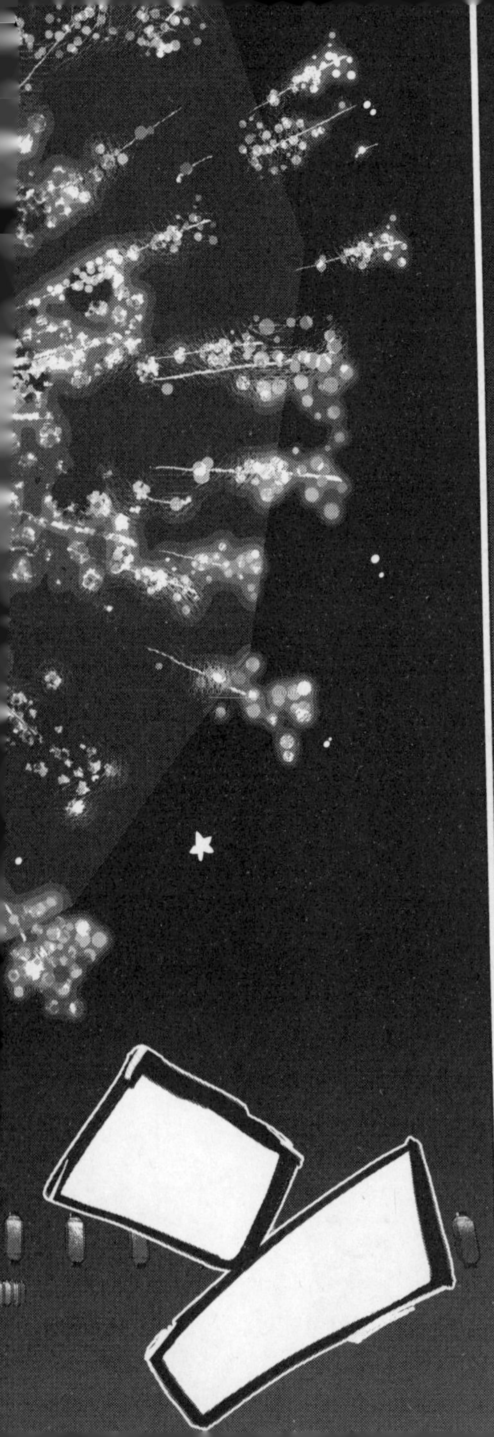

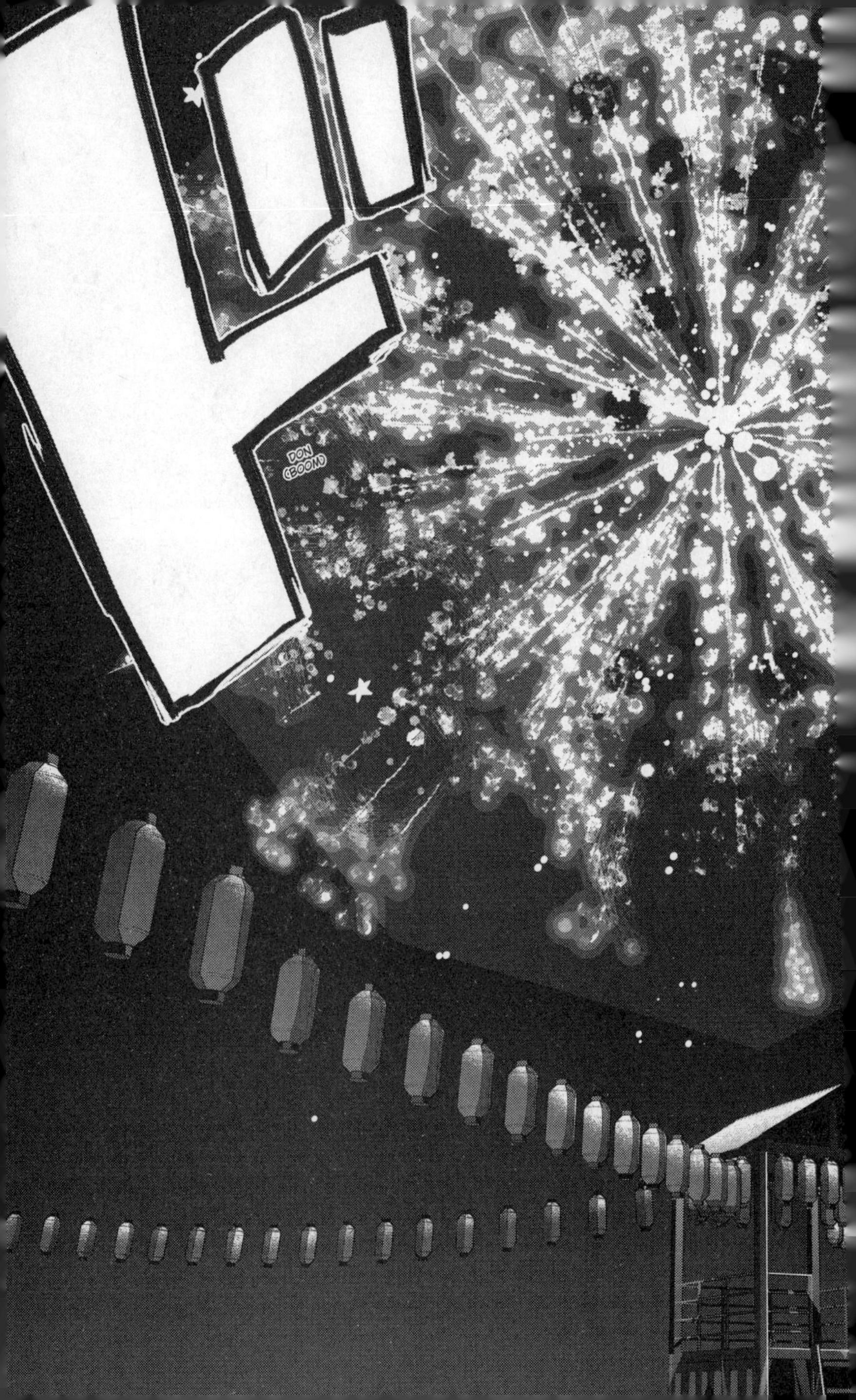
DON
(BOOM)

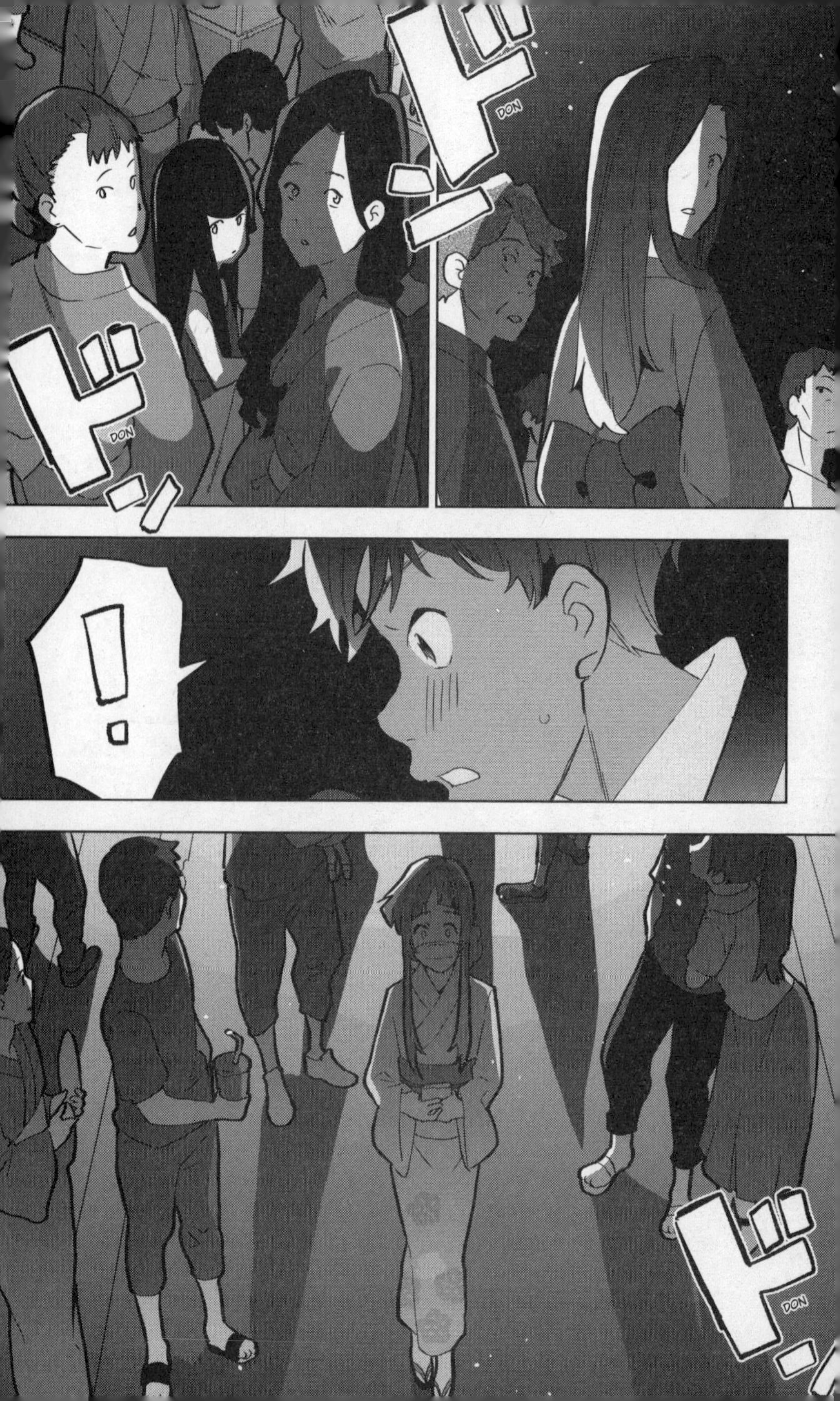
ドン
DON
ドン
DON
!
ドン
DON

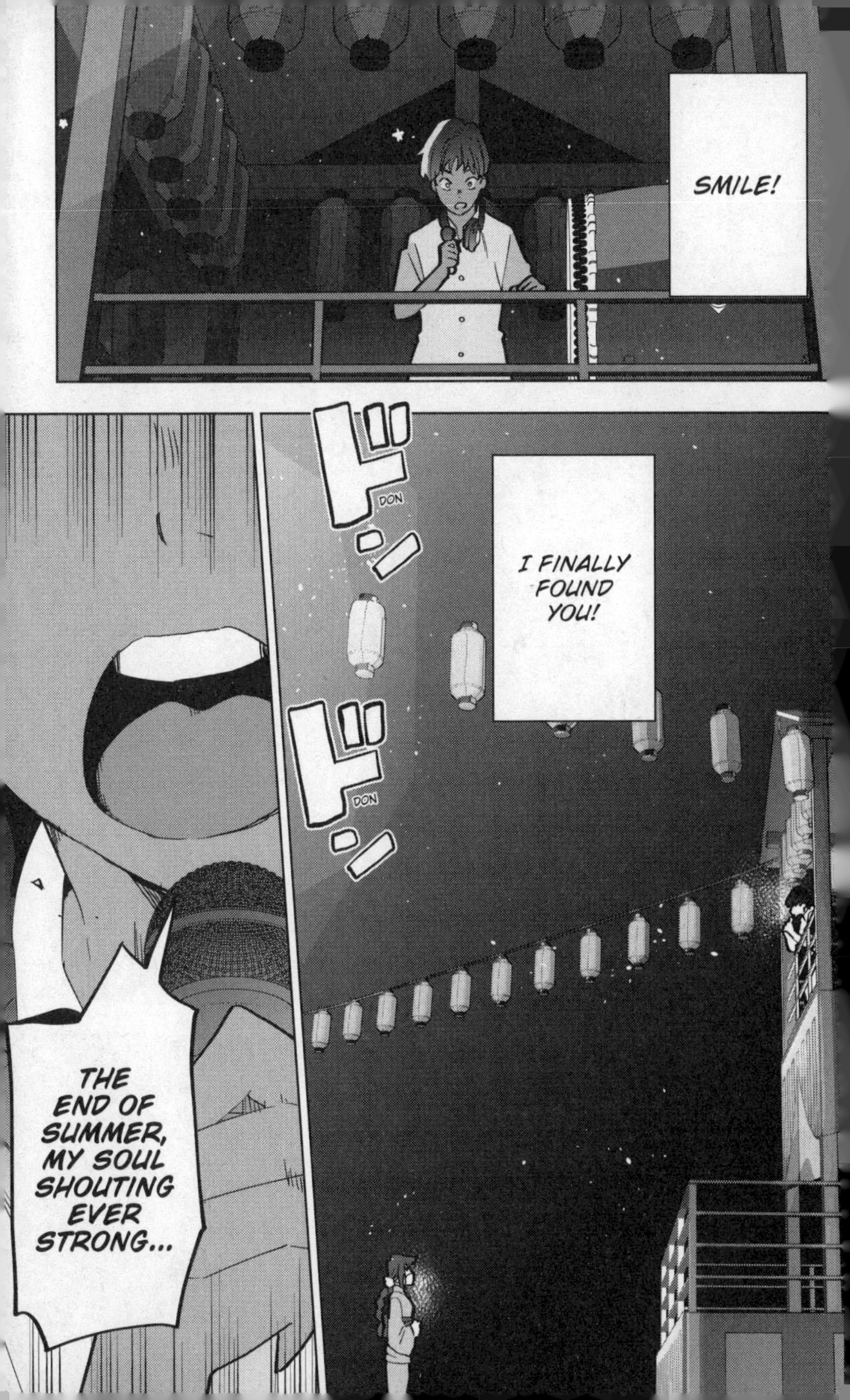
SMILE!
I FINALLY FOUND YOU!
ドーン
DON
ドーン
DON
THE END OF SUMMER, MY SOUL SHOUTING EVER STRONG...

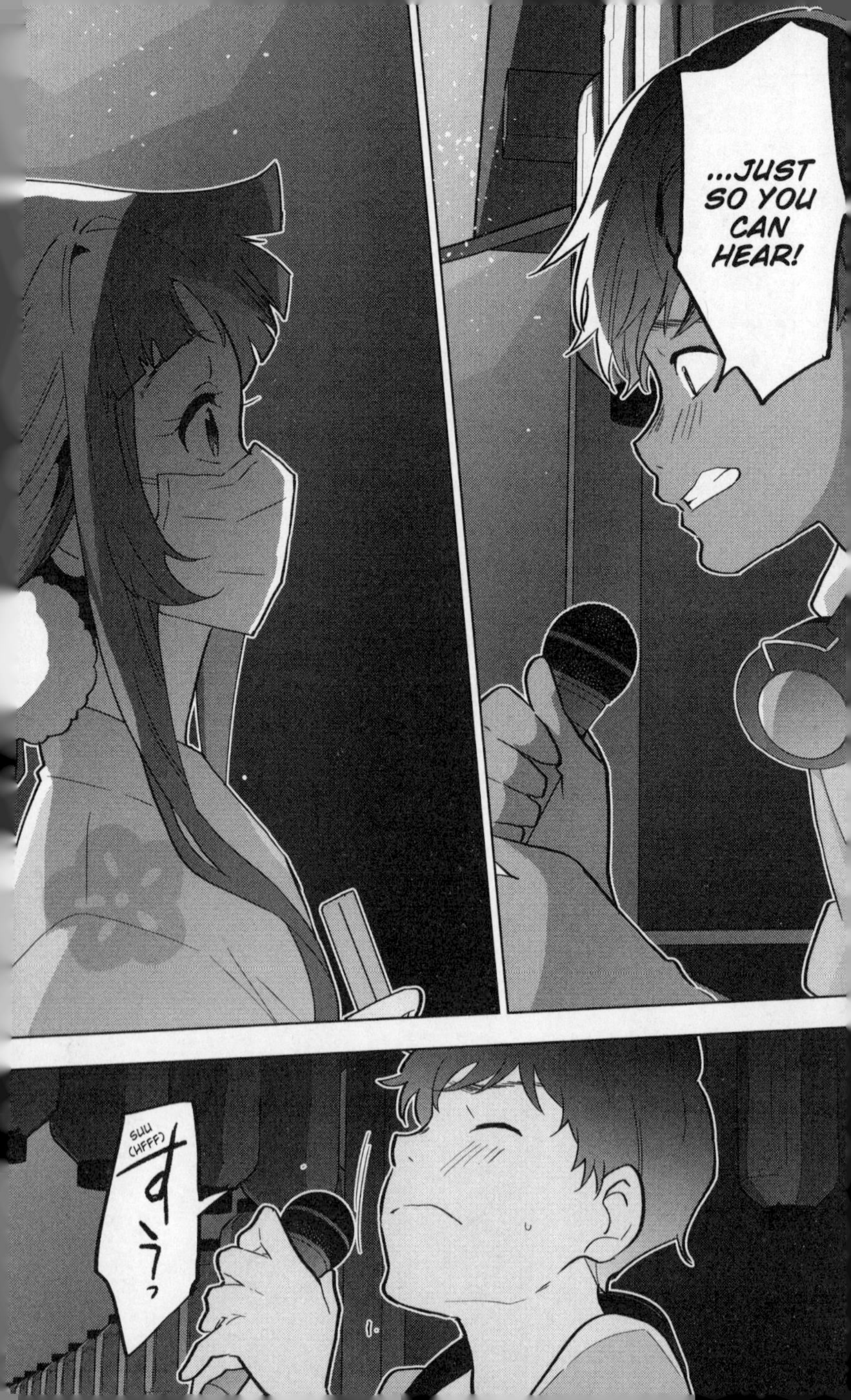
...JUST SO YOU CAN HEAR!
SUU (HFFF)
すぅっ

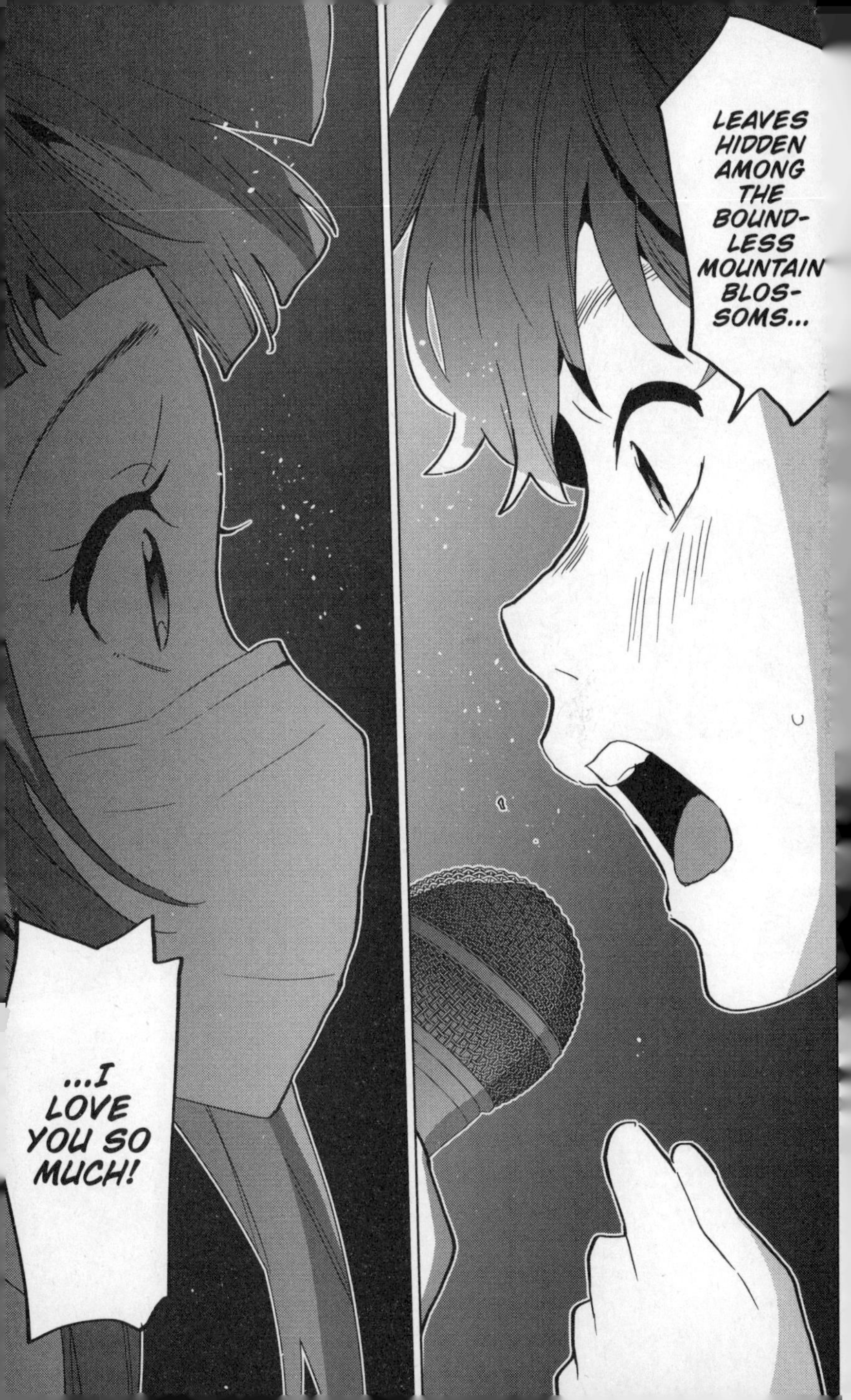
LEAVES HIDDEN AMONG THE BOUNDLESS MOUNTAIN BLOSSOMS...
...I LOVE YOU SO MUCH!

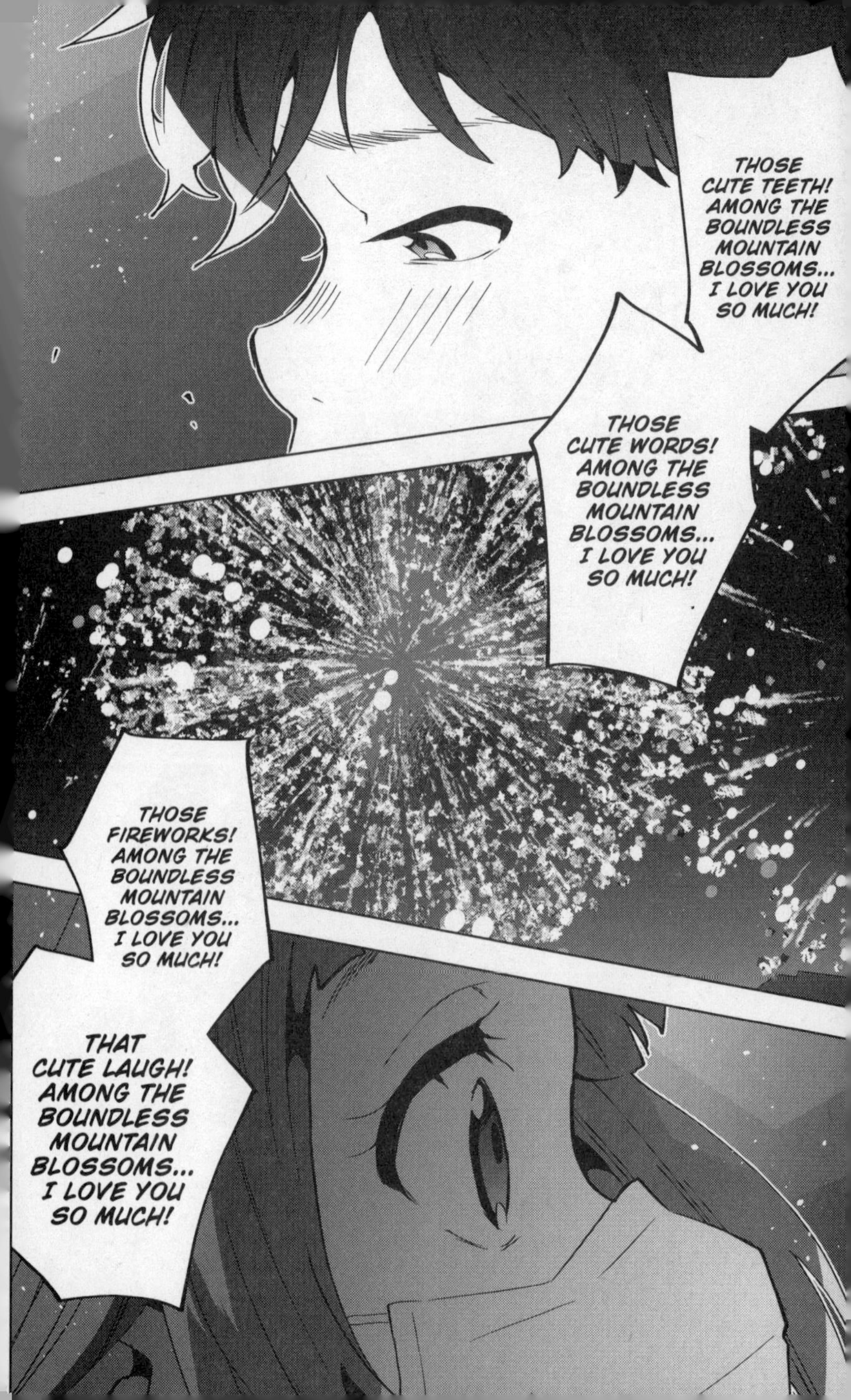
THOSE CUTE TEETH! AMONG THE BOUNDLESS MOUNTAIN BLOSSOMS... I LOVE YOU SO MUCH!
THOSE CUTE WORDS! AMONG THE BOUNDLESS MOUNTAIN BLOSSOMS... I LOVE YOU SO MUCH!
THOSE FIREWORKS! AMONG THE BOUNDLESS MOUNTAIN BLOSSOMS... I LOVE YOU SO MUCH!
THAT CUTE LAUGH! AMONG THE BOUNDLESS MOUNTAIN BLOSSOMS... I LOVE YOU SO MUCH!

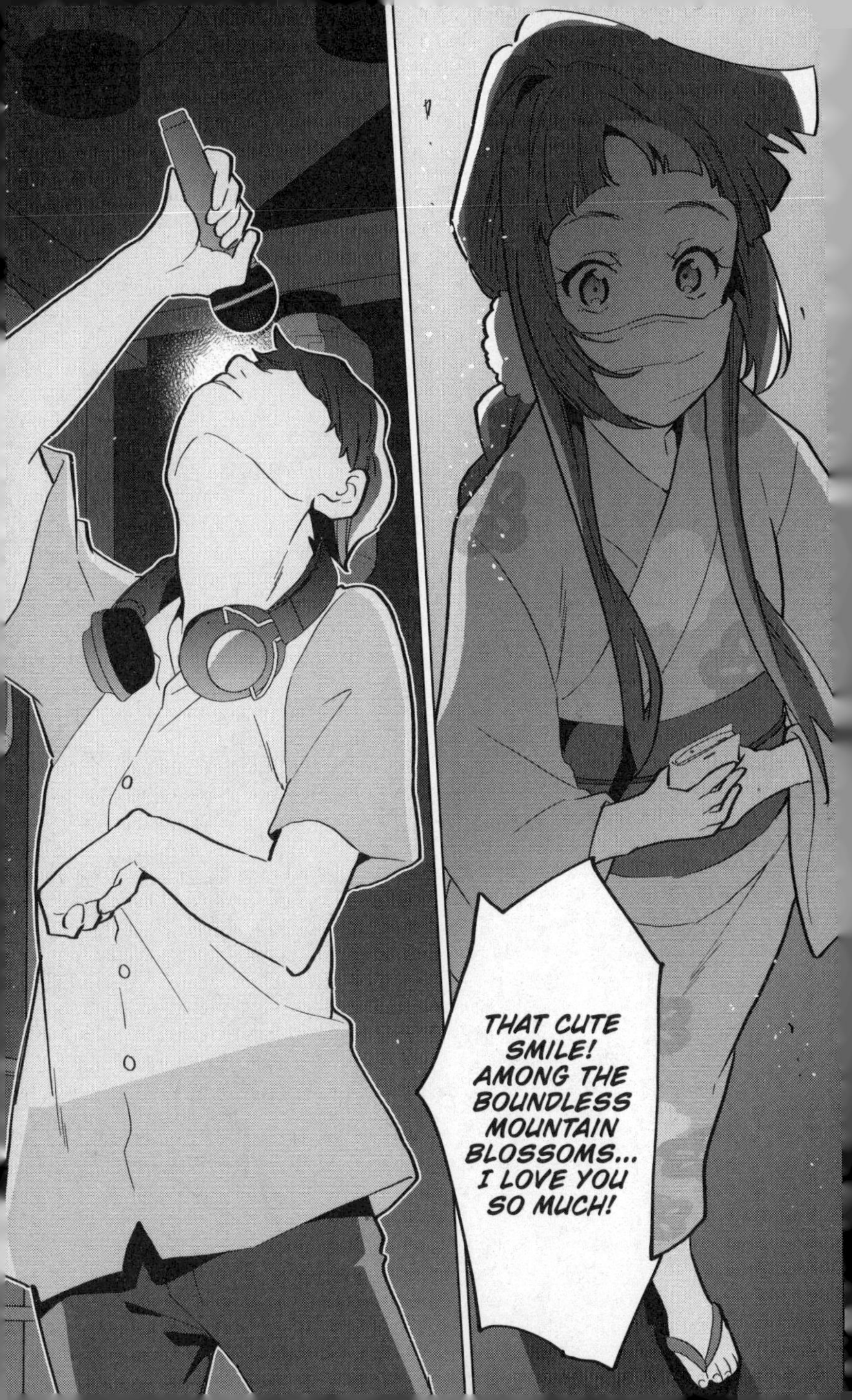
THAT CUTE SMILE! AMONG THE BOUNDLESS MOUNTAIN BLOSSOMS... I LOVE YOU SO MUCH!

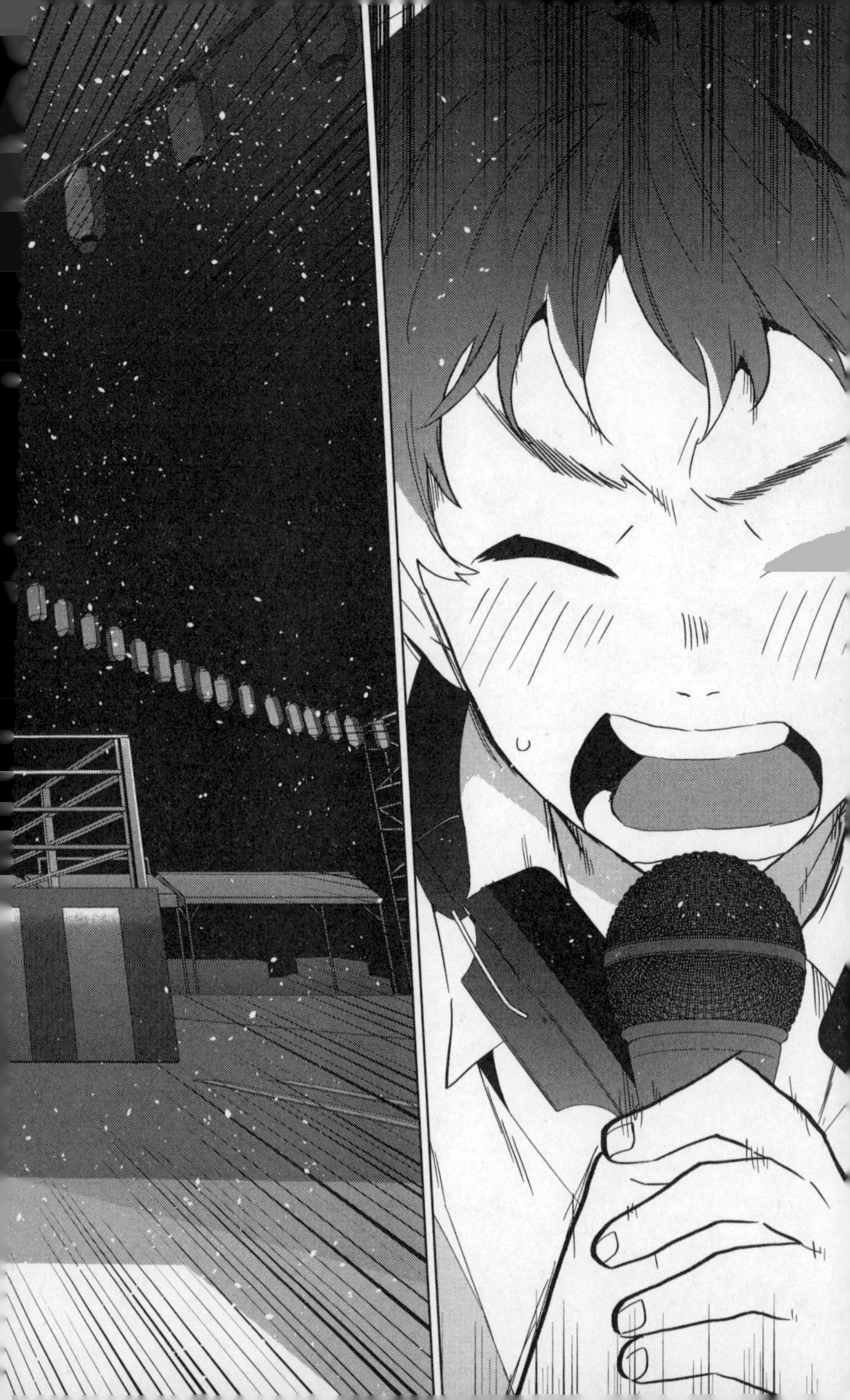

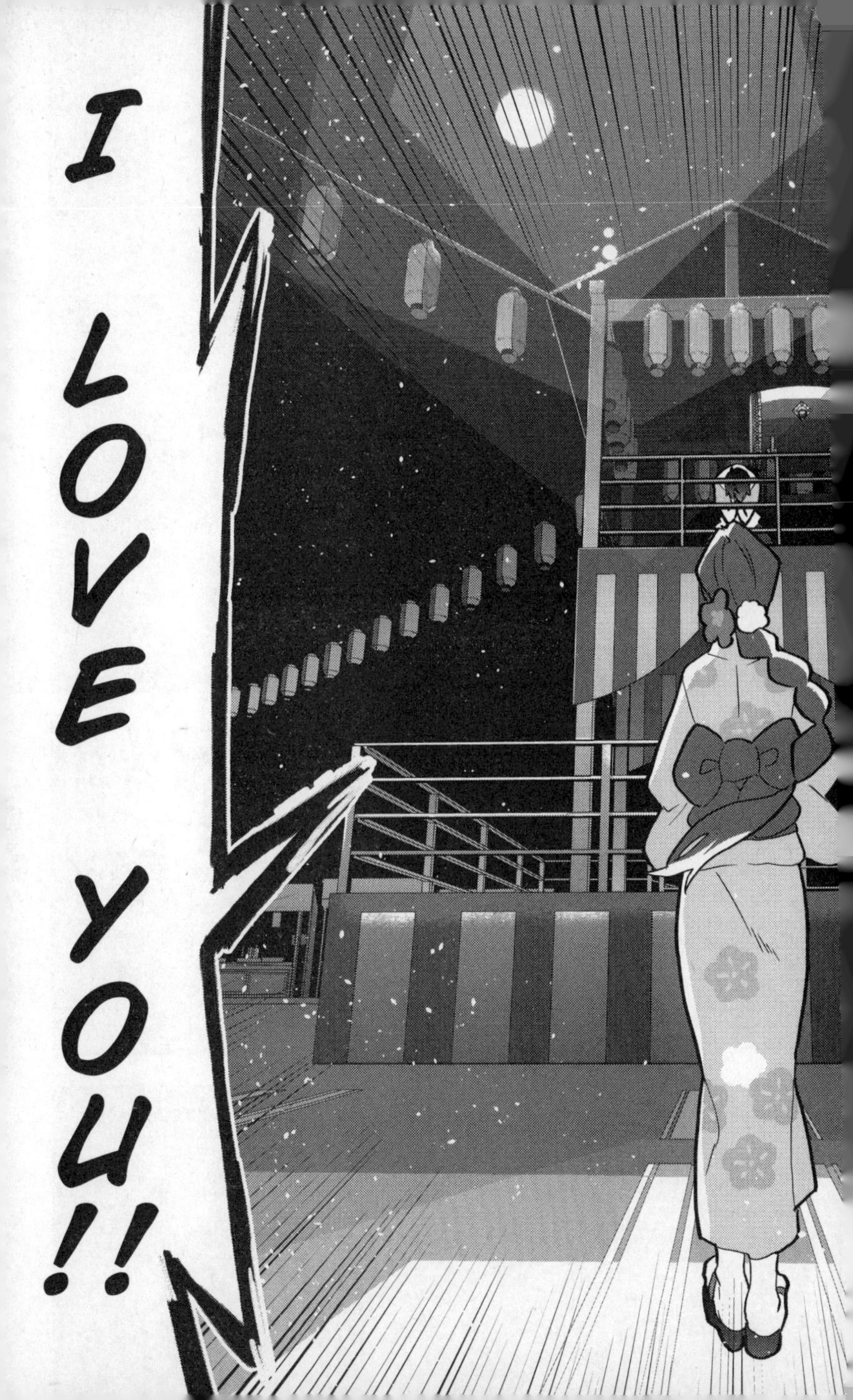
I LOVE YOU!!

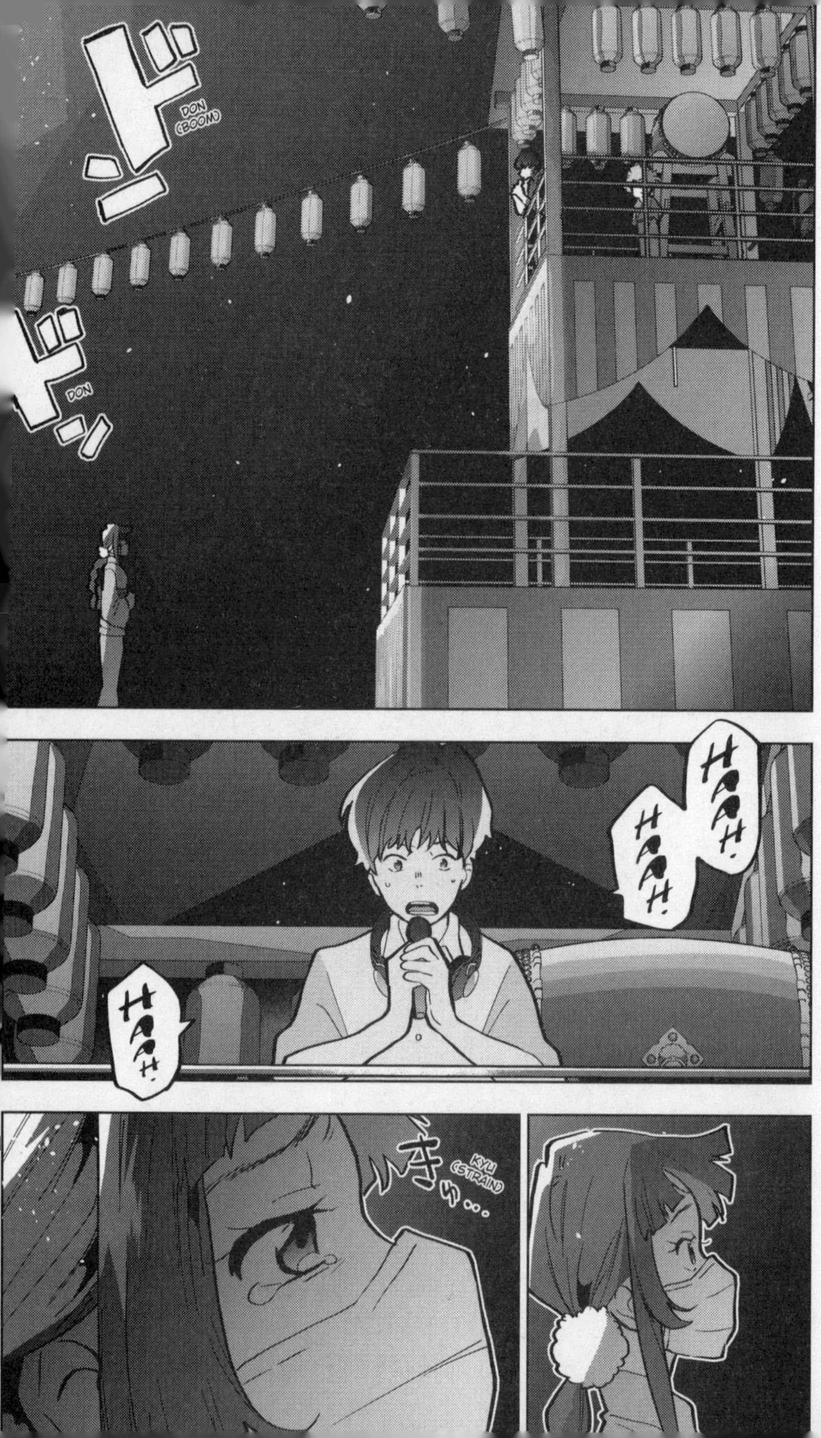
DON (BOOM)
DON
HAAH! HAAH!
HAAH!
きゅ…
KYU (STRAIN)

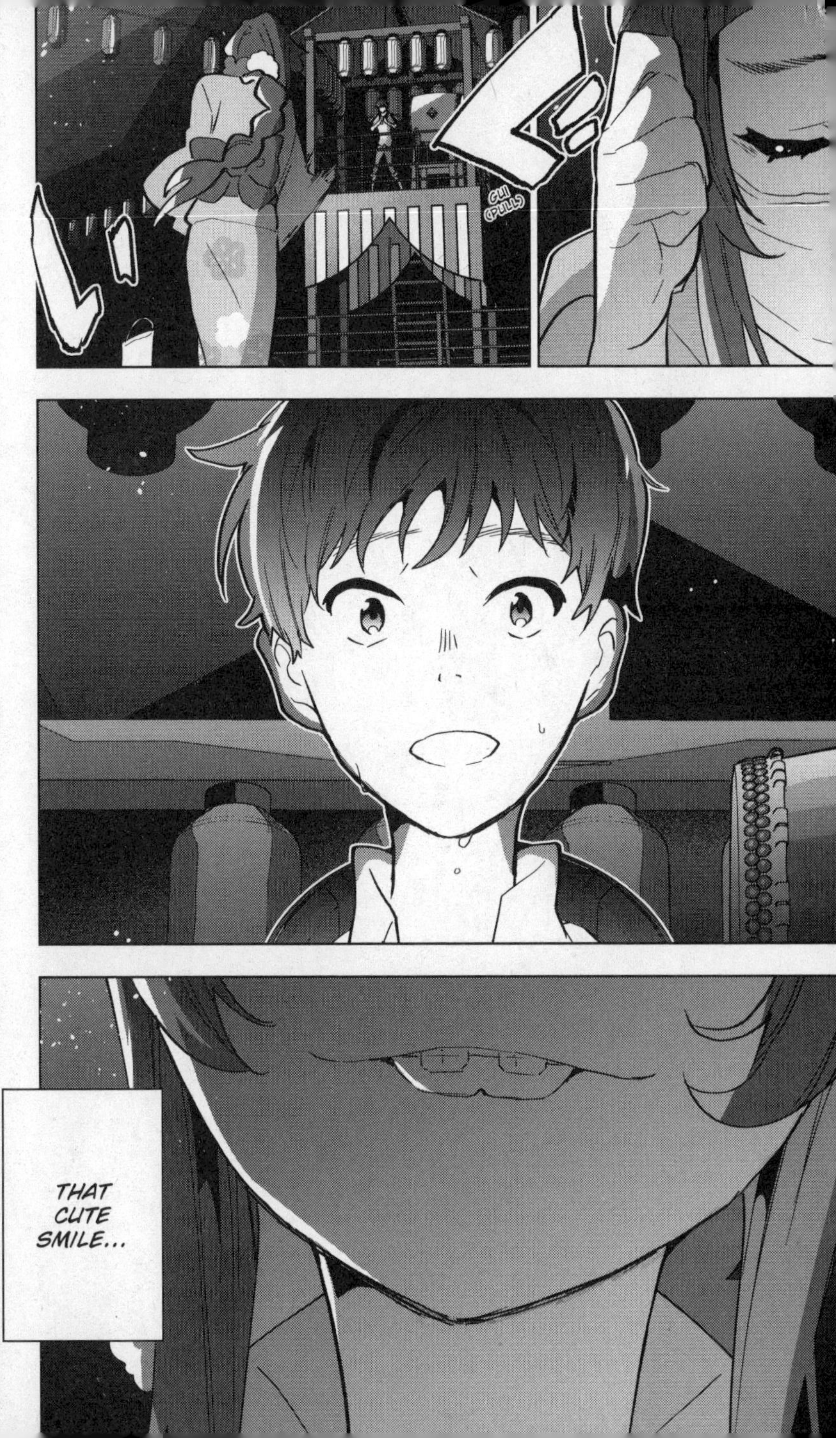
GUI
(PULL)
THAT CUTE SMILE...

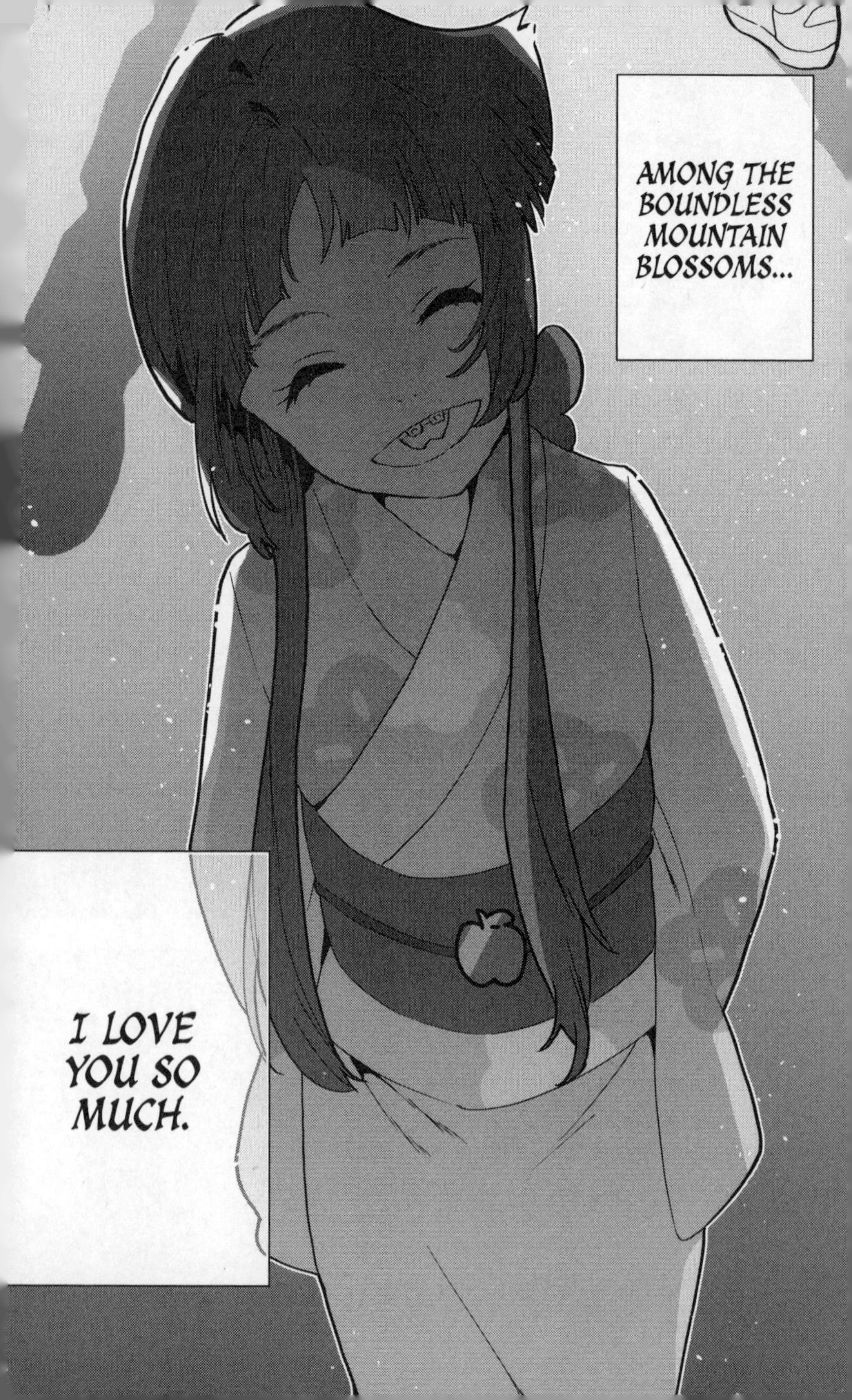
AMONG THE BOUNDLESS MOUNTAIN BLOSSOMS...
I LOVE YOU SO MUCH.

Words Bubble Up Like Soda Pop ———— *The End*

Words Bubble Up Like Soda Pop

Afterword

| Imo Oono |

We had the chance to get quite a bit in depth with the story of Fujiyama and Sakura in the manga version. I made sure they acted in a way that was consistent with the animated film while putting the story together. It was tough, but a lot of fun the whole way.

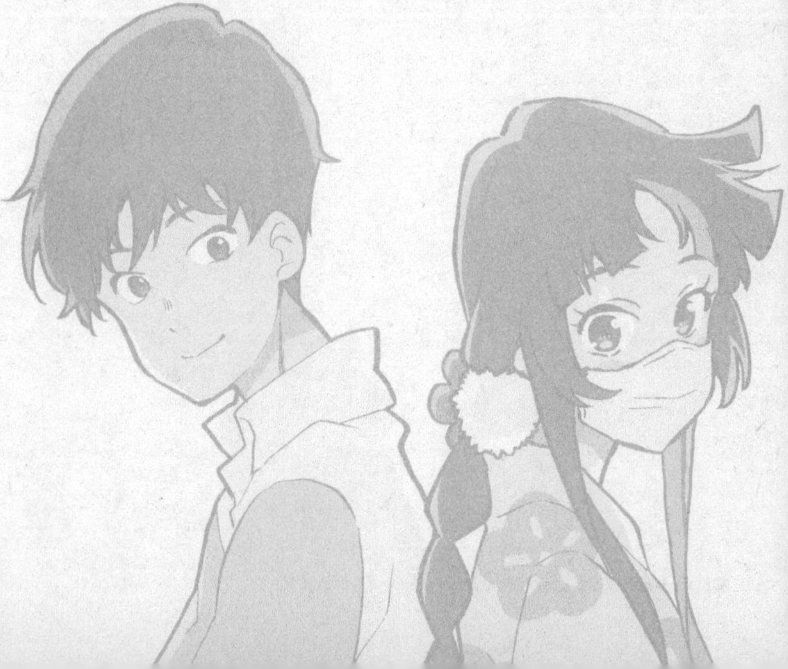

| Kyohei Ishiguro (Director/Screenwriter) |

I didn't depict the story of young Fujiyama and Sakura in the anime film or novelization in very much detail. All I had was the rough outlines of a plot, which I wrote for Taeko Onuki when I asked her to perform the song that appears in the film. This was expanded for the purposes of this manga, and if you read this after watching the film, I think it'll help you understand Sakura's song more, making it an even more moving experience. Fujiyama and Sakura, Cherry and Smile—the familiar stories of youth play across generations. Listen to them sing, and you can recall those fireworks in full bloom that they saw anytime you want to. That's how deeply connected music and memories can be.

The haiku in this work were contributed by the following writers:
Karan Kurose
Mizuho Ohtsuka - Ai Ijuin - Fumiya Owase - Shoto Ito
Akane Sugimoto - Rei Totsuka - Kouki Nakayama - Shuhei Nishida
Minori Nozawa - Aina Hasegawa - Yuina Hara - Ryo Matsunaga
Eifu Narita - Yutarou Nemoto
Daisuke Kumagai - Takeshi Yokouchi
Yuho Hashimoto - Satoshi Goto - Yumi Iwata - Yu Kawai
Kyohei Ishiguro

Words Bubble Up Like Soda Pop

3

Art by **Imo Oono**
Original Story by **FlyingDog**
Background Assistance by **Studio Cocolo**

Translator: **Kevin Gifford** • Letterer: **Bianca Pistillo**

CIDER NO YONI KOTOBA GA WAKIAGARU Vol. 3
©Imo Oono 2021
©2020 フライングドッグ／サイダーのように言葉が湧き上がる製作委員会
First published in Japan in 2021 by KADOKAWA CORPORATION, Tokyo.
English translation rights arranged with KADOKAWA CORPORATION, Tokyo
through TUTTLE-MORI AGENCY, INC., Tokyo.
English translation © 2024 by Yen Press, LLC

Yen Press
150 West 30th Street, 19th Floor
New York, NY 10001

Visit us!

yenpress.com • facebook.com/yenpress • twitter.com/yenpress
yenpress.tumblr.com • instagram.com/yenpress

First Yen Press Edition: January 2024
Edited by Yen Press Editorial: Mark Gallucci
Designed by Yen Press Design: Eddy Mingki, Wendy Chan

Yen Press is an imprint of Yen Press, LLC.
The Yen Press name and logo are trademarks of Yen Press, LLC.

Library of Congress Control Number: 2023933157

ISBNs: 978-1-9753-6443-4 (paperback)
978-1-9753-6444-1 (ebook)

1 3 5 7 9 10 8 6 4 2

WOR

Printed in the United States of America